day trips® from san antonio

fourth edition

getaway ideas for the local traveler

paris permenter & john bigley

gpp®

travel

Guilford, Connecticut

All the information in this guidebook is subject to change. We recommend that you call ahead to obtain current information before traveling.

ISBN 978-0-7627-7307-7

Printed in the United States of America
Distributed by National Book Network

contents

southeast

day trip 01

day trip 02

day trip 03

south

day trip 01

day trip 02

southwest

day trip 01

west

day trip 01

day trip 02

day trip 03

northwest

day trip 01

day trips from san antonio

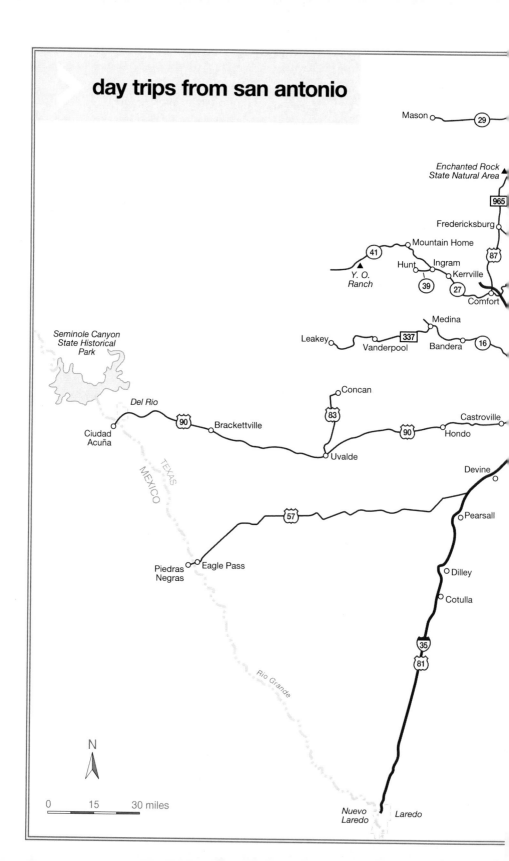

Mason

29

Enchanted Rock
State Natural Area

965

Fredericksburg

Mountain Home

87

41

Hunt

Ingram

Kerrville

Y. O.
Ranch

39

27

Comfort

Medina

Leakey

337

Seminole Canyon
State Historical
Park

Vanderpool

Bandera

16

Concan

Del Rio

83

Castroville

90

Brackettville

90

Hondo

Ciudad
Acuña

Uvalde

Devine

MEXICO   TEXAS

57

Pearsall

Piedras
Negras

Eagle Pass

Dilley

Cotulla

Rio Grande

35

81

N

0   15   30 miles

Nuevo
Laredo

Laredo

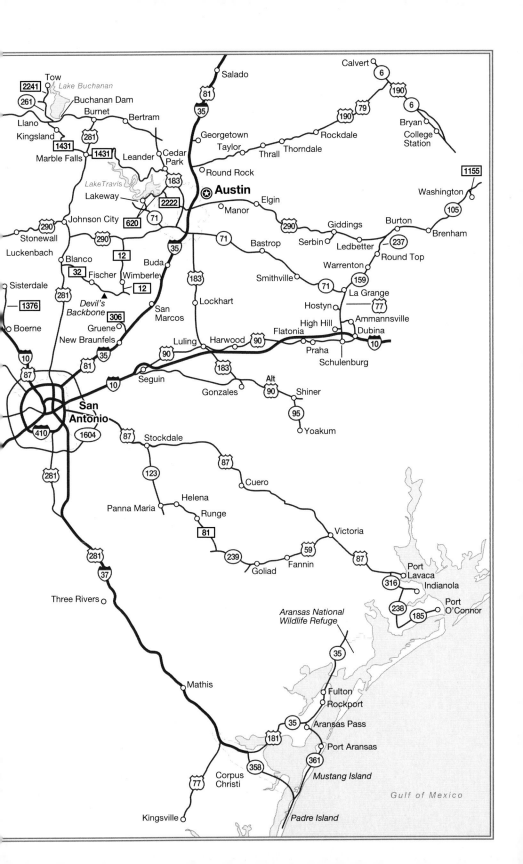

about the authors

John Bigley and **Paris Permenter** are a husband-wife team of travel writers who make their home in the Hill Country west of Austin. They are the authors of *Insiders' Guide: San Antonio in Your Pocket, Insiders' Guide to San Antonio,* and *Day Trips from Austin* (GPP Travel).

introduction

Welcome to San Antonio—the Alamo City and the gateway to South Texas.

Most people have a mental image of Texas as miles of rugged, uncivilized land where the outlines of cattle and lonely windmills stretch above the horizon. But that's just one side of the Lone Star State, also known as the "land of contrast." Texas also boasts high-tech cities, piney woods, sandy beaches, rolling hills, and fertile farmland—much of it within a two-hour drive of San Antonio.

With its semitropical climate and lush vegetation, San Antonio offers a south-of-the-border atmosphere with north-of-the-border amenities. Because the city lies at the juncture of the Hill Country, farmland, and brush country that stretches to the border with Mexico, *Day Trips from San Antonio* spans terrain ranging from farmland to rocky hills. This difference in topography is the result of an ancient earthquake that created the Balcones Fault, which runs north to south and created a buckling of the land to the west, forming what is known as the Hill Country. The fault line, slightly west of I-35, forms the dividing line between the eastern agricultural region and the Hill Country, one of the state's most popular tourism areas.

The region covered in *Day Trips from San Antonio* is as diverse as the more than 30 cultures that helped found the state. In fact, the influences of these pioneers are still apparent today in the many festivals and ethnic foods that vacationers come here to enjoy. You can head to the urban areas of Austin or Corpus Christi, or to small towns where it's not uncommon to hear German, Czech, Spanish, or even Alsatian spoken on the street. You also can get away from it all with a quiet walk along miles of undeveloped beach on Padre Island, or take a birding cruise along the Intracoastal Waterway of the Rockport-Fulton area. Most day trip recommendations also include information about overnight accommodations to make your visit more relaxing and unhurried, so you'll have plenty of time to watch a Texas-size sunset or sunrise over the Gulf waters.

Many of the attractions lie along the route taken by the "Winter Texans" who flock here during the cooler months. So whether you're heading for the Rio Grande Valley or the Gulf Coast, you'll find a wealth of useful tips and information inside. Be sure to check the sections marked "Especially for Winter Texans," as well as Appendix B, which will help you identify special services, festivals, and parks aimed at making you feel right at home.

using this guide

Day Trips from San Antonio is organized by general direction from San Antonio: north, northeast, east, southeast, south, southwest, west, and northwest. For brochures and maps on San Antonio–area attractions, call (800) 447-3327 or (201) 207-6700; contact the **San Antonio Convention and Visitors Bureau,** 203 South St. Mary's St., Suite 200, San Antonio, TX 78205; or see www.visitsanantonio.com.

Highway designations: Federal highways are designated US. State routes use TX for Texas. Farm-to-market roads are indicated by FM, park roads are shown by PR, and ranch roads are labeled RR. County roads (which are not on the Texas state map) are identified as CR.

Hours: In most cases, hours are omitted in the listings because they are subject to frequent changes. Instead, phone numbers appear for obtaining up-to-date information.

Attractions: We have noted when admission is free, but fees may be charged for special events or additional services. Be sure to call ahead to check the rates, as prices can vary widely depending upon the time of year you plan to visit.

Restaurants: Restaurant prices are for a single entrée and beverage (excludes cocktails).
$ less than $10
$$ $10 to $20
$$$ more than $20

Accommodations: Room prices are for a double-occupancy room during peak season, not including tax.
$ less than $75
$$ $75 to $150
$$$ more than $150

travel tips

To get the most out of each day trip, here are some travel tips to keep in mind.

Carry a Road Map. Although we've included directions, it's best to carry a Texas road map as you travel. It's also advisable to carry a county map for a better look at farm-to-market (FM) roads and ranch roads (RR). You can get brochures on Texas attractions and a free copy of the *Texas State Travel Guide* from the **Texas Department of Transportation,**

P.O. Box 5064, Austin, TX 78763-5064, or by calling (800) 888-TEX or visiting www.travel tex.com. The travel guide is available in print and online. The guide is coded to a free Texas state map provided by the Highway Department. State maps are also available from any of the tourist information centers located on routes into Texas and at the Texas State Capitol in Austin. The tourist information centers are open daily, except for Thanksgiving, Christmas, and New Year's Day.

The expansiveness of Texas sets it apart from other states. Note the scale of the map. With 266,807 square miles of land, Texas is the second largest state in the country. One inch on the state road map spans 23 miles.

Driving Varies with Terrain. The two-hour time limit that constitutes a "day trip" here has been stretched for the westernmost trips in this book. You won't find many towns en route from San Antonio to the Mexican border, and there's little traffic to slow your drive. To the east, population is more dense, and day trips involve quiet, slow drives along farm-to-market and ranch roads.

For questions about travel in Texas, call the Texas Department of Transportation's travel assistance line, (800) 452-9292.

Avoid Midday Heat. During summer the Texas heat is hotter than sizzling fajitas. In warm weather it's best to drive in the early morning hours or after sunset. If you are traveling with pets, never leave them in an enclosed car; temperatures soar to ovenlike heights in just minutes.

Heed Road Signs and Weather Warnings. Always be on the lookout for road signs, and if you see a notice, observe it. Obey flash flood warnings: A sudden rainstorm can turn a wash into a deadly torrent. The Hill Country north and west of San Antonio is the most dangerous region for flash flooding. Never cross a flooded roadway; it may be deeper than you think.

Watch Out for Stray Livestock. When driving through open-ranch cattle country on farm-to-market or ranch roads, be on the lookout for livestock and deer wandering across the road, especially near dusk.

You'll find that Texans are friendly folk who wave on country roads and nod as they pass you on the sidewalk. Talk to local citizens as you wind through the back roads for even more travel tips and a firsthand look at the varied cultures that make up the pieces of your journey.

north

day trip 01

north

Some of the most scenic highways in the Hill Country await you as you meander through rugged canyons and wooded valleys. Huge cypress trees line sparkling Hill Country streams, and hilltop pullovers command spectacular views. Here, small towns attract resident artisans who display their wares in galleries and small shops.

blanco

Formerly a "Wild West" kind of town, the community was originally the seat of Blanco County. Although the county seat eventually moved to nearby Johnson City, where it remains today, local residents have restored Blanco's old limestone courthouse, located at the intersection of US 281 and TX 165. Stop by for brochures and shopping.

Around the courthouse square are several art galleries and antiques shops aimed at weekend visitors, many of whom stop to camp at the Blanco State Park south of town.

getting there

To reach Blanco, follow US 281 north of San Antonio for 51 miles, past miles of cattle ranches and Hill Country vistas.

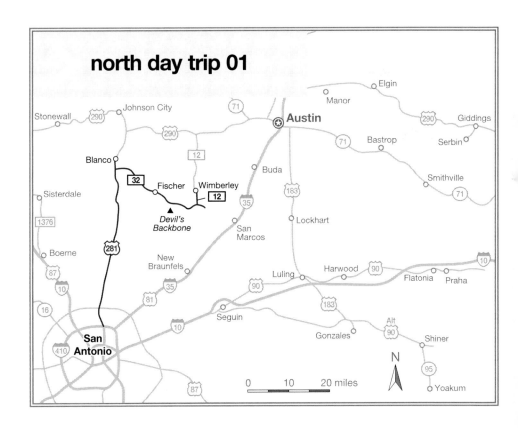

north day trip 01

where to go

Blanco Bowling Club. 310 East Fourth St.; (830) 833-4416. Housed in 1940s buildings, the bowling club and the adjacent cafe have changed little with the passing years. The 9-pin game is still set up by hand as it has been for generations. The bowling club opens at 7:30 p.m. Mon through Fri (except during football season, when everyone's at the Friday-night high school game). To bowl you must be a league member. Free admission.

Blanco State Park. South of Blanco on US 281; (830) 833-4333; www.tpwd.state.tx.us. During the Great Depression the Civilian Conservation Corps built 2 stone dams, a group pavilion, stone picnic tables, and an arched bridge in this 104-acre riverside park. Today the park is popular with swimmers, anglers, and campers. Open daily.

where to shop

Brieger Pottery and Hill Country Lavender. 408 Fourth St.; (830) 833-2294; www.brieger pottery.com and www.hillcountrylavender.com. This downtown pottery studio features handmade stoneware; it also includes the year-round retail store for Hill Country Lavender,

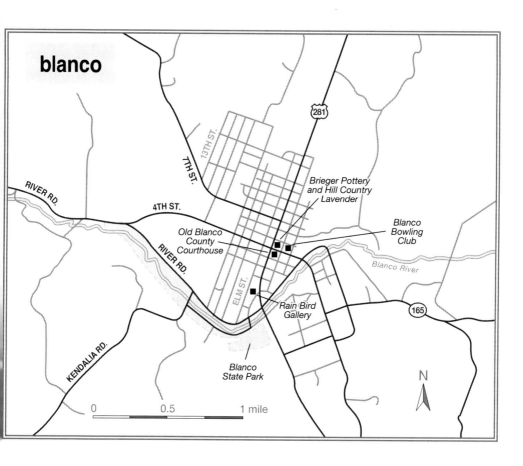

blanco

Blanco's well-known lavender farm located outside of town. The farm offers seasonal special events, including cut-your-own lavender days. Open daily.

Rain Bird Gallery. 103 Main St.; (830) 833-5900; www.rainbirdgalleryonline.com. One of the largest art galleries in the Hill Country, Rain Bird is located in a historic church and features both local and international artists. On the fourth Saturday of every month, the gallery hosts a Meet the Artist event. Open Wed through Sun.

where to eat

Blanco Bowling Club Cafe. 310 East Fourth St.; (830) 833-4416. This is a traditional Texas diner, with a linoleum floor and Formica tables, and chairs filled with locals who come here at the same time every day. Chicken-fried steak is the specialty; on Friday nights there's a catfish plate as well. Stop by in the morning for huge glazed twists and doughnuts made from scratch. Open daily for breakfast, lunch, and dinner (no dinner on Sun). $.

musical chairs with the county seat

*Built in 1888, the former **Blanco County Courthouse** has been one of the most used buildings in the county—for everything except as a courthouse, that is. The year after its construction, an election moved the county seat to Johnson City. The courthouse was used a total of four years for its original purpose, then it went into a long career of different uses. For two different periods, the building served as a schoolhouse; it also became a bank. Later it served the community as a town hall, library, opera house, and even the office of the local newspaper. From 1937 to 1961 the building served as a hospital, but later it became a Wild West museum and then a barbecue restaurant. Today the building houses the visitor center and is used for community events.*

fischer

A short drive on Fischer Store Road takes you right into the community and to the store for which the road is named. Through the years the store has served many purposes, acting as a bank and post office in addition to a mercantile. Today the store is open Wednesday through Sunday and is a nice place to grab a soft drink before continuing on your day trip.

While you're at the store, you'll notice some buildings next door. The red building is home to the Fischer Bowling Club, a 9-pin bowling league. Next door you'll see Fischer Hall, an old-fashioned dance hall that's still popular for wedding and reunion rentals.

getting there

It's just a short, winding drive through the country from Blanco to the tiny hamlet of Fischer. Retrace your drive south on US 281 for a couple of miles to the intersection of RR 32. Take a left and enjoy a quiet ride through miles of ranch land and rolling hills.

where to go

Devil's Backbone Scenic Drive. The Devil's Backbone Scenic Drive stretches along RR 32 from Fischer to the intersection of RR 12, your turnoff for Wimberley. There aren't any steep climbs or stomach-churning lookouts; a high ridge of hills provides a gentle drive with excellent views along the way. There's very little traffic, and a beautiful picnic spot is on the left, just a few miles out of Fischer. This stretch of road is often cited as one of the most scenic drives in Texas and is well known for its fall color.

wimberley

Wimberley's history goes back to the 1850s, when a resourceful Texas Revolution veteran named William Winters opened a mill here. As was tradition at the time, he named the new community Winters' Mill. When Winters died, John Cade bought the mill, and the town became Cade's Mill. Finally, in 1870, a wealthy Llano man named Pleasant Wimberley rode into town. Tired of Indian raids on his horses in Llano, he moved in, bought the mill, and changed the town's name one last time.

The small town of Wimberley is one of those "shop 'til you drop" kinds of places. Even with only 3,800 residents, the town boasts dozens of specialty stores, art galleries and studios, and accommodations ranging from river resorts to historic bed-and-breakfasts.

Wimberley is a quiet place, except when the shops open their doors on Monday, Thursday, Friday, and weekends. The busiest time to visit is the first Saturday of the month, from March through December. This is Market Day, when nearly 500 vendors set up to sell antiques, collectibles, and arts and crafts.

Many visitors come to enjoy the town's two water sources: the Blanco River and clear, chilly Cypress Creek. Both are filled with inner-tubers and swimmers during hot summer months. The waterways provide a temporary home for campers and vacationers who stay in resorts and cabins along the shady water's edge.

getting there

At the end of the Devil's Backbone, RR 32 intersects with RR 12. Take a left on RR 12, then drive 5 miles. This road drops from the steep ridge to the fertile valley that's home to the Blanco River and Cypress Creek.

where to go

Wimberley Chamber of Commerce. Wimberley North Shopping Center, RR 12 past Cypress Creek; (512) 847-2201; www.wimberley.org. Stop by the chamber offices on weekdays to load up on brochures, maps, and friendly shopping tips.

Pioneertown. 7-A Ranch Resort, 1 mile west of RR 12 on CR 178, at the intersection of CR 179; (512) 847-2517; www.7aranchresort.com. See a medicine show, tour a general store museum, or spend some time at the town jail in this Wild West village. There's also an old log fort, cowboy shows, and a western cafe. A narrow-gauge railway winds 1 mile along the Wimberley Valley. Open daily during the summer months; closed Labor Day through Memorial Day.

where to shop

Like nearby Blanco, Wimberley is home to many artists who've relocated to Texas's serene Hill Country. Specialty shops abound, selling everything from imports to sculptures and

flower power

*Is it spring? Grab the car keys in one hand, your camera in the other, and get ready for a bloomin' good time! Starting in late March and extending into early summer, wildflowers line the roadways throughout Central and South Texas. The best way to find the top fields is with a quick call to the Texas Department of Transportation's **wildflower hotline** (800-452-9292). The hotline is active from mid-March until early May, and you can request information by region (Central Texas and Hill Country cover most of this book's scope). Maps showing the best spots for viewing wild-flowers are available through the Texas Department of Transportation website (www .dot.state.tx.us/travel/flora_conditions.htm).*

antiques. Arts and crafts are especially well represented. Plan to shop Fri through Mon. Some stores are open all week, but most close midweek, especially during cooler months.

Rancho Deluxe. On the square, 14010 RR 12; (877) 847-9570 or (512) 847-9570; www .ranchodeluxe.net. Bring the cowboy look to your home with this shop's western merchandise. You'll find everything from spurs to Mexican sideboards, and from horns to hand-crafted furniture. Open daily.

Wimberley Glass Works. 6469 RR 12; (800) 929-6686; www.wgw.com. Watch demonstrations on the art of hand-blown glass and shop for one-of-a-kind creations. Open daily (glass blowing Tues through Sun).

Wimberley Market Days. 601 FM 2325; (512) 847-2201; www.shopmarketdays.com. Organized by the Wimberley Lions Club, Market Days holds the distinction as the oldest outdoor market in the Hill Country and the second oldest in the Lone Star State. With nearly 500 vendors, this 1-day extravaganza is held on the first Saturday of every month from March through December. Open 7 a.m. to 4 p.m. Free admission; charge for parking.

Wimberley Stained Glass Shop. On the square; (512) 847-3930; www.wimberley stainedglass.com. Highlighted by handcrafted Tiffany lamp reproductions, this shop also features custom-leaded doors, window panels, and sun catchers. Open daily.

where to eat

Brewster's Pizza. 9595 RR 12, Suite 4; (512) 847-3299; www.brewsterspizza.com. Located 5 miles south of Wimberley's town square, Brewster's is a great place to grab a pizza and a beer since it is also the home of the Wimberley Brewing Company, offering a nice selection of handcrafted beers and ales. Closed Mon. $$.

where to stay

Wimberley is filled with bed-and-breakfast accommodations that range from historic homes in town to ranches in the surrounding Hill Country to camps alongside Cypress Creek. For information on these many accommodations, give one of the reservation services a call: **Hill Country Accommodations,** (800) 926-5028 or (512) 847-5388, http://texasvacation .com; **All Wimberley Lodging,** (800) 460-3909, www.texashillcountrylodging.com; and **Texas Hill Country Retreats,** (800) 918-8788, www.texashillco.com. For brochures on Wimberley's other accommodations, call the chamber of commerce at (512) 847-2201.

day trip 02

north

>>> **lbj country:**
johnson city, stonewall, luckenbach,
fredericksburg, enchanted rock
state natural area

The memory of one of Texas's most famous politicians, Lyndon Baines Johnson, still looms here over hills and valleys and in local lore. While the larger-than-life Johnson was president in the 1960s, the Hill Country became the focus of attention as world leaders gathered at the Johnson Ranch, dubbed the "Texas White House," for discussion, politicking, and debate.

johnson city

LBJ brought the attention of the world to his hometown; the most popular stop here is the LBJ Boyhood Home, managed by the National Park Service. LBJ was five years old in 1913 when his family moved from their country home near the Pedernales River to this simple frame house. The visitor center provides information on this location, nearby Johnson Settlement, and other LBJ attractions. Park admission is free of charge, a stipulation of the late president.

getting there

From San Antonio, drive north on US 281 through Blanco (see North Day Trip 01 for Blanco stops). From Blanco, it's a 14-mile drive on US 281 to Johnson City.

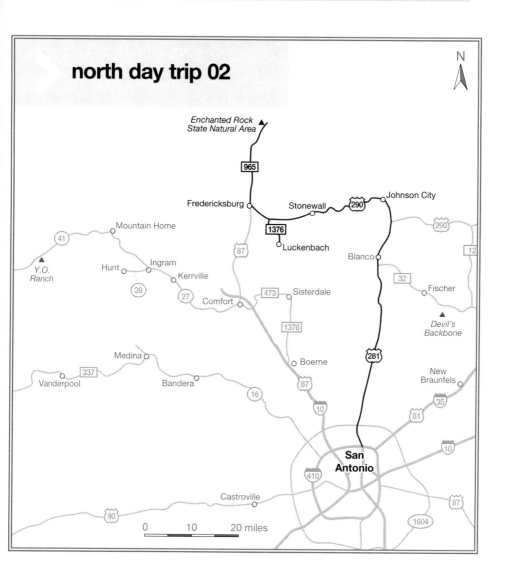

north day trip 02

N

Enchanted Rock State Natural Area

965

Fredericksburg — Stonewall — 290 — Johnson City

Mountain Home
290
41
1376
87
Luckenbach
12
Y.O. Ranch
Hunt
Ingram
Blanco
Kerrville
32
39
27
473
Sisterdale
Fischer
Comfort
1376
Devil's Backbone
Medina
281
Vanderpool
337
Bandera
Boerne
New Braunfels
16
87
35
10
81
San Antonio
10
410
Castroville
87
90
1604
0   10   20 miles

where to go

Johnson City Visitors Center. 100 East Main St.; (830) 868-7684; www.johnsoncity-texas.com. The visitor center, located in the historic Withers-Spauldings Building downtown, includes displays on the history of Johnson City as well as free maps and brochures. The center also offers free Wi-Fi access to visitors. Open daily.

The Exotic Resort Zoo. Four miles north of Johnson City on US 281; (830) 868-4357; www.zooexotics.com. Unusual species (including many endangered animals) roam the 137 acres of wooded Hill Country. In this park, leave the driving to someone else and enjoy a guided ride aboard a safari truck. Professional guides conduct tours of the ranch and provide you with information on animal behavior and other topics as you feed the friendly park residents. After the tour, you can see some wildlife up close at the petting zoo. Kids enjoy petting child-size miniature donkeys, baby deer, llamas, baby elks, and even a kangaroo at this special area. Open daily 9 a.m. to 6 p.m.

LBJ National Historic Park. South of US 290 at Ninth Street; (830) 868-7128; www.nps .gov/lyjo. Park at the visitor center and go inside for brochures and a look at exhibits. From the center, you can walk to two historic areas: Johnson Settlement and the LBJ Boyhood Home. Open daily. Free admission.

> **LBJ Boyhood Home.** LBJ was a schoolboy when his family moved here in 1913. The home is still furnished with the Johnsons' belongings. Guided tours run every half hour (except during the lunch hour).

> **Johnson Settlement.** The settlement gives visitors a look at the beginnings of the Johnson legacy. These rustic cabins and outbuildings once belonged to LBJ's grandfather Sam Ealy Johnson and his brother Tom. The two cattle drivers lived a rugged life in the Hill Country during the 1860s and 1870s. An exhibit center tells this story in pictures and artifacts. You also can tour the brothers' cabins and see costumed docents carrying out 19th-century chores.

Pedernales Falls State Park. About 9 miles east on FM 2766; (830) 868-7304; www .tpwd.state.tx.us. A favorite summer getaway, this 4,800-acre state park is highlighted by gently cascading waterfalls. Swimming, fishing, camping, and hiking are available. This park is susceptible to flash flooding; a warning on the park website tells visitors, "If you are in the river area and notice the water beginning to rise, you should leave the river area immediately." Open daily.

Texas Hills Vineyard. RR 2766, 1 mile east of US 290/281 on RR 2766, the road to Pedernales State Park; (830) 868-2321; www.texashillsvineyard.com. Texas wines produced with an Italian influence are the specialty of this vineyard. Open Mon through Fri 10 a.m. to 5 p.m., Sat 10 a.m. to 6 p.m., and Sun noon to 5 p.m. for tastings.

where to shop

Whittington's Jerky. 602 US 281 South; (877) 868-5501 or (830) 868-5500; www .whittingtonsjerky.com. This factory produces true Texas jerky; stop by for free samples or to shop for jerky and other food items. The store features a large selection of Texas souvenirs, from kitchenware to books. Open daily.

where to eat

Silver K Cafe. 209 East Main St.; (830) 868-2911; www.silverkcafe.com. This restaurant boasts "rustic elegance with Texas pride" and it lives up to that claim. Housed in the Old Lumberyard Complex, which was formerly home to a lumber company, this restaurant offers Texas fare for lunch, from chicken-fried steak to honey-pecan fried chicken. Dinner adds Louisiana shrimp and grits, Angus steaks, and more, while Saturday night brings a fine-dining menu with items such as lobster and white truffle linguine. Silver K is also known for its live music on Thurs and Sun. $$–$$$.

where to stay

The Exotic Zoo Bed and Breakfast. Four miles north of Johnson City on US 281; (830) 868-4357; www.zooexotics.com. The Exotic Resort Zoo, known for its guided safari tours and petting zoo, operates a 4-cabin bed-and-breakfast on the property. Two cabins include kitchenettes; they all include access to 2 swimming pools, a hot tub, barbecue area, and fire pit for evening bonfires. The cabins overlook the animal areas, and guests can also fish on a stocked lake, paying only for those fish caught. There is a 7-day cancellation policy on cabin rentals. $$$.

stonewall

US 290 passes through miles of peach orchards, and during early summer, farm-fresh fruit is sold at roadside stands throughout the area. Stonewall is also the home of the LBJ National and State Historic Parks, encompassing the LBJ Ranch.

getting there

From Johnson City, head west on US 290 to the tiny community of Stonewall, the capital of the Texas peach industry.

where to go

Grape Creek Vineyards. Four miles west of Stonewall on US 290; (830) 664-2710; www .grapecreek.com. The fertile land of the Pedernales Valley is a natural for vineyards, and you'll find acres of beautiful grapevines at this winery that produces cabernet sauvignon and chardonnay varieties. The winery is open daily; call for tour times. Free admission.

LBJ National and State Historic Parks. Fourteen miles west of Johnson City on US 290; (830) 644-2252; www.nps.gov/lyjo and www.tpwd.state.tx.us. These two combined parks together span approximately 700 acres. The area is comprised of three main sections: the visitor center, the LBJ Ranch and tour, and the Sauer-Beckmann Farm. The most scenic

peach fun

Stonewall is called the "Peach Capital of Texas," and every June the town is ripe with fun and festivities. The third weekend of June is set aside for a celebration of the Hill Country's sweetest product at the annual **Peach JAMboree,** *a time when the small community shares its fuzzy treasure. The festivities are genuine Texas fun, from a rodeo with bareback riding, calf roping, team roping, and bull riding, to a parade and a baking contest at the fire station. Other activities include a fiddlers' contest (open to competitors), a washer-pitching tournament, and, of course, the Gillespie County Peach Queen Pageant. The sweetest event is the Peach Show and Auction, with plenty of prize-winning examples of Stonewall's crop.*

Gillespie County, including Stonewall and nearby Fredericksburg, is filled with orchards where you can pick your own peaches. These shady groves yield their fruit until late July and offer a dozen varieties of peaches. The earliest to ripen are the cling peaches, ones whose fruit clings to the pit. As the summer progresses, varieties such as Red Skin, Loring, and Harvest Gold begin to mature.

route to the LBJ Park falls along RR 1, paralleling the wide, shallow Pedernales River. (Exit US 290 a few miles east of Stonewall.)

During Johnson's life, the ranch was closed to all but official visitors. In hopes of catching a glimpse of the president, travelers often stopped along RR 1, located across the river from the "Texas White House," the nickname of the Johnsons' home. Today the parks draw visitors from around the world, who come for a look at the history behind the Hill Country, the presidency of LBJ, and a working Texas ranch.

Make your first stop the **state park visitor center** for a look at displays on LBJ's life, including mementos of President Johnson's boyhood years. Attached to the visitor center is the **Behrens Cabin,** a dogtrot-style structure built by a German immigrant in the 1870s. Inside, the home is furnished with household items from more than a century ago. Nearby is the **Sauer-Beckmann Living Historical Farm.** The two 1918 farm homes are furnished in period style. Outside, children can have a great time petting the farm animals. From here, it's just a short walk back to the visitor center.

While you're at the visitor center, obtain a driving permit for a self-guided drive of the **LBJ Ranch.** In your car, you'll travel across the president's ranch, making a stop at the one-room **Junction School,** where Johnson began his education. Other stops include a look at the reconstructed birthplace home and the family cemetery where the former president and First Lady are buried. The next stop is the **Texas White House** and the president's airstrip. In the onetime aircraft hangar, you'll now find a national park visitor center. Along with some displays and a small gift shop, the center also sells tickets ($2 for adults) for guided tours of LBJ's office in the Texas White House.

After returning to your car, the next stop is the **cattle barns,** still surrounded by ancestors of LBJ's herd, noted with a trademark *LBJ* emblazoned on their horns.

Although the park does not have overnight facilities, there are picnic areas and hiking trails for day use. Open daily. Free admission (fee for Texas White House tours).

Torre di Pietra. 10915 East US 290; (830) 644-2829; www.texashillcountrywine.com. This family-owned winery carries on a long Texas tradition of wine-making in a setting that evokes Italy. In addition to a selection of semidry, red, and sweet wines as well as ports, the winery produces liquid-filled chocolates containing the Torre di Pietra product. Along with tastings, the winery draws visitors with live music on the shaded patio every Sat. Open daily.

luckenbach

This town was founded in 1852 by Jacob, William, and August Luckenbach. The brothers opened a post office at the site and called it South Grape Creek. In 1886 a man named August Engel reopened the post office and renamed it Luckenbach in honor of the early founders.

In 1977 Waylon Jennings and Willie Nelson's popular country-western song "Luckenbach Texas (Back to the Basics)" made this community a Texas institution. The town had entered the music scene in 1973 when Jerry Jeff Walker recorded an album called *Viva Terlingua* in Luckenbach's dance hall, and it later went on to produce more Texas classics such as Gary P. Nunn's "London Homesick Blues (Home with the Armadillo)."

Today the town is primarily composed of a small general store that serves as a beer joint, souvenir stand, and general gathering place. Nearby, a large dance hall fills nightly with live music and plenty of boot-scootin' action.

getting there

To reach Luckenbach, leave Stonewall on US 290. Turn left on FM 1376 and continue for about 4.25 miles. Don't expect to see signs pointing to the turnoff for Luckenbach Road; they are often stolen as fast as the Highway Department can get them in the ground. After the turn for Grapetown, take the next right down a narrow country road. Luckenbach is just around the bend.

where to shop

Luckenbach General Store. 412 Luckenbach Town Loop; (888) 311-8990, ext. 23; www.luckenbachtexas.com. The old post office is today a combination general store and beer joint, the walls covered with scrawled names penned by Luckenbach fans. The store, built in 1851, sells town souvenirs and is open daily. In front of the store, you'll find a statue of Hondo Crouch, who along with Guich Koock and Kathy Morgan, bought the town in 1970.

fredericksburg

Once the edge of the frontier and home to brave German pioneers who faced many hardships, including hostile Comanche Indians, Fredericksburg is now a favorite with antiques shoppers, history buffs, and fans of good German food.

US 290 runs through the heart of the downtown district, becoming Main Street within the city limits. Originally the street was designed to be large enough to allow a wagon and team of mules to turn around in the center of town. Today Main Street is filled with shoppers who come to explore the stores and restaurants of downtown Fredericksburg. Stop by the visitor center at 106 North Adams for brochures and maps.

Fredericksburg welcomes all visitors—just look at the street signs for proof. Starting at the Adams Street intersection, head east on Main Street and take the first letter of every intersecting street name: They spell ALL WELCOME. Drive west on Main Street starting after the Adams Street intersection, and the first letters of the intersecting streets spell COME BACK.

That welcoming spirit extends from the excellent restaurants to the unique boutiques that line Main Street to the hundreds of cozy bed-and-breakfast establishments that dot Gillespie County. Unlike traditional bed-and-breakfasts, where the owners or managers reside on the premises, guest houses are usually managed by a reservation service. After checking in with the service, guests receive directions and keys. Breakfast, which can range from a simple continental meal to a spread of sausage wraps and homemade pastries, often awaits in the refrigerator. But perhaps nowhere else is the visitor's welcome so obvious as at Fredericksburg's many festivals.

Fredericksburg is a prime destination for day-trippers looking for antiques, gifts, books, Texas wines, and one-of-a-kind purchases. The shops along Fredericksburg's Main Street and nearby side streets offer travelers a weekend bursting with shopping opportunities, no matter what their tastes.

getting there

Retrace your steps from Luckenbach, and continue west on US 290 to Fredericksburg.

where to go

Fredericksburg Chamber of Commerce. 302 East Austin; (888) 997-3600 or (830) 997-6523; www.fredericksburg-texas.com. Stop by the chamber offices for brochures, maps, and information on a self-guided walking tour of historic downtown buildings, many of which

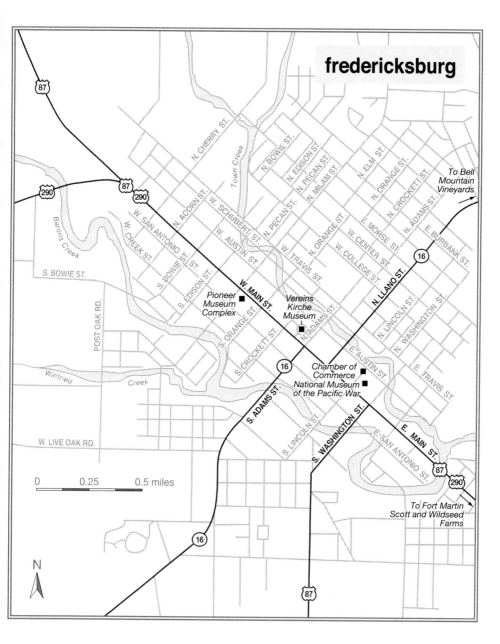

now house shops and restaurants. The staff here also can direct you to bed-and-breakfast facilities in the area. Open Mon through Sat.

Bell Mountain Vineyards. TX 16 North, 14 miles from Fredericksburg; (830) 685-3297; www.bellmountainwine.com. Tour the château-type winery that produces chardonnay,

Riesling, pinot noir, and several private-reserve estate varieties. Guided tours and tastings are offered every Sat from Mar through mid-Dec. Free admission.

Fort Martin Scott. 1606 East Main St., 2 miles east of Fredericksburg on US 290; (830) 997-9895. Established in 1848, this was the first frontier military fort in Texas. Today the original stockade, a guardhouse, and a visitor center with displays on local Indians are open to tour, and historical reenactments keep the history lesson lively. Ongoing archaeological research conducted here offers a glimpse into the fort's past. Reenactments involving costumed Indians, infantrymen, and civilians are scheduled at least once a month. Plans are under way for the construction of a Texas Rangers Heritage Center at the site. Open Tues though Fri 10 a.m. to 5 p.m.

National Museum of the Pacific War. 340 East Main St.; (830) 997-8600; www.pacific warmuseum.org. This historic park (formerly the Admiral Nimitz State Historical Park) is composed of several sections: the historic Nimitz Steamboat Hotel, which is now the Admiral Nimitz Museum; the Japanese Garden of Peace; Pacific Combat Zone; George H. W. Bush Gallery; Plaza of Presidents; Memorial Courtyard; and the Nimitz Education and Research Center.

This complex was first named for Admiral Chester Nimitz, World War II commander in chief of the Pacific (CinCPac) and Fredericksburg's most famous resident. He commanded 2.5 million troops from the time he assumed command 18 days after the attack on Pearl Harbor until the Japanese surrendered.

The Nimitz name was well known in the area even years earlier. Having spent time in the merchant marines, Captain Charles H. Nimitz, the admiral's grandfather, decided to build a hotel here, adding a structure much like a ship's bridge to the front of his establishment. Built in 1852, the Nimitz Steamboat Hotel catered to guests who enjoyed a room, a meal, and the use of an outdoor bathhouse.

Today the former hotel houses the **Admiral Nimitz Museum,** a 3-story museum honoring Admiral Nimitz and Fredericksburg's early residents. Many exhibits are devoted to World War II, including several that illustrate the Pacific campaign. In addition to displays that record the building's past, several early hotel rooms, the hotel kitchen, and the bathhouse have been restored.

Behind the museum lies the **Japanese Garden of Peace,** a gift from the people of Japan. This classic Japanese garden includes a flowing stream, a raked bed of pebbles and stones representing the sea and the Pacific islands, and a replica of the study used by Admiral Togo, Nimitz's counterpart in the Japanese forces.

Nearby, the **Pacific Combat Zone** is a 3-acre outdoor exhibit area filled with displays recalling the struggles that took place during the war. Guided tours show visitors the hangar deck of an aircraft carrier; a South Pacific PT boat base with the world's only combat-proven, restored PT boat; and an island battlefield, modeled on the Japanese defenses at Tarawa. Tours of this outdoor exhibit take place on the hour between 10 a.m. and 4 p.m.

fredericksburg's wine industry

Dawn breaks over a dew-crystallized vineyard. Nearby, the vintner arrives for an early start to the day. In the distance, pickup trucks meander down the ranch road, greeted by the calls of onlooking cattle and goats.

It's another day in Texas wine country.

Much of the Lone Star State's fast-growing wine industry is centered in the Hill Country near Fredericksburg, founded by German settlers who planted the Vitis vinifera grapes that thrived in the Mediterranean-like climate of their new home. It would be a century before production would begin on a serious scale, but the roots of the Texas wine industry had been planted.

This community remembers its old-world heritage with German-style build-ings, shops, and restaurants. Those roots are also evident at the downtown **Fredericksburg Winery** *(247 W. Main St.; 830-990-8747; www.fbgwinery .com). Its signature labels, like the Texas chardonnay Adelsverein (named for the Society of Noblemen founded by German princes to help emigrants to the newly formed Republic of Texas), feature artwork and a little history. Like many local wineries, this is a family-run operation, headed by no-nonsense Cord Switzer (look for the man in the gimme cap), along with his wife Sandy, broth-ers Jene and Burt, and mother "Oma," charged with labeling each bottle by hand.*

Fourteen miles north of Fredericksburg you'll find **Bell Mountain Vineyards** *(463 Bell Mountain Rd.; 830-685-3297; www.bellmountainwine.com), located in Texas's first designated wine-growing area. Or head east, where "bouquet" describes not only wine but wildflowers.*

Farther east stands Stonewall, home to Lyndon Baines Johnson's "Texas White House" and also to **Grape Creek Vineyards** *(4 miles west of Stonewall on US 290; 830-644-2710; www.grapecreek.com), where acres of climbing vines yield the prize-winning cabernet Trois.*

Nearby, **Becker Vineyards** *(10 miles east of Fredericksburg off US 290; 830-644-2681; www.beckervineyards.com), with 46 acres of French vinifera vines, boasts Texas's largest underground wine cellar. It's filled with specialties such as the 2002 Viognier, an elegant wine with a hint of violets and peach, served at a dinner for Australia's prime minister at President Bush's Prairie Chapel Ranch, and the 2002 Cabernet Sauvignon Reserve, poured at a White House dinner.*

The newly expanded **George H. W. Bush Gallery** features the story of the Pacific War. One of the major exhibits is the HA-19, one of five Japanese two-man submarines. Interactive computer installations take visitors to the fall of Bataan, one of many displays the museum says makes a visit here a "high impact experience."

Finally, the outdoor **Plaza of the Presidents** features monuments to 10 presidents from FDR to the first President Bush, each of whom had a role in World War II. Open daily.

Pioneer Museum Complex. 325 West Main St.; (830) 990-8441; www.pioneermuseum .net. This collection of historic old buildings includes an 1849 pioneer log home and store, the old First Methodist Church, and a smokehouse and log cabin. Also on the premises you'll see a typical 19th-century "Sunday house." Built in Fredericksburg, Sunday houses catered to farmers who would travel long distances to do business in town, often staying the weekend. With the advent of the automobile, such accommodations became obsolete. Today the old Sunday houses scattered throughout the town are used as bed-and-breakfasts, shops, and even private residences. They are easy to identify by their small size and the fact that most have half-story outside staircases. Open Tues through Sat 10 a.m. to 5 p.m. Admission includes the Vereins Kirche Museum as well.

Vereins Kirche Museum. Marketplatz on Main Street, across from the courthouse; (830) 997-7832; www.pioneermuseum.net. You can't miss this attraction: It's housed in an exact replica of an octagonal structure erected in 1847. Back then the edifice was used as a church as well as a school, fort, meeting hall, and storehouse. The museum is sometimes called the Coffee Mill (or Die Kaffe-Muehle) Church because of its unusual shape. Exhibits here focus on Fredericksburg's German heritage, plus Indian artifacts from archaeological digs. Open Tues through Sat 10 a.m. to 5 p.m. You can purchase a ticket for the Vereins Kirche only or a combination ticket for admission to the Pioneer Museum Complex.

Wildseed Farms. Seven miles east of Fredericskburg on US 290; (800) 848-0078; www .wildseedfarms.com. This attraction holds the record as the largest family-owned wildflower seed farm in the United States. There's a self-guided walking tour through the colorful grounds as well as a market center featuring all types of gift items. Open daily 9:30 a.m. to 6 p.m. Free admission.

where to shop

Fredericksburg's many specialty shops offer antiques, linens, Texana, art, and collectibles. Most stores are housed in historic buildings along Main Street.

Charles Beckendorf Gallery. 105 North Adams St.; (800) 369-9004 or (830) 997-5955; www.beckendorf.com. This downtown gallery showcases the locally known work of artist Charles Beckendorf and is a good place to pick up prints of regional scenes, from one-room schoolhouses to brilliant fall landscapes. Open daily.

Fredericksburg Herb Farm. 405 Whitney St.; (800) 259-HERB or (830) 997-8615; www .fredericksburgherbfarm.com. These herb gardens produce everything from teas to potpourris, which are sold in the large gift shop Tour the grounds, then visit the shop for a look at the final product in the form of soaps, candles, and more. A bed-and-breakfast and a spa are also located on-site. Closed Mon.

Whistle Pik Galleries. 425 East Main St.; (800) 999-0820 or (830) 990-8151; www.whistle pik.com. This fine-arts gallery features bronzes, limited-edition prints, and original artwork. Special events throughout the year showcase artists in a variety of media. Open Mon through Sat 10 a.m. to 5:30 p.m.

where to eat

Altdorf German Biergarten and Restaurant. 301 West Main St.; (830) 997-7865; www.altdorfbiergarten-fbg.com. Take a break from shopping and enjoy some good German food in a traditional outdoor *biergarten*. Sandwiches, steaks, burgers, and Mexican food are served here as well. There's also dining in an adjacent stone building erected by the city's pioneers. The restaurant is open for lunch and dinner every day except Tues. $–$$.

August E's. 203 East San Antonio St.; (830) 997-1585; www.august-es.com. One of Fredericksburg's most sophisticated dining options, the Zagat-rated August E's features nouveau Texas cuisine in a relaxed setting offering both outdoor deck dining and a main dining room that was formerly a historic train depot. The restaurant is especially known for its dry-aged prime Angus steaks as well as its fresh, never frozen, seafood that is shipped in daily. Open Tues through Sun for dinner, Wed through Sat for lunch. $$$.

Ausländer Biergarten and Restaurant. 323 East Main St.; (830) 997-7714; www.the auslander.com. This popular German eatery has served up schnitzel, sausage, and suds for over two decades. Opt for indoor or outdoor dining with a selection that includes traditional bratwurst, Wiener schnitzel, Jager schnitzel, and even Texas schnitzel, topped with a spicy ranchero sauce. The beer garden features an extensive selection of beverages accompanied by live music. Open daily except Wed, 11 a.m. to 9 p.m. $$.

The Cabernet Grill—Texas Wine Country Restaurant. 2805 South TX 16; (830) 990-5734; www.cottonginlodging.com. Located just a few minutes south of downtown at the Cotton Gin Village, this restaurant offers elegant dining in a Texas-style environment. The restaurant is surrounded by historic cabins, each available for a bed-and-breakfast stay, as well as a waterfall and pond. Inside, the menu reflects Texas tastes, starting with Shiner Bock–battered onion rings and pecan-crusted crab cakes and continuing with entrees including grilled Bandera quail, Gulf shrimp ranchero, and many cuts of steak. Open for dinner Tues through Sat. $$$.

Fredericksburg Brewing Company. 245 East Main St.; (830) 997-1646; www.yourbrewery
.com. This downtown brewery is known for its ales and lagers but is equally notable for its
casual restaurant, housed in an 1890 building, which also includes a *biergarten*. Next door,
a "bed-and-brew" offers accommodations complete with a 4-brew tasting each night. Open
Mon and Thurs 11:30 a.m. to 9 p.m., Fri and Sat 11 a.m. to 10 p.m., and Sun 11:30 a.m.
to 7 p.m. $–$$.

Hill Top Cafe. US 87, 10 miles north of Fredericksburg; (830) 997-8922; www.hilltopcafe
.com. This local favorite is known not only for its Cajun and Greek food (especially Sunday
brunch), but also for its live music on Fri and Sat nights. Open Tues through Sun for lunch
and dinner. $$.

Peach Tree Tea Room. 210 South Adams St.; (830) 997-9527; www.peach-tree.com.
Enjoy a lunch of quiche, soup, or salad in this tearoom, whose name is synonymous with
Fredericksburg. This restaurant is extremely popular, so consider reserving a table, espe-
cially on weekends. After dining, save time for a look around the extensive gift shop. Open
for lunch daily. $.

where to stay

Fredericksburg is the capital city of Texas bed-and-breakfast inns, with accommodations
in everything from Sunday houses to local farmhouses to residences just off Main Street.
Several reservation services provide information on properties throughout the area.

Gastehaus Schmidt. 231 West Main St.; (830) 997-5612; www.fbglodging.com. This ser-
vice represents 100 bed-and-breakfast accommodations, including cottages, log cabins,
and a 125-year-old rock barn. $–$$$.

Hangar Hotel. 155 Airport (south of town); (830) 997-9990; www.hangarhotel.com. This
stylish hotel is perfect for airplane or history buffs. Built to look like a 1940s aircraft hangar,
the hotel is located right at the Fredericksburg airport; you can sit out on the balcony and
watch private planes come and go. The stylish touches continue in the rooms, down to
chairs covered in bomber-jacket leather. The hotel includes an "officer's club" bar and an
adjacent '40s-style diner. $$–$$$.

Magnolia House. 101 East Hackberry; (800) 880-4374 or (830) 997-0306; www.magnolia-
house.com. This historic bed-and-breakfast, constructed in 1923, offers guests a full breakfast. Offering 5 guest rooms, the inn is located 7 blocks from Main Street. Complimentary
high-speed Internet access available. $$–$$$.

Sunday House Inn and Suites. 501 East Main St.; (830) 997-4484; www.sundayhouseinn
andsuites.com. Located on the eastern edge of town, this modern facility includes a restaurant, pool, and cable TV. Guests receive free wireless Internet as well as daily continental
breakfast. $$–$$$.

especially for winter texans

If you're traveling by RV or trailer, spend some time at the 113-site **Lady Bird Johnson Municipal Park,** just southwest of Fredericksburg. Campsites have electrical, water, sewer, and cable TV hookups. There's a 14-day limit on camping from April through September. The park also has a self-guided nature trail. Pick up a checklist of birds or insects found in the region.

The park, located 3 miles south of Fredericksburg on TX 16, sports an 18-hole golf course, 6 tennis courts, and badminton and volleyball courts. There's also a 17-acre lake for fishing. For more information, call (830) 997-4202.

enchanted rock state natural area

Whether you're a climber or just looking for a good picnic spot, drive out to **Enchanted Rock State Natural Area** (830-685-3636; www.tpwd.state.tx.us). This natural area features the largest stone formation in the West. Nationally, this 640-acre granite outcropping takes second only to Georgia's Stone Mountain. According to Native American legend, the rock is haunted. Sometimes, as the rock cools at night, it makes a creaking sound, which probably accounts for the story.

People of all ages in reasonably good physical condition can enjoy a climb up **Enchanted Rock.** The walk takes about an hour, and hikers are rewarded with a magnificent view of the Hill Country. In warm weather (Apr through Oct), start your ascent early in the morning before the relentless sun turns the rock into a griddle.

Experienced climbers can scale the smaller formations adjacent to the main dome. These bare rocks are steep and dotted with boulders and crevices, and their ascent requires special equipment.

Picnic facilities and a primitive campground at the base of the rock round out the offerings here. No vehicular camping is permitted. Buy all your supplies in Fredericksburg; there are no concessions here. To prevent overcrowding, a limited number of visitors are allowed in the park during peak periods. (The busiest times are fall and spring.) Arrive early. Open daily, except when the park is closed for public hunts.

getting there

Enchanted Rock State Natural Area is located 18 miles north of Fredericksburg on RR 965.

northeast

day trip 01

old-world fun:
new braunfels, gruene

Fun abounds year-round along the track of this day trip, whether it be splashing in water parks and scenic Hill Country rivers, boot-scootin' at famous Gruene Hall, or soaking up German heritage at Wurstfest in New Braunfels.

new braunfels

If you're looking for a romantic getaway in a historic inn or a weekend of outdoor fun, New Braunfels is the place. Just half an hour northeast of San Antonio on I-35, this town of 52,000 offers something for every interest, from antiques and water sports to German culture.

In the 1840s a group of German businessmen bought some land in Texas, planning to parcel off the acreage to German immigrants. Led by Prince Carl of Germany's Solms-Braunfels region, the group came to Texas to check on their new purchase. They discovered that it was more than 300 miles from the Texas coast, far from supplies in San Antonio, and located in the midst of Comanche Indian territory. Prince Carl sent a letter warning other settlers not to come, but it was too late—almost 400 already had set sail for Texas. The prince saved the day by buying another parcel of land, this one in the central part of the state. Called "The Fountains" by the Indians, it offered plentiful springs and agricultural opportunities. The Germans soon divided the land into farms, irrigating with springwater. The settlement they founded was named New Braunfels in honor of their homeland.

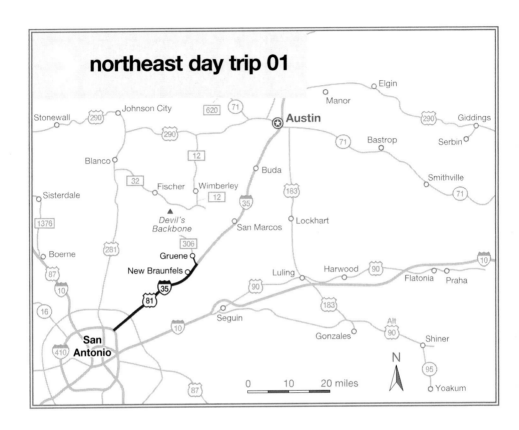

New Braunfels has never forgotten these ties to the old country. Even today German is spoken in many local homes. Every November the town puts on its lederhosen for Wurstfest, one of the largest German celebrations in the country. During these 10 days, you can polka the night away, listen to well-known yodelers and accordionists, or dine on schnitzel at this family-friendly festival. The entire community of New Braunfels is filled with activities during the Wurstfest weeks, with events that range from arts and crafts shows to boating regattas. The New Braunfels Conservation Society conducts several special tours of Conservation Plaza during weekends, touring restored German buildings including a general store, music studio, cabinet shop, and the Church Hill School.

The German settlers were a practical lot, and they saved old items of every description. Everything from handmade cradles to used bottles and jars were kept and passed down through generations. Eventually, many of those objects found their way into area antiques shops. Because of this, New Braunfels touts itself as the "Antique Capital of Texas."

The early settlers of New Braunfels also were attracted by the Comal and Guadalupe Rivers. Today swimmers, rafters, inner-tubers, and campers are drawn to these shady banks. The 2-mile-long Comal holds the distinction of being the world's shortest river. Its

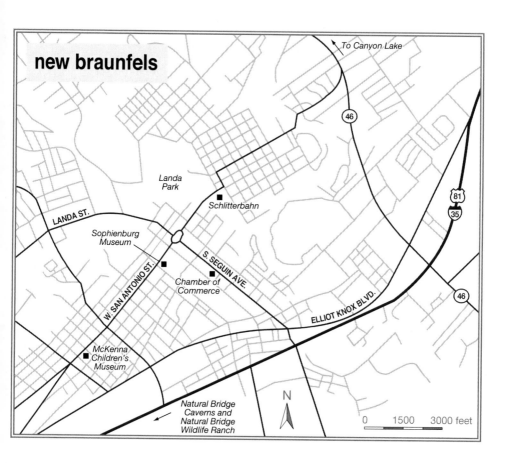

crystal-clear waters begin with the springs in downtown Landa Park, eventually merging with the Guadalupe River, home to many local outfitters. Located on the River Road scenic drive, the outfitters provide equipment and transportation for inner-tubers and rafters of all skill levels who like nothing better on a hot Texas day than to float down the cypress-shaded waters.

getting there

From San Antonio, head north on I-35 for 35 miles.

where to go

New Braunfels Chamber of Commerce. 390 South Seguin Ave.; (800) 572-2626; www .nbcham.org. Drop by for maps, brochures, shopping information, and friendly hometown advice about the area. Open daily.

Canyon Lake. FM 306, northwest of town; (800) 528-2104; www.canyonlakechamber
.com. With 80 miles of protected shoreline, Canyon Lake is very popular with campers,
bicyclists, scuba divers, and boaters. The lake has 7 parks with boat ramps and picnic
facilities.

Heritage Village–Museum of Texas Handmade Furniture. 1370 Church Hill Dr., in
Conservation Plaza; (830) 629-6504; www.nbheritagevillage.com. This 19th-century home
contains cedar, oak, and cypress furniture handcrafted by early German settlers. Open 1 to
4 p.m.; closed Mon from Feb through Nov.

Landa Park. Landa and San Antonio Streets; (830) 221-4350. Named for Joseph Landa,
New Braunfels' first millionaire, this downtown park includes a miniature train, a glass-
bottom boat cruise, a golf course, and a 1.5-acre spring-fed swimming pool. This is the
headwaters of the Comal River, where springs produce 8 million gallons of pure water every
hour. Picnicking is welcome in the park, but no camping. Free admission.

Lindheimer Home. 491 Comal Ave.; (830) 608-1512. Located on the banks of the Comal
River, this home belonged to Ferdinand Lindheimer, a botanist who lent his name to more
than 30 Texas plant species. Now restored, it contains early memorabilia from Lindheimer's
career as both botanist and newspaper publisher. A backyard garden is filled with examples
of his native flora discoveries. Open Tues through Fri 10 a.m. to 2:30 p.m., Sat and Sun 2
to 5 p.m., but hours are seasonal; call before you go.

McKenna Children's Museum. 801 West San Antonio St.; (830) 620-0939; www.nb
children.org. Bring the kids to enjoy hands-on fun at this interactive museum that features a
television studio. Open daily in summer, Tues through Sat the remainder of the year.

Natural Bridge Caverns. RR 3009, southwest of New Braunfels; (830) 651-6101; www
.naturalbridgecaverns.com. Named for the rock arch over the entrance, this cave is one
of the most spectacular in the area. The largest cave in central and southern Texas, it has
wide, well-lit trails, perfect for introducing young visitors to the beauties of this underground
world. Most visitors take the Discovery Tour; tours depart at least every 30 minutes and last
about 75 minutes. The tours take visitors through enormous rooms that look like the playing
fields of prehistoric dinosaurs, rooms with names like the Castle of the White Giants. And for
the most active members of your party, there are the Adventure Tours, for which guests are
outfitted in spelunking gear. These moderate-to-hard tours includes rappelling and crawling
through passageways to view rarely seen cave features such as a 14-foot "soda straw," one
of the largest such formations in North America. You'll need to make special reservations
for these tours. Open daily year-round; phone for tour times.

Natural Bridge Wildlife Ranch. 26515 Natural Bridge Caverns Rd., next to the caverns;
(830) 438-7400; www.wildliferanchtexas.com. From I-35 south of New Braunfels, take RR

wurstfest

*November's **Wurstfest** holds the title as one of the country's largest German celebrations, an event filled with plenty of old-world atmosphere. At family-friendly Wurstfest, a salute to sausage (not to mention plenty of suds and song), you can polka the night away, listen to well-known yodelers and accordionists, and dine on schnitzel.*

The entire community of New Braunfels is filled with activities during the Wurstfest weeks, with events that range from arts and crafts shows to boating regattas to organized walks, runs, and bike rides.

3009 west. From TX 46 west of town, you also can take a left on RR 1863 for a slightly longer but more scenic route.

For more than a century this property has operated as a family ranch, and since 1984 it has showcased exotic species, today holding the title as the oldest and most visited safari park in the state. More than 50 native, exotic, and endangered species roam the grounds. The ranch offers a drive past zebras, gazelles, antelopes, ostriches, and more. You'll be given animal feed when you arrive, so be prepared for the animals to come right up to the car for a treat. (And watch out, or the ostrich will put his head inside the car in search of that food!) A large cat run gives jaguars and cougars plenty of room to stroll, and another area houses 3 species of primates, scarlet macaws, and other exotic birds. A walking area holds some species that require a little more attention, such as reticulated giraffes, Bennett wallabies, and Patagonian cavies. Children love the petting zoo for the chance to get face to face with pint-size, friendly animals. Open daily.

River Road. This winding drive stretches northwest of the city for 18 miles from Loop 337 at the city limits to the Canyon Lake Dam. It's lined with river outfitters and beautiful spots where you can pull over and look at the rapids, which delight rafters, canoeists, and inner-tubers.

Rockin' R River Rides. 1405 Gruene Rd.; (800) 55-FLOAT or (830) 629-9999; www .rockinr.com. You can take a river ride here anytime between Mar and Oct. Excursions range from family tubing trips to white-water thrillers. This company also operates a campground, Camp Hueco Springs, on River Road.

Schlitterbahn Waterpark Resort New Braunfels. 305 West Austin St.; (830) 625-2351; www.schlitterbahn.com. From I-35 take the Boerne exit (Loop 337) to Common Street, then turn left and continue to Liberty Street. This water park ranks first in Texas and is tops in the United States among seasonal water parks. With 65 acres, over 40 rides, and 3 miles of tubing fun, it is the largest water theme park in the state. Schlitterbahn, which means "slippery road" in German, is also the largest tubing park in the world, with 9 tube chutes, 2 uphill water coasters, 17 water slides, 5 playgrounds, and more. The Comal River supplies 24,000 gallons a minute of cool springwater and also provides the only natural river rapids found in a water theme park.

Among the most colorful rides are the Soda Straws, huge Plexiglas-enclosed slides that take riders from the top of a 27-foot concrete soda glass to a pool below. There's the steep 60-foot Schlittercoaster, the mile-long Raging River tube chute, the 6-story Master Blaster uphill water coaster (voted "World's Best Waterpark Ride") for daredevils, and a 50,000-gallon hot tub with a swim-up bar and a gentle wave pool for the less adventurous. Plan to spend a whole day here, and bring a picnic if you like. Open May through Sept.

Sophienburg Museum. 401 West Coll St.; (830) 629-1572; www.sophienburg.com. For a look at the hardworking people who settled this rugged area, spend an hour or two at the Sophienburg. Named for the wife of settlement leader Prince Carl, the museum displays a reproduction of an early New Braunfels home, a doctor's office (complete with medical tools), a blacksmith's shop, and carriages used by early residents, along with other exhibits. Open Tues through Sat 10 a.m. to 4 p.m.

where to shop

Downtown Antique Mall. 209 West San Antonio St.; (830) 620-7233; www.thedowntown antiquemall.com. Located 1 block south of the town square, this spacious emporium has 12,000 square feet of antiques shopping. Housed in a restored historic building, over 40 dealers are represented, offering furniture, art, jewelry, books, Depression glass, and other collectibles. Open daily.

New Braunfels Marketplace. Exits 187 and 189 off I-35; (830) 620-6806; www.nbmarket place.com. What started out as a single factory store has become a destination for bus-loads of shoppers from Houston and Dallas. Goods from sportswear to books to leather goods are featured in the many shops. Open daily.

where to eat

Naegelin's Bakery. 129 South Seguin Ave.; (830) 625-5722; www.naegelins.com. Naege-lin's has operated on the same spot since 1868. The original building is gone now, replaced by the current structure in 1942. The store's specialty is apple strudel, a 2-foot-long creation that is certain to make any pastry lover's mouth water. During the holidays, some of Nae-gelin's best sellers are *springerle,* a licorice cookie, and *lebkucken,* a frosted gingerbread cookie. Open Mon through Sat. $.

New Braunfels Smokehouse. 1090 North Business 35, at TX 46 and US 81; (830) 625-2416; www.nbsmokehouse.com. If you get the chance to attend Wurstfest, you'll undoubtedly sample the product of this smokehouse. For this fall event, New Braunfels Smokehouse produces between 40,000 and 60,000 pounds of sausage. That sausage is the specialty of the house, but the restaurant has a little of everything, including smoked ham and barbecued brisket. A large gift shop up front offers Texas specialty foods and cookbooks. Open daily. $–$$.

Oma's Haus. 1248 FM 1101, Suite 200, 1 block east of I-35 on TX 46; (830) 625-3280; www.omashaus.com. This restaurant serves a wide selection of German dishes in a family atmosphere. The menu includes chicken and pork schnitzel, and a specialty of the house called Oma's Pride, a spinach-filled pastry shell. For the less adventurous, chicken-fried steak and chicken breast also are offered. Open for lunch and dinner daily. $$.

where to stay

New Braunfels has plenty of accommodations for everyone, including numerous chain motels along I-35. Check with the chamber of commerce at (800) 572-2626.

Faust Hotel. 240 South Seguin Ave.; (830) 625-7791; www.fausthotel.com. A New Braunfels tradition, this renovated 1929 4-story hotel features a bar that's popular with locals and visitors. The lobby is appointed with beautiful antique furnishings. $$.

Prince Solms Inn. 295 East San Antonio St.; (800) 625-9169 or (830) 625-9169; www .princesolmsinn.com. Built in 1900, this quiet bed-and-breakfast has 2 suites and a guest parlor downstairs; upstairs there are 8 guest rooms. All rooms are furnished with period antiques. $$$.

The Resort at Schlitterbahn. 305 West Austin St.; (830) 608-8520; www.schlitterbahn .com/resort. You can extend your visit to Schlitterbahn Waterpark with a stay at the resort, totaling nearly 240 guest rooms. You'll find apartments as well as motel rooms. The Schlitterbahn Unlimited Stay and Play Package includes a free water park ticket on the day you check in, with unlimited use of the water park until the day you check out for every registered guest staying on resort property. The package also offers extended access to popular attractions such as the Boogie Bahn surf ride and Master Blaster uphill water coaster before or after park hours. Also included are the use of resort-only pools and hot tubs, along with free Wi-Fi, on-site resort parking, and shuttle transportation to the parks. $$–$$$.

especially for winter texans

Heidelberg Lodges. 1020 North Houston Ave.; (830) 625-9967; www.heidelberglodges .com. Located near the headwaters of the Comal River, this scenic family resort is popular in the summer with swimmers, snorkelers, and scuba divers. During the off-season it's home to Winter Texans, who are welcomed with potluck dinners and get-togethers. Accommodations include A-frame cottages and motel units. Call for long-term winter rates. $$–$$$.

gruene

Although it has the feel of a separate community, Gruene actually sits within the northern New Braunfels city limits. Like Waxahachie and Refugio, the pronunciation of Gruene is one of those things that sets a real Texan apart. To sound like a local, just say "Green" when referring to this weekend destination.

In the days when cotton was king, Gruene was a roaring town on the banks of the Guadalupe River. Started in the 1870s by H. D. Gruene, the community featured a swinging dance hall and a cotton gin. Prosperity reigned until the boll weevil came to Texas, with the Great Depression right on its heels. Gruene's foreman hanged himself from the water tower, and H. D.'s plans for the town withered like the cotton in the fields. Gruene became a ghost town.

One hundred years after its founding, investors began restoring Gruene's historic buildings, and little by little businesses began moving into the once-deserted structures. Now Gruene is favored by antiques shoppers, barbecue and country music lovers, and those looking to step back into a simpler time. On weekdays you may find Gruene's streets quiet, but expect crowds every weekend.

Gruene is compact, with everything within easy walking distance. Park your car and enjoy a slow stroll along these historic streets as you do some shopping and dining.

getting there

In New Braunfels, exit I-35 on FM 306 and head west for 1.5 miles to Hunter Road. Turn left and continue to Gruene.

where to go

The Grapevine. 1612 Hunter Rd.; (830) 606-0093; www.grapevineingruene.com. This wine-tasting room specializes in Texas vintages. On most days, 20 different wines are available for tasting. In addition to wines, the tasting room also sells cheeses and crackers that can be enjoyed on the front porch or in the garden. On Thursday during the spring, fall, and summer, a certified wine specialist conducts free sessions. The Grapevine also often has live jazz. Open daily.

Gruene Hall. 1281 Gruene Rd.; (830) 606-1281; www.gruenehall.com. The oldest continuously operated dance hall in Texas is as lively today as it was when it was built in 1878. Dances and concerts are regularly held here (even though the hall still offers only natural air-conditioning), and it is also open to tour. Burlap bags draped from the ceiling dampen the sound, and 1930s advertisements decorate the walls. The hall opens at 11 a.m. most days. On weekdays there's usually no cover charge for evening performances; weekend cover charges vary with the performer. Call for a schedule of events.

Gospel Brunch with a Texas Twist. 1281 Gruene Rd.; (830) 606-1281; www.gruene hall.com. Gruene Hall hosts this event on the second Sunday of every month. Put your hands together and enjoy the sounds of gospel at this New Orleans–inspired event that includes brunch and, for an extra charge, libations. Seating is limited, so reservations are a must.

Gruene River Raft Company. 1404 Gruene Rd.; (888) 705-2800 or (830) 625-2800. See the Guadalupe at your own pace—during a leisurely inner-tube ride or on an exciting white-water raft journey—with this outfitter.

where to shop

Buck Pottery. 1296 Gruene Rd.; (830) 629-7975; www.buckpottery.com. Here you can watch crafters make pottery in the back room. This shop sells dinnerware, gift items, and outdoor pots, all made with unleaded glazes. Open Mon through Sat 10 a.m. to 6 p.m. and Sun 11 a.m. to 5 p.m.

Gruene Antique Company. 1607 Hunter Rd.; (830) 629-7781; www.grueneantiqueco .com. Built in 1904, this was once a mercantile store. Today it's divided into several vendor areas and filled with antiques. Open daily 10 a.m. to 9 p.m.

Gruene General Store. 1610 Hunter Rd.; (800) 974-8353 or (830) 629-6021; www.gruene generalstore.com. This shop brings back memories of small-town life during Gruene's heyday as a cotton center. It was the town's first mercantile store, built in 1878 to serve the families that worked on the cotton farms. It also served as a stagecoach stop and a post office. Today, instead of farm implements and dry goods, this general store sells cookbooks, fudge, and Texas-themed clothing. Belly up for a soda from the old-fashioned fountain and have a taste of homemade fudge.

Gruene Haus Country Store. 1297 Gruene Rd.; (830) 620-7454. Built in the 1880s, this shop was the former home of H. D. Gruene's foreman. Linens, lace runners, silk bluebon-nets, gifts for cat lovers, and decorative accessories are offered for sale. Open daily.

Gruene Market Days. 1700 block of Hunter Road; (830) 832-1721; www.gruenemarket days.com. More than 100 arts and crafts vendors sell their wares during Market Days, a time when this small burg swells with shoppers. The event is juried, and artisans are care-fully selected; all items sold are made by the vendors themselves. Look for everything from candles to metal art, furniture to crafts at this popular fair. Market Days are held February through November on the third Saturday and Sunday of the month, and a Christmas market takes place on the first weekend in December. Open 10 a.m. to 5 p.m.

Lone Star Texas Eclectic. 1613 Hunter Rd.; (830) 609-1613; www.lonestaringruene .com. Bring the cowboy look home with accessories from this shop. Lamps, dinnerware, and folk art are offered for sale. Open daily.

where to eat

The Gristmill River Restaurant and Bar. 1287 Gruene Rd.; (830) 625-0684; www.grist millrestaurant.com. Housed in the ruins of a century-old cotton gin, this restaurant serves chicken, chicken-fried steak, catfish, burgers, and other Texas favorites. You can eat inside or outside on the deck overlooking the Guadalupe River. Open daily. $$.

Huisache Grill & Wine Bar. 303 West San Antonio St.; (830) 620-9001; www.huisache .com. A longtime favorite with day-trippers looking for more than traditional Texas fare, the Huisache (pronounced "WEE-satch") offers everything from soups and salads to entrees in an elegantly comfortable, historic 1920s structure. Many dishes feature regional ingredients; try the ham and gouda sandwich with sweet caramelized onions for lunch, or pecan-dusted pork chops with apple brandy butter sauce for dinner. Open for lunch and dinner. $$–$$$.

where to stay

Gruene Mansion Inn. 1275 Gruene Rd.; (830) 629-2641; www.gruenemansioninn.com. Guests at this inn stay in restored 1870s cottages on a bluff overlooking the Guadalupe River. Eight lovely rooms are decorated with period antiques. A 2-night rental is required on weekends. $$$. No credit cards.

day trip 02

northeast

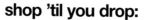

shop 'til you drop:
san marcos, buda

Bring your credit card on this day trip, as it leads to some of Texas's finest outlet shopping destinations. Ever-expanding outlet malls, featuring world-famous labels, line I-35 as you head north to San Marcos, drawing shoppers from both Texas and Mexico.

san marcos

Like neighboring New Braunfels, San Marcos is best known for its pure springwaters. The San Marcos River, which has been used by humans for more than 13,000 years, flows through town, providing the city with beautiful swimming and snorkeling spots and a family educational park.

Permanent settlement of the area began in 1845. Today San Marcos is a popular tourist town and the home of Texas State University (formerly Southwest Texas State University).

This community is a shopping stop for many travelers. San Marcos is home to the largest outlet malls in Texas, and they bring devoted shoppers by the busload from as far as Dallas, Houston, and Mexico. In fact, the malls rank as one of the top tourist attractions in Texas! These mega-shopping stops are located alongside I-35 at exit 200. Whether you're in search of clothing or china, children's toys or summer luggage, you'll find it at these Texas-size malls.

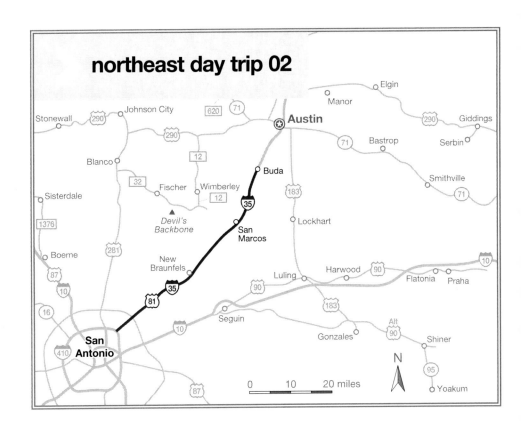

northeast day trip 02

getting there

San Marcos is located 51 miles north of San Antonio on I-35. You can head straight there on the interstate highway or take Northeast Day Trip 01 through New Braunfels and Gruene and then continue 16 miles from those communities to San Marcos.

where to go

Tourist Information Center. 617 I-35, on the northwest side of town; (888) 200-5620 or (512) 393-5930; www.toursanmarcos.com. Traveling from the north, take exit 204B (C. M. Allen Parkway); from the south, take exit 205. Stop here for brochures on area attractions and accommodations, as well as free maps. Open daily. Free admission.

Aquarena Center. 921 Aquarena Springs Dr.; (800) 999-9767 or (512) 245-7570; www .aquarena.txstate.edu. Take the Aquarena Springs exit from I-35 and follow signs west of the highway. This resort dates from 1928, when A. B. Rogers purchased 125 acres at the headwaters of the San Marcos River to create a grand hotel. He added glass-bottom boats to cruise Spring Lake, fed by more than 200 springs that produce 150 million gallons daily.

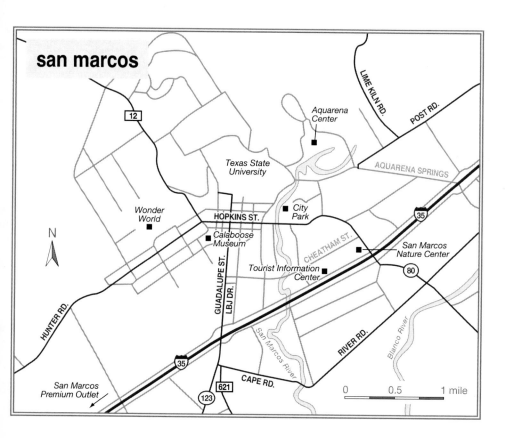

Pristine artesian water is home to many fish (including some white albino catfish) and various types of plant life. Today visitors can still enjoy a cruise on the glass-bottom boats and see the site of an underwater archaeological dig that unearthed the remains of Clovis Man, one of the hunter-gatherers who lived on the San Marcos River more than 13,000 years ago.

Formerly a family amusement park, today Aquarena Center, operated by Texas State University, focuses on ecotourism, with exhibits and activities aimed at introducing visitors of all ages to the natural history and natural attractions of this region. This family park features half-hour glass-bottom boat rides, an endangered-species exhibit, a wetlands boardwalk, and plenty of educational fun. The park offers special guided trips that focus on endangered species, archaeological sites, bird watching, and the flora and fauna of the area. Open daily, although hours change seasonally. Free admission; fee for boat rides.

The Calaboose Museum of African American History. 200 West Martin Luther King Dr.; (512) 353-0124. Housed in the 1873 building that served as Hays County's first jail, this museum preserves the history of the African Americans of San Marcos. Along with an extensive collection of books and artifacts, the museum also schedules frequent educational programs and public events. Open Sat afternoon and by appointment. Donation.

Centex Wing Museum. 1841 Airport Dr.; (512) 396-1943. Operated by the Central Texas Wing of the Commemorative Air Force, the museum is housed in a vintage wooden hangar at the San Marcos Municipal Airport. This collection contains World War II artifacts and several historic aircraft. A unique display is a replica of the CAF Japanese "Kate," built for the movie *Tora! Tora! Tora!* Open Mon, Wed, Fri, and Sat 9 a.m. to 4 p.m. Donation.

City Park. 170 Bobcat Dr. Concessioners here rent inner tubes so that you can float down the San Marcos Loop. The floating excursion, in 72-degree water, takes about an hour and a half. Snorkeling is popular here as well, and you might see a freshwater prawn (which can reach 12 inches in length), the rare San Marcos salamander, or one of 52 kinds of fish. Free admission.

John J. Stokes San Marcos River Park. From TX 80, turn right on River Road for about 1 mile, then turn left on County Road to the island where the park is located. Operated by the City of San Marcos, this day-use park is also known as Thompson's Island and is located across the river from the A. E. Wood State Fish Hatchery. The park offers river access but no facilities. Free admission.

LBJ Museum of San Marcos. 131 North Guadalupe St., across from the courthouse; (512) 353-3300; www.lbjmuseum.com. This museum showcases LBJ's educational ties to the region, from his years at Texas State University to his teaching days in Cotulla to the signing of the Education Bill. Open Thurs through Sat 10 a.m. to 5 p.m. Free admission.

San Marcos Nature Center. 430 Riverside Dr., next to the Tourist Information Center; (512) 393-8448; www.ci.san-marcos.tx.us. This nature center, located in Crook Park, is a cooperative program of the City of San Marcos and Texas State University. The center focuses on the San Marcos River Watershed ecosystem with both indoor and outdoor exhibits, including a Butterfly House. Open Tues through Sat 10 a.m. to 6 p.m. Free admission.

The Wittliff Collections at the Alkek Library. Albert B. Alkek Library, Texas State University; (512) 245-2313; www.thewittliffcollections.txstate.edu. Located on the 7th floor of the Albert B. Alkek Library, the Wittliff Collections include the Southwestern Writers Collection, which showcases the writers of the region and explores the impact the land made on their work. It includes over 100 writers, including J. Frank Dobie, Cormac McCarthy, and John Graves. Also featured is a music collection with items ranging from a handmade songbook created by an 11-year-old Willie Nelson to a fiddle played by Western Swing legend Bob Wills. The Lonesome Dove room includes every draft of Bill Wittliff's *Lonesome Dove* screenplay as well as costumes, props, and more from the television miniseries that starred Robert Duvall and Tommy Lee Jones. The Southwestern and Mexican Photography Collection traces the history of photography from the 19th century to the present in both Mexico and the southwestern United States. Open daily, but call ahead to verify hours and schedule changes due to the academic calendar. Free admission.

Wonder World. Exit at Wonder World Drive on the south side of San Marcos and follow signs for about a mile; (877) 492-4657 or (512) 392-3760 for group and tour reservations; www.wonderworldpark.com. A guided tour lasting nearly 2 hours covers the entire park, including the 7.5-acre **Texas Wildlife Park,** Texas's largest petting zoo. A miniature train chugs through the animal enclosure, stopping to allow riders to pet and feed white-tailed deer, wild turkeys, and many exotic species.

The next stop on the tour is **Wonder Cave,** created during a 3.5-minute earthquake 30 million years ago. The same earthquake produced the Balcones Fault, an 1,800-mile line separating the western Hill Country from the flat eastern farmland. Within the cave is the actual crack in the two land masses, with huge boulders lodged in the fissure. At the end of the cave tour, take the elevator ride to the top of the 110-foot Tejas Tower, which offers a spectacular view of the Balcones Fault and the contrasting terrain it produced.

The last stop is the **Anti-Gravity House,** a structure employing optical illusions and a slanted floor to create the feeling that you're leaning backward. In this house, water appears to run uphill, yet another illusion. Open daily; hours vary seasonally.

where to shop

Centerpoint Station. 3946 I-35 South at exit 200, south of San Marcos; (512) 392-1103; www.centerpointstation.com. This charming shop, built like an old-fashioned general store, is filled with Texas and country collectibles, T-shirts, gourmet gift foods, cookbooks, and more. Up front, a counter serves sandwiches, malts, and ice cream.

San Marcos Premium Outlet. 3939 I-35 South at exit 200, south of San Marcos; (512) 396-2200; www.premiumoutlets.com. This open-air mall features more than 140 shops that sell direct from the factory. Luggage, shoes, leather goods, outdoor gear, china, kitchen goods, and other specialties are offered for sale. Chartered buses from as far as Dallas and Houston stop here regularly. An expansion brought some of the beauty of Europe to San Marcos. Check out the gondoliers on the mall's Grand Canal as well as reproductions of some of Venice's most notable buildings, including the Doge's Palace and the Campanile. Open daily.

Tanger Factory Outlet Center. 4014 I-35 South at exit 200, south of San Marcos; (512) 396-7446; www.tangeroutlet.com. More than 100 shops feature name-brand designers and manufacturers in this open-air mall. Housewares, footwear, home furnishings, leather goods, perfumes, and books are offered. Open daily.

where to eat

Cool Mint Cafe. 415 Burleson St.; (512) 396-COOL; www.coolmintcafe.com. Located in a mint-tinted house, this restaurant focuses on wholesome food served in a 1920s Arts and Crafts–style setting. Fruits, vegetables, and herbs are sourced from Hill Country farmers, all used to prepare dishes such as grilled quail, stacked sweet potato enchiladas, and trout with buckwheat noodles. Open for lunch and dinner Tues through Sat and brunch on Sun; closed Mon. $$$.

where to stay

Crystal River Inn. 326 West Hopkins St.; (888) 396-3739 or (512) 396-3739; www.crystal riverinn.com. The Crystal River Inn offers visitors elegant Victorian accommodations in rooms named for Texas rivers. Owners Cathy and Mike Dillon provide guests with a selection of special packages, including tubing on the San Marcos River and a popular weekend murder mystery, where costumed guests work to solve a mystery using clues based on actual events in San Marcos history. $$–$$$.

buda

Buda is one of the most mispronounced communities in Texas (and with names like Gruene, Leakey, and Boerne around, that's saying a lot). To sound like a local, just say "b-YOU-da." The name has caused more than one foreign visitor to come here expecting an old-world Hungarian settlement. Though possibly a reference to Budapest, the name is more likely of Spanish origin. According to legend, several widows cooked in the local hotel restaurant that was popular with employees of the International–Great Northern Railroad. The Spanish word for "widow" is *viuda*. Since the *v* is pronounced as a *b* in Spanish, Buda may be a phonetic spelling for *viuda*.

Buda is still a railroad town, with double tracks running parallel to Main Street.

getting there

From San Marcos, it's an easy 15-minute drive north on I-35 to Buda, a former railroad town located on Loop 4 (Main Street) west of the highway.

where to shop

Many Buda stores are closed Mon through Wed, although some are open by appointment. Most shops are located in a 2-block stretch of Main Street.

Cabela's Buda. 15570 I-35; (512) 295-1100; www.cabelas.com. This Texas-size outdoors store is an attraction for everyone. The 185,000-square-foot store features a large freshwater aquarium as well as a "mountain" exhibit dotted with trophy animals of all types. The store also has an indoor archery range, a restaurant, live bait, and RV parking. Open daily.

day trip 03

northeast

capital fun:
austin

Maybe it's the college student population that tops 50,000 at just one of the city's universities. Maybe it's the live music industry that has made this city a haven for fans and performers alike. Or maybe it's just geography, with the city situated on a downtown lake and perched at the edge of a rambling Hill Country lake that offers everything from windsurfing to nude sunbathing.

Whatever the reason, there's one thing for certain: Austin is a town that doesn't want to grow up. Like a perpetual teenager, the capital of Texas is brash, sassy, and sometimes just downright silly. Sure, the city is home to both high-tech industry and countless state officials, but residents use any excuse to toss off the ties and three-piece suits. They don elaborate costumes for an annual party in Pease Park to celebrate (believe it or not) the birthday of Eeyore, the pal of Winnie the Pooh. But those costumes are just a dress rehearsal for the Halloween party that takes place on Sixth Street, mobbed by 20,000 to 70,000 merrymakers each year.

austin

Austin began in 1835 as a small village named Waterloo, settled by Jacob Harrell along the banks of Waller, Shoal, and Barton Creeks, tributaries of the Colorado River. At the time, the territory was the home of the Comanche and Tonkawa Indians and fell under the governance of Mexico.

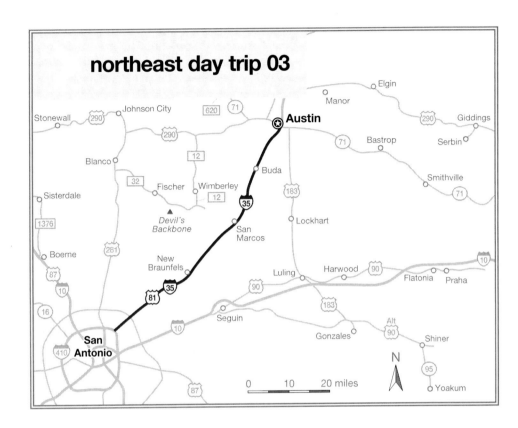

northeast day trip 03

As Harrell constructed a stockade for protection of the new settlement, the Texas War of Independence was under way. The next year, the Republic of Texas declared its independence from Mexico. Harrell's friend, Mirabeau B. Lamar, became vice president of the new nation and soon visited Waterloo on a buffalo hunt. The beauty and natural resources of Waterloo impressed Lamar.

Months after his visit, Lamar succeeded war hero General Sam Houston as president of the republic. As one of Lamar's first acts, Waterloo became the capital city, and its name was changed to Austin in honor of Stephen F. Austin, one of the first colonizers of Texas. The new capital did not meet the approval of Sam Houston, who thought the city was too close to Mexico and too far from the Gulf Coast to serve as the seat of the young nation's government.

The constant threat of attack by both Indians and Mexican troops caused concern in the new capital throughout Lamar's term of office. When Sam Houston was again elected president of the republic in 1841, he decided the government should be relocated to the security of his namesake city, Houston, and sent the Texas Rangers to obtain the state's papers.

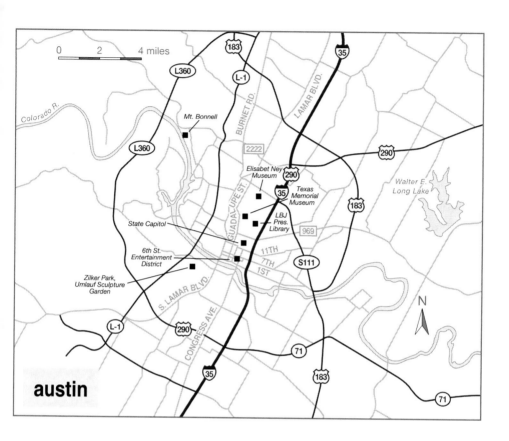

The residents of Austin quickly worked to stop the action in a move called the Archive Wars. The citizens captured the papers from the Texas Rangers and returned them to Austin, although for the next several years the government operated out of Houston. Austin eventually became the seat of government for the state as Texas joined the Union in 1845. Statewide referendums in 1850 and 1872 settled the matter.

Austin experienced steady growth, and in 1871 the railroad came to town. Soon the railroad hauled granite blocks from the western Hill Country community of Marble Falls to downtown Austin to construct a new state capitol, dedicated in 1888.

For years the city was plagued by flooding along the Colorado River. In 1938 the Lower Colorado River Authority began constructing a series of dams along the Texas length of the Colorado River, forming the chain of Highland Lakes, including Austin's Lady Bird Lake (formerly known as Town Lake) and Lake Austin.

Lake Austin begins at the foot of the Hill Country and flows for 22 miles through the western part of the city. Although high-priced residential structures are scattered along the shores, much of the countryside is still preserved in public parks. Lake Austin empties into Lady Bird Lake, a narrow stretch of water that slices through the center of downtown.

Beautifully planted greenbelts compose the shoreline, which includes 15 miles of hike and bike trails. Although swimming and motorboating are prohibited, visitors can rent canoes near the lakeside Hyatt Regency Austin Hotel. The calm waters of Lady Bird Lake draw collegiate rowing teams from around the country to train in the warm climate.

Attractions abound on both sides of the Colorado River, most just a few minutes off I-35. A bit north of the river and within five minutes of the interstate are the best two shows in town: the Texas Legislature and the University of Texas. The legislature meets in the State Capitol from January through May in odd-numbered years. Even when this body is not in session, you can take a free tour of the historic building and watch the hustle and bustle of state government.

From the capitol, it's a 10-minute walk north on Congress Avenue to Martin Luther King Boulevard and the southern edge of the University of Texas campus. This sprawling institution boasts students and faculty from around the world and some of the finest educational facilities in the country. The centerpiece of the university is the Main Tower, illuminated by orange lights whenever the University of Texas Longhorns win. The tower stands in the open mall, which includes the large Student Union building where students and the general public can grab a low-priced lunch.

Guadalupe (pronounced in Austin as "GWAD-a-loop") Street divides the educational campus from a commercial strip called the Drag, the stretch of Guadalupe that runs from Martin Luther King Boulevard to 26th Street. The area is always crowded and fun, filled with shops and eateries that cater to every student need. The People's Renaissance Market, just across the street from the Student Union, is an open-air bazaar where crafters sell their wares. It's especially popular with Austinites for Christmas shopping.

Most of the University of Texas grounds are closed to motorized traffic, but you can park at the LBJ Presidential Library and Museum, located on the north side of campus. Before touring the Presidential Library, walk to the fountain for an unparalleled view of both the university and downtown Austin.

As your day draws to a close, head back to Lady Bird Lake. During summer months people flock to the shoreline near the Ann W. Richards Congress Avenue Bridge at Lady Bird Lake to witness the nightly departure of Mexican free-tailed bats from the Bat Colony. Austin boasts the largest urban population of bats in the nation.

Finally, spend your evening on Sixth Street, Austin's entertainment district that runs from Congress Avenue east to I-35. It's lined with restaurants, bars, and clubs featuring nightly music performed by Austin musicians. Friday and Saturday evenings are crowded. Be forewarned: Many clubs don't crank up the music until the wee hours.

getting there

You can extend Northeast Day Trips 01 and 02, heading north of San Marcos on I-35 for 30 miles. If you drive directly from San Antonio on I-35, it's an 81-mile journey.

where to go

Visitor Information Center. 209 East Sixth St.; (512) 478-0098 or (866) GO-AUSTIN; www .austintexas.org. Stop here for tour tickets, bus routes, and dining and attractions informa- tion. Open weekdays 9 a.m. to 5 p.m., Sat and Sun 9:30 a.m. to 5:30. Free admission.

Austin Children's Museum. 201 Colorado St.; (512) 472-2499; www.austinkids.org. The museum has operated in Austin since 1983 but in 1997 moved to the 19,000-square-foot Dell Discovery Center, named for Austin computer mogul Michael Dell. Hands-on activities for educational fun fill the dynamic, multilevel facility. Infants and toddlers crawl through a Hill Country landscape, while older visitors measure wind speed, slide down a time tower, or experiment with audio technology in a sound studio. Open Tues, Thurs, Fri, and Sat 10 a.m. to 5 p.m.; Thurs 10 a.m. to 8 p.m.; and Sun noon to 5 p.m. Fee, but free on Sun 4 to 5 p.m.

Austin Museum of Art–Laguna Gloria. 3809 West 35th St.; (512) 458-8191; www.amoa .org. This Mediterranean-style villa, located on Lake Austin, was built in 1916. Today the elegant structure is home to a museum that hosts changing exhibits of 20th-century art. Open Tues and Wed noon to 4 p.m., Thurs through Sun 10 a.m. to 4 p.m.

Austin Nature and Science Center. 301 Nature Center Dr., west of Zilker Park; (512) 974-3888; www.ci.austin.tx.us/ansc. The Hill Country's smallest residents, from field mice to raccoons, are featured at this popular ecological stop. All animals here have been injured and can no longer live in the wild. Along with exhibits on local wildlife, the center sponsors special workshops and festivities such as Hummingbird Day and Safari Day. Open Mon through Sat 9 a.m. to 5 p.m. and Sun noon to 5 p.m.

Austin Overtures. Tickets sold at Visitor Information Center, 209 East Sixth St., or by phone, (512) 659-9478; or online at www.austinovertures.com. These sightseeing tours of Austin and the Hill Country depart daily. The Austin tour looks at the capital city in a 90-min- ute narrated tour following a 30-mile route past some of the city's many highlights. Riders can pair an Austin Overtures ticket with a Capital Metro bus ticket for a hop-on, hop-off experience. Reservations are recommended for these popular tours.

Austin Zoo & Animal Sanctuary. 10808 Rawhide Trail; (512) 288-1490; www.austinzoo .org. Bring along the kids to this privately owned zoo, located near Oak Hill, to enjoy pony rides, train rides, a petting zoo, and plenty of exotic creatures. Young visitors can purchase animal food to feed some of the inhabitants by hand. Open daily; hours vary seasonally.

Bat Colony. Congress Avenue Bridge at Lady Bird Lake; (512) 478-0098. Austin is well known as home of its seasonal visitors: 1.5 million Mexican free-tailed bats that reside under the Ann W. Richards Congress Avenue Bridge during the summer months. Crowds gather along the banks of Lady Bird Lake every night at sundown to watch the bats leave their perch to feast upon the insects of the Hill Country. The best viewing is from the hike and bike trail, the bridge, or a free bat-viewing area in the parking lot of the *Austin*

American-Statesman building at 305 South Congress Ave. The peak spectator months are July and August. For more on the bats, check out the information kiosks at the Four Seasons Hotel at 98 San Jacinto Blvd. and the *Austin American-Statesman* parking lot on the south shore. Free admission.

The Bob Bullock Texas State History Museum. 1800 North Congress Ave., at the intersection of Martin Luther King Boulevard; (888) 369-7108 or (512) 936-8746; www.the storyoftexas.com. A favorite stop with visitors to the nearby State Capitol, this expansive museum includes 3 floors of Texas-related exhibits and audiovisual shows. The museum offers many interactive exhibits on the history of Texas as well as an IMAX theater. The museum has a parking garage on the south side of the building on 18th Street, just off North Congress Avenue. Open Mon through Sat 9 a.m. to 6 p.m. and Sun noon to 6 p.m.

Capital Cruises. 208 Barton Springs Rd., at the Hyatt Regency boat dock; (512) 480-9264; www.capitalcruises.com. Enjoy a sightseeing excursion on Lady Bird Lake or, during the warm-weather bat season, a bat-watching cruise 30 minutes before sunset. Call for schedule.

Elisabet Ney Museum. 304 East 44th St.; (512) 458-2255; www.ci.austin.tx.us/elisabet ney. German immigrant Elisabet Ney was considered Texas's first sculptress, and this stone building served as her studio and home. It's filled with her statues, working drawings, and personal belongings. Ney's work also can be seen in the entrance of the State Capitol. Open Wed through Sun noon to 5 p.m. Free admission.

French Legation Museum. 802 San Marcos St.; (512) 472-8180; www.frenchlegation museum.org. Located in East Austin a few blocks from I-35, this unique museum is Austin's oldest remaining building. Its chief interest, however, lies in its role as the former French Legation during the years when Texas was an independent republic. Behind the home stands an authentic reproduction of an early Creole kitchen. Open Tues through Sun 1 to 5 p.m.

Governor's Mansion. 1010 Colorado St.; (512) 463-5516; www.txfgm.org. Texas governors had enjoyed the opulence of this grand home since 1856, but sadly it was severely damaged by a fire in 2008. Work is under way to restore the mansion to its former glory; at present, estimates are for the Governor's Mansion to reopen in 2012.

Hike and Bike Trails. Few metropolitan areas boast more fitness-conscious folks than Austin. Residents and visitors alike enjoy more than 50 miles of trails, including many popular and always busy trails around Lady Bird Lake. Download trail maps on the Parks and Recreation Department website at www.ci.austin.tx.us/parks/trails.htm.

Jourdan-Bachman Pioneer Farms Living History Park. 10621 Pioneer Farms Dr., northeast of town; (512) 837-1215; www.pioneerfarms.org. Here children can watch daily chores of the period being carried out with authentic tools. The farm hosts special events such as A Taste of Texas Past, with old-time cooking methods and recipes. Open Fri through Sun 10 a.m. to 5 p.m.

Lady Bird Johnson Wildflower Center. 4801 LaCrosse Ave. (take Loop 1 0.8 mile south of Slaughter Lane); (512) 292-4100; www.wildflower.org. This unique institution is the only one in the nation devoted to the conservation and promotion of native plants and flowers. The center was the dream of Lady Bird Johnson, wife of the late president. Mrs. Johnson was also responsible for the beautiful bluebonnet and wildflower plantings along the interstate highways in Texas. The center, located on a 279-acre site in an $8 million facility, includes a children's discovery room, gallery, gift shop, and the Wildflower Cafe. Visitors can take a self-guided educational tour of the grounds; groups of 10 or more may arrange for a guide. The center acts as an information clearinghouse, distributing numerous fact sheets on more than 100 native species. Annual events include landscaping seminars and workshops. The center is open Tues through Sat 9 a.m. to 5:30 p.m. and Sun noon to 5:30 p.m.

McKinney Falls State Park. Seven miles southeast of Austin on US 183; (512) 243-1643; www.tpwd.state.tx.us. This easily accessible, 744-acre state park is home to some low waterfalls that make it a favorite summertime getaway. The park also includes picnic facilities. Open daily.

Mount Bonnell. 3800 Mount Bonnell Rd. Climb up for a look across Lake Austin and the outlying Hill Country from atop one of the city's best lookouts. The view is located 1 mile past the west end of West 35th Street. Closes at 10 p.m. daily. Free admission.

O. Henry Home and Museum. 409 East Fifth St.; (512) 472-1903; www.ci.austin.tx.us/ohenry. The short-story writer O. Henry (aka William Sidney Porter) lived in Austin for several years and resided in this small home. Today the author's belongings are on display in furnished rooms. Open Wed through Sun noon to 5 p.m. Free admission.

Sixth Street. This entertainment district is one of the first introductions many visitors get to Austin, but it's just as popular with residents. Fri and Sat nights are often standing room only

live music capital of the world

Austin has earned its nickname thanks to the large number of live music venues scattered throughout the city. On any given night, about 100 venues ranging from concert halls to alternative bars to honky-tonks move to the sound of live music. The city has drawn many well-known names, who select Austin not just for performances, but for their home. Today Austin is home to the Dixie Chicks, Shawn Colvin, Willie Nelson, Asleep at the Wheel, Don Walser, and others.

in an entertainment district that's sometimes compared to New Orleans's Bourbon Street. Here blues rather than jazz is king, and it's found in little clubs such as Momo's, Maggie Mae's, and the 311 Club. They're all well received by music fans in this city that gave Janis Joplin her start years ago, as well as favorites such as Willie Nelson, Stevie Ray Vaughn, and the Fabulous Thunderbirds.

Texas Capitol Complex. The Texas Capitol Complex is the heart of downtown Austin. It's a sprawling mix of office buildings and shady green spaces. At the center of it all is the iconic capitol building itself, a favorite stop for Austin visitors.

Capitol Complex Visitor Center. 112 East 11th St.; (512) 305-8400; www.tspb .state.tx.us. Start your visit to the Texas State Capitol with a stop by the Capitol Visitor Center, located on the southeast corner of the grounds. Housed in the 1857 General Land Office, the oldest government office building in the state, this was once the workplace of short-story writer O. Henry. Today the restored building features exhibits on Texas history, and guided tours depart from here every half hour to tour the State Capitol. The center also includes a Texas Travel Center with information about statewide travel. Open Mon through Sat 9 a.m. to 5 p.m. and Sun noon to 5 p.m. Free admission.

Texas State Capitol. 11th Street and Congress Avenue; (512) 463-0063; www .capitol.state.tx.us. This restored building is truly a building of Texas-size proportions. Taller than its national counterpart, the pink granite structure is filled with history and legend. There are exhibits on the building and the state, and guided tours are available from the Capitol Complex Visitor Center. Visitors must pass through airport-like security measures. Open Mon through Fri 7 a.m. to 10 p.m. and weekends 9 a.m. to 8 p.m.; extended hours during the legislative session, held January through May in odd-numbered years. Free admission.

Texas State Library. 1201 Brazos St.; (512) 463-5480; www.tsl.state.tx.us. Located in the Lorenzo de Zavala Archives and Library Building just east of the State Capitol, this library contains both the state archives and the genealogical records of Texas. Parking is available in the Capitol Visitors Parking Garage located between 12th, 13th, Trinity, and San Jacinto Streets. Open Mon through Fri 8 a.m. to 5 p.m. Free admission.

Treaty Oak. 503 Baylor St. This 600-year-old oak captured the nation's attention in 1989 when it was poisoned. It was once called the finest example of a tree in North America. Today one-third of the original tree is gone.

Umlauf Sculpture Garden and Museum. 605 Robert E. Lee Rd.; (512) 445-5582; www .umlaufsculpture.org. Take a peaceful walk through this garden, featuring the works of Charles Umlauf, former professor emeritus at the University of Texas. Located off Barton

Springs Road, near Zilker Park, the garden displays about 60 sculptures, and the museum exhibits about an equal number of smaller pieces. A video provides a look at the life of the sculptor. Open Wed through Fri 10 a.m. to 4:30 p.m. and weekends 1 to 4:30 p.m.

The University of Texas at Austin. (512) 475-7348; www.utexas.edu. The University of Texas (best known simply as "UT") has the largest student population of any US university. Practically a city within a city, the campus includes several visitor attractions. Parking is at a premium in this area.

The Blanton Museum of Art. 200 East Martin Luther King Blvd.; (512) 471-7324; www.blantonmuseum.org. This museum is located on the southern boundary of UT and includes 17,000 works of art. It also holds the distinction of being the largest university-owned art museum in the United States. Paid parking is available in the Brazos Garage on Brazos Street and Martin Luther King Jr. Boulevard. Open Tues through Fri 10 a.m. to 5 p.m., Sat 11 a.m. to 5 p.m., and Sun 1 to 5 p.m. Fee, but free on Thurs.

Harry Ransom Center. Guadalupe and 21st Streets; (512) 471-8944; www.hrc .utexas.edu. Located on the UT campus, this research center is noted for its copy of the Gutenburg Bible, one of only 48 known to exist. The center also houses a collection of photographic and film materials, including the world's first photograph. Paid parking is available in the Dobie Center parking garage on the corner of 21st and Whitis. Open Tues, Wed, and Fri 10 a.m. to 5 p.m.; Thurs 10 a.m. to 7 p.m.; and weekends noon to 5 p.m. Free admission.

Lyndon Baines Johnson Library & Museum. 2313 Red River St. (from I-35, exit west at 26th Street); (512) 721-0200; www.lbjlibrary.org. Located on the east side of campus, this facility serves as a reminder of the Hill Country's most famous resident, Lyndon Baines Johnson. The library is filled with more than 35 million historic documents, housed in archival boxes and available for scholarly research. The first two floors offer films on Johnson's life and career, as well as exhibits featuring jeweled gifts from foreign dignitaries and simpler handmade tokens from appreciative Americans. Visitors also can take in special displays of political, civil rights, and educational memorabilia. The top floor holds a reproduction of LBJ's Oval Office, furnished as it was during his term. Free parking available in front of the museum. Open daily 9 a.m. to 5 p.m. Free admission.

Texas Natural Science Center. 2400 Trinity St.; (512) 471-1604; www.utexas .edu/tmm. This complex includes the Texas Memorial Museum, the Vertebrate Paleontology Laboratory, the Non-vertebrate Paleontology Laboratory, and the Texas Natural History Collections. Look for exhibits on everything Texan, from dinosaur bones found in the Lone Star State to historic displays on the Native Americans who lived on this land. Paid parking available at the San Jacinto (SJG) parking garage located at 2500 San Jacinto Blvd. just north of the museum. Open Mon through Thurs 10 a.m. to 5 p.m., Fri 9 a.m. to 4:45 p.m., Sat 10 a.m. to 4:45 p.m., and Sun 1 to 4:45 p.m. Free admission.

Wild Basin Wilderness Preserve. 805 North Loop 360; (512) 327-7622; www.wildbasin .org. This 227-acre preserve offers a good look at the natural side of the Hill Country. More than 2 miles of trails wind through the brush; there's also an easy access trail. Open Tues through Sun 9 a.m. to 4 p.m.

Zilker Park. 2100 Barton Springs Rd.; (512) 472-4914; www.ci.austin.tx.us. From I-35, take the Riverside Drive exit west and continue to Barton Springs Road. Follow Barton Springs Road to the park. Located just south of Lady Bird Lake, this 355-acre city park is a favorite with joggers, picnickers, swimmers, soccer teams, and kite flyers. One of almost 200 parks in Austin, Zilker is the largest and most popular of the well-used facilities. The park was originally the site of temporary Franciscan missions in 1730 and was later used as a gathering place by Native Americans. Today the park includes several distinct gardens, the city's most famous swimming hole, the Zilker Zephyr miniature train for the kids, dinosaur tracks, canoeing, hike and bike trails, picnicking, and a nature center. Hours vary by attraction so be sure to call ahead. Free; fee for pool and train.

Barton Springs Pool. 2101 Barton Springs Rd.; (512) 867-3080. This beautiful spring-fed pool tempts visitors to take a dip in the 68-degree, crystal-clear waters all year long. Open daily; hours vary seasonally.

Hartman Prehistoric Garden. 2220 Barton Springs Rd.; www.hartmanprehistoric garden.com. This 1.5-acre garden features ancient plants, including many rare and unusual species that evolved by the Cretaceous period, approximately 100 million years ago. The garden features replicas of original dinosaur tracks, 2 large dinosaur sculptures, limestone cliffs, and more. Open daily 7 a.m. to sunset. Free; fee for parking on weekends and holidays.

Splash! The Beverly S. Sheffield Education Center. 2201 Barton Springs Rd.; (512) 478-3170. This small nature museum, housed in the old Barton Spring Pool Bathhouse, focuses on the Edwards Aquifer, which supplies water to the adjacent Barton Springs Pool and all of Austin. Among the displays are a simulated limestone cave, small exhibits of local aquatic life such as the endangered Barton Springs salamander, and interactive exhibits. Open Tues through Sat 10 a.m. to 5 p.m. and Sun noon to 5 p.m. Free admission.

Zilker Botanical Garden. 2220 Barton Springs Rd.; (512) 477-8672. The Zilker Botanical Garden includes several distinct gardens, as well as a Swedish log cabin dating from the 1840s. A Xeriscape Demonstration Garden displays more than 50 native and low-water-use trees, shrubs, groundcovers, and wildflowers resistant to

Central Texas's hot summers. Nearby, the Cactus and Succulent Garden features mostly native West Texas cactus and succulents. The Isamu Taniguchi Oriental Garden is highlighted by blooming cherry trees from mid-March through mid-April, followed by blossoming water lilies into the fall months. The Mabel Davis Rose Garden features beds ranging from the latest All-America Rose Society award winners to the antique shrub roses of the Republic of Texas collection; peak blooming times are April to June and October. The Herb and Fragrance Garden contains dozens of culinary and fragrant plants among the raised beds. The Hamilton Parr Memorial Azalea Garden, in bloom during March and April, contains dazzling azalea beds surrounding a shaded flagstone patio. The Douglas Blachly Butterfly Trail showcases local flowers and plants that attract numerous species of Texas butterflies; visitors can view Austin's attractive butterflies and migrating species as well. Open daily 7 a.m. to 7 p.m. Mar to early Nov, 7 a.m. to 5:30 p.m. the rest of the year. Free admission.

where to shop

Bookpeople. 603 North Lamar Blvd.; (512) 472-5050; www.bookpeople.com. This mega-store spans 4 floors with more than 300,000 titles, 2,000 magazines and newspapers, and plenty of space just to hang out and browse. An espresso bar fills the first floor with the scent of fresh brew. Open daily 9 a.m. to 11 p.m.

Central Market Austin–North Lamar. 4001 North Lamar Blvd.; (512) 206-1000; www .centralmarket.com. More than just a grocery store, this market is the original Central Market and ranks as a top tourist destination in Austin, drawing 2 million guests a year. The store is an international smorgasbord of produce, wines, meats, fish, and seasonings from around the globe. Regularly scheduled cooking classes offer visitors the chance to learn techniques from the pros. Open daily 8 a.m. to 10 p.m.

Clarksville Pottery. 4001 North Lamar Blvd.; (512) 454-9079; www.clarksvillepottery .com. Shop for handmade stoneware from bowls and goblets to decorative ware at this fine crafts gallery. Open Mon through Sat 10 a.m. to 6:30 p.m. and Sun noon to 4 p.m.

Kerbey Lane and Jefferson Square. West 35th Street at Kerbey Lane. This shopping enclave is a favorite for those looking for unique gift items, collectibles, and fashions. Located off Austin's medical district, the shops line Kerbey Lane and the open-air Jefferson Square center. Most shops open Mon through Sat.

Renaissance Market. 23rd and Guadalupe Streets; no phone. Tucked right off the Drag in the University of Texas area, this open-air market is filled with the work of Austin artisans who sell handmade jewelry, woodcrafts, tie-dye shirts, glasswork, toys, pottery, and more one-of-a-kind items. This market claims to be Texas's only continuously operating open-air arts and crafts market. The number of artists varies by season, reaching a crescendo in the weeks before the holidays and a low point during the Christmas break, when UT students are few and far between. Open daily.

South Congress Avenue. Austin's best imports, antiques, and funky merchandise can be acquired on South Congress Avenue, just south of Lady Bird Lake. This eclectic district is definitely for those looking for something a little different, whether that means a mariachi costume or wood carvings, hand-carved furniture or 1970s disco polyester getups. Most shops open Mon through Sat and Sun afternoons.

where to eat

Chuy's. 1728 Barton Springs Rd.; (512) 474-4452; www.chuys.com. Chuy's takes great pride in being a restaurant that definitely fits into the "Keep Austin Weird" theme. With the name, you might expect Chinese food, but you'll get Tex-Mex in a funky decor featuring multitudes of those Elvis-on-black-velvet paintings. The food is great, but watch out for the spiciest dishes—they're ultra hot, even for seasoned Tex-Mex lovers. Open for lunch and dinner daily. $.

County Line on the Hill. 6500 West Bee Cave Rd.; (512) 327-1742; www.countyline .com. This popular barbecue eatery combines the menu fare of side-of-the-road joints with the elegance of a lakeside restaurant. Both indoor and outdoor tables are available; menu offerings include brisket, sausage, chicken, and more, accompanied by large side orders and homemade desserts. $$$.

Fonda San Miguel. 2330 West North Loop; (512) 459-4121; www.fondasanmiguel.com. Austin is home to many excellent Tex-Mex eateries, but this restaurant specializes in true Mexican cuisine, such as shrimp Veracruz and *pescado al mojo de ajo*. Open for dinner daily and brunch on Sun. $$$.

Green Pastures. 811 West Live Oak; (512) 444-4747; http://greenpasturesrestaurant .com. This South Austin eatery is a favorite for wedding receptions and power meals but also makes a romantic retreat. The restaurant is housed in a historic mansion and features continental fare. Open daily 11 a.m. to 2 p.m. and 6 to 10 p.m. $$$.

Hudson's on the Bend. 3509 RR 620 North; (512) 266-1369; www.hudsonsonthebend .com. This well-known eatery is a favorite for those looking for continental fare with a Texas twist. Dishes such as smoked quail are prepared with a gourmet touch. The restaurant itself, located near Lake Travis's Mansfield Dam, is housed in a stone home surrounded by gardens. Open Tues through Sun for dinner only. Reservations are suggested. $$$.

Hut's Hamburgers. 807 West Sixth St.; (512) 472-0693; www.hutsfrankandangies.com. This lively diner serves up some of Austin's most popular burgers, just as it has since 1939. Choose from more than 20 types of burgers, or enjoy chicken-fried steak, a salad, or the daily special. One of the specialties of the house is an order of Texas-size onion rings. Open for lunch and dinner daily. $.

Iron Works BBQ. 100 Red River St.; (512) 478-4855; www.ironworksbbq.com. This former foundry is still decorated with branding irons, and diners flock here to enjoy plates of juicy barbecue. If you have a big appetite, order the ribs. Open Mon through Sat for lunch and dinner. $–$$.

Jeffrey's. 1204 West Lynn; (512) 477-5584; www.jeffreysofaustin.com. One of the most noted Austin restaurants is Jeffrey's, known for its gourmet continental cuisine. The restaurant opened in 1975 when owners Ron and Peggy Weiss created a unique bistro celebrating the varied cuisines they enjoyed as they traveled the world. Since then, Jeffrey's has become a landmark for smart Austin dining. Their menus are seasonally-driven, offering a changing palate of nightly specials, delivered with impeccable service and flair. $$$.

Matt's El Rancho. 2613 South Lamar Blvd.; (512) 462-9333. This restaurant is a longtime Austin favorite offering up traditional Tex-Mex as well as Mexican dishes. Both indoor and outdoor seating are available. Open daily for dinner only. $$–$$$.

Scholz Garten. 1607 San Jacinto; (512) 474-1958; www.scholzgarten.net. Dine on burgers or chicken-fried steak in the beer garden of this restaurant that dates from 1866, making it the oldest restaurant and banquet facility in Texas. A popular hangout for legislative types. Open for lunch and dinner Mon through Sat. $–$$.

Threadgill's. 6416 North Lamar Blvd.; (512) 451-5440; www.threadgills.com. Janis Joplin used to sing in this restaurant back in the early '60s. Today the place, affectionately called "Old No. 1" since it was the first Threadgill's, is best known for its home-style cooking, including jumbo chicken-fried steaks, fried chicken, and vegetables like Grandma used to make. Open Mon through Sat 11 a.m. to 10 p.m. and Sun 10 a.m. to 9:30 p.m. $–$$.

Trudy's Texas Star. 409 West 30th St.; (512) 477-2935; www.trudys.com. This popular university-area restaurant feeds you Tex-Mex for breakfast, lunch, and dinner. The green chicken (meaning the sauce, not the chicken) enchiladas are the best in town. Open for dinner only Mon through Thurs and breakfast, lunch, and dinner Fri through Sun. $–$$.

where to stay

Barton Creek Resort and Spa. 8212 Barton Club Dr.; (866) 572-7369 or (512) 329-4000; www.bartoncreek.com. This luxurious resort is a favorite with golfers, offering 4 championship courses to satisfy even the most dedicated player. Other amenities include a driving range, a putting green, lighted tennis courts, both indoor and outdoor pools, and a spa. $$$.

The Driskill Hotel. 112 East Sixth St.; (800) 252-9367 or (512) 474-5911; www.driskillhotel .com. Built in 1886 by cattle baron Jesse Driskill, this is Austin's oldest hotel. Its 177 rooms and beautiful lobby recall an elegant age in the city's history. The hotel sits within easy walking distance of the State Capitol and the Sixth Street entertainment district. Two restaurants and bars offer food and refreshments to guests preferring to "stay in." $$$.

Four Seasons Hotel Austin. 98 San Jacinto Blvd.; (512) 478-4500; www.fourseasons.com/austin. Located on the northern edge of Lady Bird Lake, this hotel offers a southwestern atmosphere and a great view of the lake. The elegant hotel is a favorite with visiting celebrities. Its back terrace is very popular with Austinites during the summer months, affording patrons one of the best looks at the city's famed bat colony. $$$.

Holiday Inn Austin–Town Lake. 20 North I-35; (512) 472-8211; www.holidayinn.com. Day-trippers who want to extend their Austin excursion with a stay along Lady Bird Lake find this hotel relaxing and well located (although not as well suited for walkers as the lakefront properties farther west). Situated on the south banks of Lady Bird Lake just off I-35, the hotel includes a restaurant and bar as well as a pool. $$$.

Hyatt Regency Austin. 208 Barton Springs Rd.; (512) 477-1234; www.austin.hyatt.com. This 447-room hotel, located on the south bank of Lady Bird Lake, has a signature Hyatt lobby, with glass elevators, a flowing stream, and a beautiful view of the capital city. The hotel is within walking distance of SoCo, the trendy South Congress Avenue restaurant, shopping, and nightlife area. $$$.

Lake Austin Spa Resort. 1705 South Quinlan Park Rd.; (800) 847-5637 or (512) 372-7300; www.lakeaustin.com. Perched on a quiet shore of Lake Austin in the rolling hills, this resort is casual elegance at its best. You'll find plenty of activities here, from mountain biking to sculling on the lake's calm waters. Activity goes hand-in-hand with relaxation at the extensive spa that's earned this resort top ranking as the #1 destination spa in North America by the readers of *Condé Nast Traveler*. $$$.

Lakeway Resort and Spa. 101 Lakeway Dr. (18 miles west of Austin on FM 620, off TX 71 on Lake Travis); (800) 525-3939; www.lakewayresortandspa.com. This resort is a quiet getaway and a favorite with those looking for a weekend of spa pampering, boating, tennis, or golf. Rooms have private patios, many with great views of the lake. Amenities include 4 championship golf courses, indoor and outdoor tennis, sailing, water sports, and more. $$$.

east

day trip 01

east

>>> **pumpjacks & pioneers:**
seguin, luling

The history of south-central Texas—from its early pioneers to the oil boom that brought this state to the national spotlight—is the focus of this easy day trip from San Antonio. Although it all lies just off bustling I-10, the sights and attractions of this trip are a step back in time.

seguin

Located on the Guadalupe River, Seguin (pronounced "se-GEEN") is named for Lieutenant Colonel Juan Seguin, a hero of the Texas Revolution. Prior to the Mexican invasion of 1837, Seguin was ordered by his superiors to destroy San Antonio. He refused, thus saving the city.

Many towns boast nicknames, from Austin's "River City" to San Antonio's "Alamo City." Seguin, though, has one of the most unusual: "The Mother of Concrete Cities." A Seguin chemist held several concrete production patents, accounting for the use of the material in more than 90 area buildings by the end of the 19th century.

The most beautiful area of Seguin is Starcke Park. It offers picnic tables under huge pecan, oak, and cypress trees and a winding drive along the Guadalupe River. The tree Seguin is best known for is the pecan. The town even calls itself the home of the "World's Largest Pecan," a statue located on the courthouse lawn at Court Street.

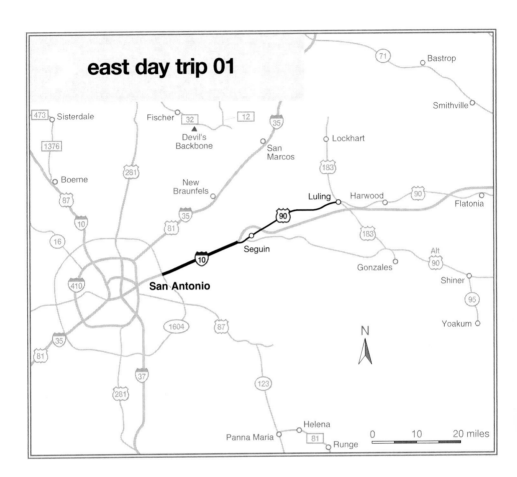

east day trip 01

getting there

You can reach Seguin via either US 90 or I-10 east of San Antonio. It's a 36-mile trip.

where to go

Tourist Information Center. 116 North Camp St.; (830) 379-6382; www.seguinchamber .com. Stop by the chamber office for brochures and maps. Open weekdays 8:30 a.m. to 5 p.m. and Sat 9 a.m. to 1 p.m. Free admission.

Heritage Museum. 114 North River St.; (830) 372-0309. This local-history museum is housed in a former grocery store. Exhibits trace the multicultural heritage of this city's early settlers. Open Tues through Fri noon to 5 p.m.

Los Nogales Museum. 415 South River St., just south of the courthouse; (830) 303-7333. The museum in Los Nogales, which means "the walnuts" in Spanish, houses local artifacts. The small brick adobe building was constructed in 1849. Next door, the Doll House is filled with period children's toys you can see through the windows. This white miniature home was built between 1908 and 1910 by local cabinetmaker Louis Dietz as a playhouse for his niece. Later he used it to promote his business. Open by appointment.

Pape's Pecan House and Nutcracker Museum. 101 South TX 123 Bypass; (830) 379-7442; www.papepecan.com. Along with processing and selling pecans, this location is home to a very unique little museum featuring over 3,000 nutcrackers from around the world. Pape's is also home to the world's largest mobile pecan. Yes, it's a pecan on wheels. Open 8 a.m. to 5 p.m. weekdays and 8 a.m. to noon Sat. Free admission.

Sebastopol House State Historical Park. 704 Zorn St.; (830) 379-4833; www.tpwd .state.tx.us. From I-35, take TX 123 South in San Marcos and follow Business 123 into Seguin. Turn right onto Court Street to 704 Zorn. This is one of the best examples of the early use of concrete in the Southwest. Sebastopol was once a large private home, constructed of concrete with a plaster overlay. Today it is open for tours and contains exhibits illustrating the construction of this historic building and its restoration in 1988. Open Fri through Sun 9 a.m. to 4 p.m.

Seguin's Lakes. Seguin is surrounded by four lakes on the Guadalupe River that offer bass, crappie, and catfish fishing, with lighted docks for night fishing. RV facilities are available as well. The lakes include **Lake Dunlap** (I-10 to TX 46 exit west of Seguin, then go 8 miles on TX 46); **Lake McQueeney** (I-10 to FM 78 exit, then go west 3 miles to FM 725, then turn right and continue for 1 mile); **Lake Placid** (I-10 to FM 464 exit, then stay on access road); and **Meadow Lake** (I-10 to TX 123 Bypass, then go south for 4 miles).

biggest small-town celebration

*Summer Seguin visitors should be ready for a red, white, and blue party known as the biggest small-town Fourth of July parade in Texas. The annual **Freedom Fiesta** has been drawing onlookers and participants since the early 1900s. Activities start in the morning with a patriotic parade, followed by food booths, arts and crafts, family entertainment, and kiddie rides for an old-fashioned street-fair atmosphere. In the evening, a street dance keeps the mood festive, as does a grand fireworks display in Max Starcke Park.*

Starcke Park. South side of town, off Austin Street; (830) 401-2480. Make time for this pleasant park, where visitors can enjoy golf, tennis, and baseball as well as many riverside picnic spots. Large water park open seasonally. Free admission.

> **Wave Pool.** Starcke Park East, south of downtown off Austin Street; (830) 401-2482. In this Texas-size pool, youngsters can cool off under the Mushroom Shower or splash in the simulated waves. Nearby, the sprawling Kids Kingdom Playscape makes another excellent stop for energetic young travelers. Open Tues through Sun, Memorial Day weekend through the end of Aug.

Texas Theatre. 427 North Austin St. This 1931 theater has been used for scenes in two movies: *Raggedy Man* and *The Great Waldo Pepper.* It still sports its original marquee and recalls the old days of small-town Texas theaters. The theater was recently restored by the Seguin Conservation Society for use as a cultural events center.

True Women Tours. Fans of Janice Woods Windle's *True Women* can take a guided tour of the sites mentioned in this best seller and seen in the television miniseries. Led by local docents, the tours take a look at sites that play an important role in the historical novel: the live-oak-shaded **King Cemetery,** the old **First Methodist Church** where two *True Women* characters were married, and the river bottom where horses were daringly rescued in the tale.

One of the most memorable stops is the **Bettie Moss King Home,** near the King Cemetery. The home, with its wraparound porch and shady lawn, saw generations of the King family and was also the childhood home of author Janice Woods Windle.

Call the Seguin Chamber of Commerce for tour times; a map for a self-guided drive is also available at the visitor center (116 North Camp St.). Fee for guided tour.

where to eat

Lola's Mexican Restaurant #2. 301 North Austin St.; (830) 386-0166. Housed in the downtown Aumont Building, Lola's prepares home-style Tex-Mex specialties like enchiladas, tacos, and menudo, with numerous daily specials. Open for breakfast and lunch Tues through Sun and dinner Fri and Sat. $–$$.

where to stay

Weinert House Bed and Breakfast. 1207 North Austin St.; (830) 372-4600; www.weinert houseseguin.com. Kick back and enjoy small-town life amid 1890s elegance in this historic Victorian home. Four guest quarters are decorated with period antiques. The Senator's Suite includes a fireplace and screened sunporch. $$.

luling

Luling is best known as an oil town. Oil was discovered here in 1922, and fields pumping this "black gold" can be seen throughout the Luling area. Even before that time the town had a reputation as "the toughest town in Texas," frequented by gunfighters such as John Wesley Hardin and Ben Thompson. Luling was also a cattle center and the end of a railroad line to Chihuahua, Mexico.

When oil was discovered, the economy of the town shifted to this profitable industry. Today dozens of oil wells pump within the city limits. As part of a beautification effort, the chamber of commerce commissioned an artist to transform several of the pump jacks into moving sculptures in the shapes of cartoon characters. There's even a Santa Claus and a butterfly to brighten up the streets.

getting there

From Seguin, continue east on I-10, or on US 90 for 21 miles to the community of Luling, located just north of I-10 at the intersection of US 183 and TX 80.

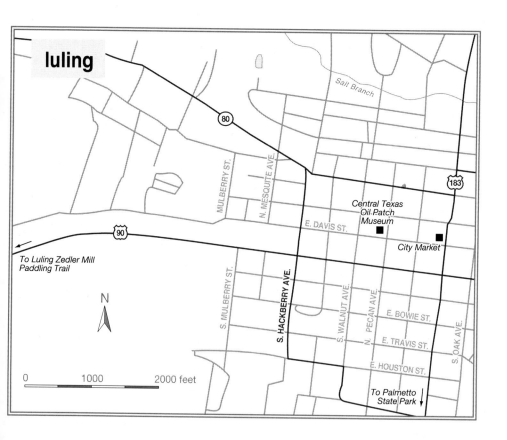

where to go

Central Texas Oil Patch Museum and Luling Area Chamber of Commerce Visitors' Center. 421 Davis St.; (830) 875-3214. Luling's oil businesses, starting with Rafael Rios No. 1 (an oil field 12 miles long and 2 miles wide), are explored in this museum. Open Mon through Fri 9 a.m. to 4 p.m. and Sat 10 a.m. to 4 p.m. Free admission.

Luling Zedler Mill Paddling Trail. Five miles west of Luling, where US 90 crosses the San Marcos River; www.tpwd.state.tx.us/fishboat/boat/paddlingtrails/inland/luling. In the 1870s both a gristmill and cotton mill were built at this site to harness the power of the San Marcos River. The cotton mill was destroyed by a flash flood, then rebuilt, only to become an electrical plant. This site became part of Texas's first paddling trail, operated by Texas Parks and Wildlife. You put into the river 6 miles upstream, then come out at Zedler Mill, located within city limits. (There's a dam beyond the mill, so be careful not to go beyond the mill.) Check the website for information on local canoe rentals, shuttles, and even GPS coordinates along the river.

Palmetto State Park. Six miles southeast of town on US 183, then southwest on PR 11 for 2 miles, along the banks of the San Marcos River; (830) 672-3266; www.tpwd.state .tx.us. Palmetto State Park is a topographical anomaly amid gently rolling farm and ranch land. According to scientists, the river shifted course thousands of years ago, leaving a huge deposit of silt. This sediment absorbed rain and groundwater, nurturing a marshy swamp estimated to be more than 18,000 years old. Now part of Palmetto State Park, the swamp is filled with palmettos as well as moss-draped trees, 4-foot-tall irises, and many bird species. Nature trails wind throughout the area.

The park has full hookups and tent sites. There's also picnicking. During the warmer months, bring along mosquito repellent. Open daily.

where to eat

City Market. 633 Davis St.; (830) 875-9019. This is small-town barbecue the way it ought to be: served up in a no-frills meat market, with ambience replaced by local atmosphere. You'll enter the restaurant through the dining room, then step in and place your order in a glassed-in room where the pits are working their smoky magic creating smoked brisket, sausage, and ribs. You can grab takeout or dine in the 2 large (and always full) dining rooms. $.

day trip 02

east

painted churches:
flatonia, praha, schulenburg,
dubina, ammannsville, hostyn,
high hill

The small German and Czech communities of this day trip are farming centers where the largest building in town is often a historic church. These places of worship are called collectively the Painted Churches of Texas, known for their elaborately painted interiors and faux details such as marbleized columns, all reminders of the homelands left behind.

The churches on this tour are open occasionally, but, if you drive by, it's worth a stop to see if you might be able to take a peek at the beautiful interiors. The Schulenburg Chamber of Commerce offers guided group tours with prior arrangement and also offers maps to the locations. You'll find more details about these churches in the PBS documentary *The Painted Churches of Texas* and on its accompanying website, www.klru.org/paintedchurches.

flatonia

This community was settled by English, German, Bohemian, and Czech immigrants, many of whom came to the United States in the 1850s and 1860s to avoid Austro-Hungarian oppression.

Flatonia hosts Market Days four times a year, featuring local merchants and artisans. Markets are held on the second Saturday in March, April, September, and October. Check the Flatonia Chamber of Commerce website at www.flatoniachamber.com.

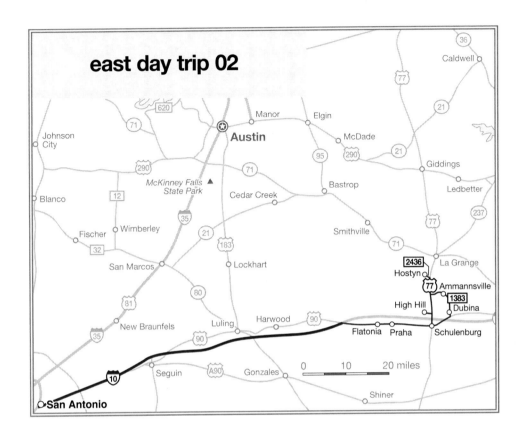

east day trip 02

getting there

From San Antonio, it's a 90-mile drive to Flatonia. Head east on I-10 past the cities of Seguin and Luling (see East Day Trip 01 for stops on this route) then take US 90 into Flatonia.

where to go

E. A. Arnim Archives and Museum. 101 Main St.; (512) 865-3920. This local-history museum contains exhibits on Flatonia's early days and its settlement by many cultural groups. Open the third Sat of the month Apr through Dec from 1 to 4 p.m. Free admission.

Flatonia Photo Pavilion. Intersection of Penn Street and Main Street. Flatonia holds a special place in the hearts of train buffs and is a favorite for rail lovers to watch trains. This elevated, open-air pavilion, located by the cross rails, provides a safe place for train viewing. Free admission.

Railroad Tower. Main Street, downtown; call (361) 865-3920 for tours. Train buffs can also enjoy a tour of the old Railroad Tower, one of the longest-standing switch towers in the state. The switch was manually operated until 1997, controlling the north–south, east–west cross rails.

praha

Praha (the Slovakian spelling for "Prague") is, like its European counterpart, home to a predominantly Czech population. Many of these residents are descendants of immigrants who came here in 1855.

getting there

From Flatonia, head east for 3 miles on US 90 to Praha.

where to go

Assumption of the Blessed Virgin Mary Church. Two miles east of US 90 on FM 1295; no phone. The main structure in Praha is the Assumption of the Blessed Virgin Mary Church, often simply called St. Mary's. Built in 1895, it is one of a half-dozen painted churches in the area. Although few examples remain today, painted churches were not unusual in the 19th century.

St. Mary's has a beautifully painted vaulted ceiling, the work of Swiss-born artist Gottfried Flury. Never retouched, the 1895 murals on the tongue-and-groove ceiling depict golden angels high over a pastoral setting.

This Praha church, as well as ones in Ammannsville and High Hill, are listed on the National Register of Historic Places. The churches are open Mon through Sat 8 a.m. to 5 p.m., although it is not guaranteed the doors will be unlocked at all times. Free admission.

schulenburg

The community of Schulenburg (meaning "school town" in German) has a long agricultural history. Carnation Milk Company's first plant was built here in 1929, and even today dairy products generate a major source of income for the area. Schulenburg is known as the "Home of the Painted Churches," although the elaborately painted structures are actually located in nearby small communities (Dubina, Ammannsville, Swiss Alp, High Hill, and Praha). These beautifully painted buildings are reminders of the area's rural traditions and ethnic background.

getting there

Continue east on US 90 for 9 miles from Praha to Schulenburg.

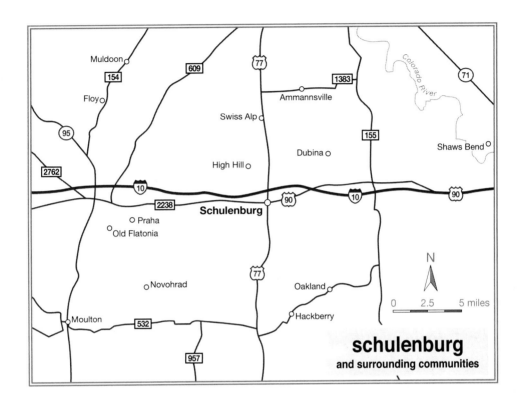

Muldoon
154
Floyo
95
2762
609
77
Swiss Alp
High Hill o
Ammannsville
1383
Dubina o
155
Shaws Bend o
Colorado River
71
10
2238
Schulenburg
90
10
90
O Praha
Old Flatonia
o Novohrad
77
Oakland
Moulton
532
Hackberry
957
N
0   2.5   5 miles

schulenburg
and surrounding communities

where to go

Painted Churches Tour. With a 2- to 3-week notice, the Schulenburg Chamber of Commerce (866-504-5294 or 409-743-4514) provides guides for groups of 10 or more. You
can always enjoy a self-guided tour; maps of the church locations are available from the
chamber at 618 North Main St. Fee for guided tour.

where to eat

Oakridge Smokehouse Restaurant. I-10 and TX 77; (800) 320-5766 or (979) 743-
3372; www.oakridge-smokehouse.com. Hungry I-10 travelers between San Antonio
and Houston know all about Oakridge Smokehouse. In business over half a century,
this family-owned company churns out barbecue and sausage to please travelers and
mail-order customers. The comfortable restaurant is popular with families, not just for its
extensive menu but also for its large gift shop up front. Open for breakfast, lunch, and
dinner daily. $–$$.

dubina

Nicknamed the "Mother of Czechs in Texas," Dubina holds the title as the first Czech settlement in the Lone Star State. Even its name—derived from the term for an oak grove—harkens back to its Czech roots.

getting there

From Schulenburg, head northeast on US 90 to the intersection with FM 1383. Turn north on FM 1383 and continue just over 2 miles to the community of Dubina.

where to go

Saints Cyril and Methodius Catholic Church. FM 1383; no phone. Built in 1909, this church is home to spectacular murals. Covered over during a 1952 remodel, the paintings were uncovered in 1981 and renovated by a local parishioner. The murals depict winged angels with elaborate stenciling. Mass is held here on Sat at 4 p.m. and Sun at 10:15 a.m.

ammannsville

Ammannsville was settled by both German and Czech immigrants in the 1870s, growing by 1900 to include multiple stores, blacksmiths, a physician's office, and two gins. Eventually the population of this agricultural community dwindled, however, and today only about 40 or so residents call Ammannsville home.

getting there

From Dubina, continue north on FM 1383, turning west as FM 1383 intersects with FM 1965 and continues as FM 1383.

where to go

St. John the Baptist Catholic Church. 7745 Mensik Rd.; (979) 743-3117. Built in 1918, this painted church has stained-glass windows illustrating the Czech history of the parish. Mass is held on Sat at 5 p.m. (in odd months), Sun at 9:30 a.m. (in even months), and Fri at 5 p.m.

hostyn

It's easy to see why this town was first named Bluff: It overlooks the Colorado River. Settled by Germans in the 1830s and joined by Czech settlers 20 years later, the name was later changed to Hostyn, after a Moravian city.

getting there

From Ammannsville, continue west on FM 1383 to the intersection with US 77, turning north to the intersection of FM 2436. Turn left on FM 2436 and continue 1 mile to the community of Hostyn.

where to go

Hostyn Grotto. FM 2436. This grotto, a replica of France's Grotto of Lourdes, was constructed in 1925 in thanks for the end of the 1924–25 drought. The grotto is located at the Holy Rosary Catholic Church; the grounds are also home to an adjoining cemetery. The cemetery is of interest not only for its Czech tombstones, but also for the graves of a father and son buried side by side—although they fought on opposing sides during the Civil War. Open during daylight hours.

high hill

This town was once a thriving community on a stagecoach line but, when bypassed by the railroad in 1874, the population began dwindling—but not before the construction of the Nativity of the Blessed Virgin Mary Church, also known as St. Mary's.

getting there

From Hostyn, return to US 77 and head south just over 5 miles to the intersection with FM 956. Turn right and head west on FM 956 for slightly more than a mile to the intersection with FM 2672. Turn left and drive south for 2.7 miles to the community of High Hill.

where to go

Nativity of the Blessed Virgin Mary Church. 2833 FM 2672; (979) 561-8455 or (979) 743-3117. This church was built in 1906 and painted 6 years later. The Gothic-style red-brick building designed by Texas architect Leo Dielmann is noted for its wooden columns painted to resemble marble, stained-glass windows, and religious statuary. The church also has a history of a European-style seating arrangement, with women on the left and men on the right. Mass is held Sat at 6:30 p.m. and Mon at 6 a.m.

day trip 03

east

suds & saddles:
gonzales, shiner, yoakum

This history-filled day trip offers a look at a historic battleground, one of Texas's most popular breweries, and one of the world's biggest leather producers.

gonzales

For many years Gonzales was the westernmost settlement in the state. In 1831 the Mexican government gave a small brass cannon to Gonzales's citizens, as protection from constant Indian attacks. Four years later, when relations between Texas and Mexico soured, more than 150 Mexican soldiers staged a battle to retrieve the weapon. The soldiers were faced with 18 Gonzaleans, who stalled the army while local citizens rolled out the small fieldpiece and prepared for action. Meanwhile, other townsfolk sewed the first battle flag of Texas, which pictured a cannon beneath the words "Come and Take It," a motto by which Gonzales is still known. The Texans fired the first shot, and the Mexican troops retreated. Although the confrontation was brief, this act began the Texas Revolution.

The site of this historic first conflict is marked by a monument located 7 miles southwest of Gonzales on TX 97. The first shots were fired a half mile north of the present monument.

Today Gonzales is a quiet town, with most activity taking place around its dual squares: Heroes Plaza and Confederate Plaza.

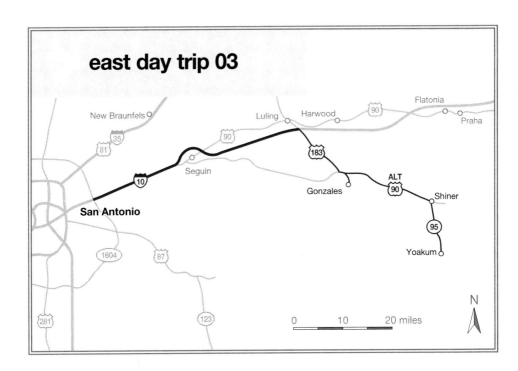

east day trip 03

getting there

From San Antonio, take I-10 East for 57 miles, then take exit 632 for US 183 South. Continue on US 183 South for 14 miles.

where to go

Gonzales Chamber of Commerce. 414 St. Lawrence St.; (888) 672-1095 or (830) 672-6532; www.gonzalestexas.com. Located in the Old Jail Museum, this office has brochures on local attractions and events. Open weekdays.

Gonzales Pioneer Village Living History Center. 2122 Joseph St., 0.5 mile north of town on US 183; (830) 672-2157; www.thepioneervillage.com. This center takes visitors back to Gonzales's frontier days. The village is composed of log cabins, a cypress-constructed house, a grand Victorian house, a smokehouse, a blacksmith shop, and a church. The village also stages reenactments, including the "Come and Take It" celebration in late September or early October. Open Tues through Fri 1 to 4 p.m., Sat 10 a.m. to 4 p.m., and Sun 1 to 5 p.m.; group tours by appointment.

Memorial Museum. 414 Smith St., between St. Lawrence and St. Louis Streets; (830) 672-6350. This museum is dedicated to the history of Gonzales. Exhibits on the town's early days include the "Come and Take It" cannon. Open Tues through Sat 10 a.m. to 5 p.m. (closed noon to 1 p.m.) and Sun 1 to 5 p.m. Free admission.

Old Jail Museum. 414 St. Lawrence St.; (830) 672-6532 (chamber of commerce); www .cityofgonzales.org. This unusual museum is housed in the old Gonzales jail, built in 1887 and used until 1975. Downstairs you can tour the room where female prisoners and men- tally ill persons once were incarcerated together. Exhibits include jail weapons created from spoons and bedsprings.

The walls of the second floor are chiseled with graffiti of past residents. The large room is rimmed with iron cells, all overlooking a reproduction of the old gallows that carried off its last hanging in 1921. According to legend, the prisoner continually watched the clocks on the adjacent courthouse, counting the hours he had left to live. He swore that he was innocent and said that if he were hanged the clocks would never keep accurate time again. Although the four clock faces have been changed since that time, none of them has ever kept the same time again. Open Mon through Fri 8 a.m. to 5 p.m., Sat 9 a.m. to 4 p.m., and Sun 1 to 4 p.m. Free admission.

where to shop

Discovery Architectural Antiques. 409 St. Francis St.; (830) 672-2428; www.discoverys .net. This truly Texas-size shop specializes in architectural antiques, salvaged doors, floor- ing, beams, stained glass, and much (much) more. With over a million items in stock at any given time, the store is actually five warehouses with items that have been salvaged from historic homes. Open Tues through Sat 9 a.m. to 5 p.m.

where to eat

Gonzales Food Market. 311 St. Lawrence St.; (800) 269-5342; www.gonzalesfoodmarket .com. What began in 1959 as a small, family-owned grocery store with a meat market is still owned by the same family—but without the groceries. Today shopping at the Gonzales Food Market means choosing among brisket, sausage, lamb ribs, beef ribs, chicken, and more, all prepared in pits on-site. You can dine in the adjoining dining room or take out. Open Mon through Sat. $.

shiner

Best known as the home of Shiner Beer, a Texas favorite produced by the tiny Spoetzl Brewery since 1909, this charming community is a quiet getaway, except during festival weekends.

getting there

Continue east from Gonzales on US 90A for 18 miles to Shiner.

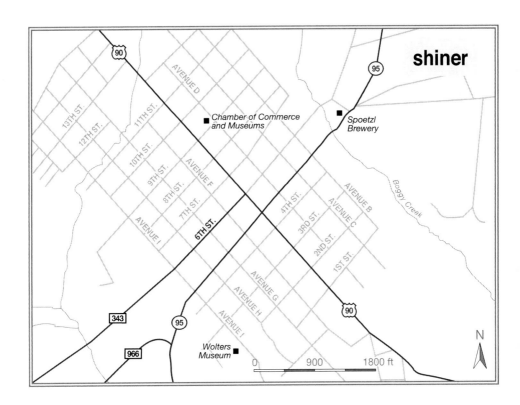

where to go

Shiner Chamber of Commerce. 817 North Avenue East; (361) 594-4180; www.shinertx
.com. Located in the historic Cigar Factory, the chamber offers brochures and maps to area
attractions. Open Mon through Fri 8:30 a.m. to 4:30 p.m. Free admission.

Cigar Factory and Green Cabin Museums. 817 North Avenue East; (361) 594-4180;
www.shinertx.com. This museum complex (including one building occupied by the chamber
of commerce) was originally the Louis Ehlers Cigar Factory. The factory, which began in
1895, once produced three types of cigars. Also at the site is the William Green Jr. Cabin, a
pioneer cabin that later served as a post office and a general store. Open Mon through Fri
8:30 a.m. to 4:30 p.m. Free admission.

Edwin Wolters Memorial Museum. 306 South Avenue I, off TX 95 South; (361) 594-
3774. This museum is filled with home implements, weapons, fossils, and even a country
store representing the community's early days. Open Mon through Fri 8 a.m. to 5 p.m. and
every second and fourth Sun 2 to 5 p.m. Free admission.

Spoetzl Brewery. 603 Brewery St., off TX 95 North; (361) 594-3383; www.shiner.com. This tiny but historic brewery was founded in 1909 by Kosmos Spoetzl, a Bavarian brewmaster. Here several Shiner beers are produced in one of the smallest commercial brew kettles in the country. Across the street, a museum and gift shop overflow with Shiner memorabilia, antiques, and photos of Spoetzl's early days. Free brewery tours on weekdays at 11 a.m. and 1:30 p.m. (additional tours at 10 a.m. and 2:30 p.m. during the summer months). Hospitality room open following tour. Gift shop open weekdays 9 a.m. to 5 p.m. and Sat 11 a.m. to 3 p.m. Free admission.

where to eat

Shiner Restaurant & Bar. 103 East Seventh St.; (361) 594-2898; www.shinerrestaurant .com. Located in the historic downtown, this elegant restaurant features everything from flame-grilled burgers to shrimp penne with pecan pesto—all accompanied, of course, by Shiner Beer if you like. Open for lunch and dinner Thurs through Sat 11 a.m. to 11 p.m. $$.

where to stay

The Old Kasper House. 219 Avenue C; (361) 594-4336; www.oldkasperhouse.com. This bed-and-breakfast is located in the former home of cotton ginner John F. Kasper and his wife, Mary. Today the 2-story Victorian home is a great small-town getaway, offering rooms with private baths. Nearby, other options include the Honeymoon Cottage, Czech Me Inn, Marenka's Cottage, and the Derrich Domov Inn, each with its own living and dining areas. All bedrooms have a private bath. $–$$.

yoakum

Yoakum was the starting point of many cattle drives along the Chisholm Trail, and in 1887 it became the junction for the San Antonio and Aransas Pass Railroad. When the railroad came to town, meat packinghouses followed. In 1919 the first tannery opened, producing leather knee pads for cotton pickers. Soon more leather businesses arrived, and eventually Yoakum earned its title as the "Leather Capital of the World." Today several leather companies produce belts, saddles, bullwhips, gun slings, and wallets.

getting there

From Shiner, drive south on TX 95 for 8 miles to US 77A. Turn right and continue for 2 miles.

where to go

Bird Sanctuary. Located at the water treatment plant just south of Yoakum on US 77A; (361) 293-2309 (Chamber of Commerce). Spanning 15 acres, this sanctuary is home to birds (50 species have been identified here) and wildflowers. You'll find a 0.3-mile trail at this site, which features everything from prairie to pecan groves to the banks of Brushy Creek. Free admission.

Yoakum Heritage Museum. 312 Simpson St.; (512) 293-7022. This 2-story museum, built as an antebellum home in the early 1900s, is filled with Yoakum memorabilia, from railroad paraphernalia to household items. The most interesting exhibit area is the Leather Room, with its displays on the leather factories. Open Tues, Thurs, and Fri 1 to 4 p.m. and Sun 2 to 4 p.m. Free admission.

Return home from Yoakum by retracing your route or by heading north on TX 95 to Flatonia. To continue on from here, go west on either I-10 or US 90. Attractions on this stretch are covered in East Day Trip 01.

day trip 04

east

lost pines:
lockhart, cedar creek, bastrop, smithville, la grange

One of Texas's natural anomalies, the Lost Pines forest is the westernmost stand of loblolly pines in America. Scientists believe that these trees were once part of the forests of East Texas, but climatic changes over the last 10,000 years account for the farmland now separating the Lost Pines from their cousins to the east.

lockhart

Lockhart is a conglomeration of the stuff of Texas legends: Indian battles, cattle drives, barbecue, cotton, and oil. This small town, located 23 miles south of Austin on US 183, contains a state park and lots of history.

The biggest event in Lockhart's past was the Battle of Plum Creek in 1840. More than 600 Comanches raided the community of Linnville and were on their way home when they passed through this area. A group of settlers joined forces with the Tonkowa Indians to attack the Comanches, driving the Indians farther west and ending the Indian attacks in the region. This battle is reenacted every May at the Chisholm Trail Roundup.

Lockhart is also well known as the home of Mebane cotton. Developed by A. D. Mebane, this strain is resistant to the boll weevil, an insect that can demolish not only whole fields, but entire economies as well.

But Lockhart's real claim to fame is its barbecue. Declared the "Barbecue Capital of Texas" by both the Texas House of Representatives and the Texas Senate, this community

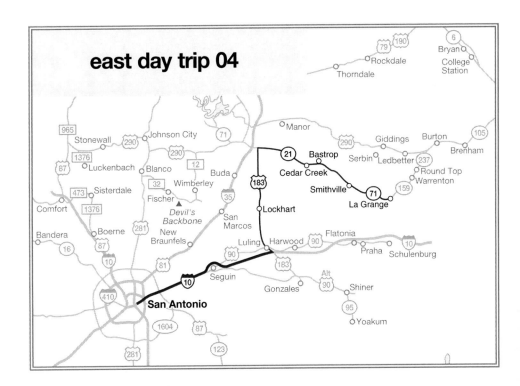

east day trip 04

is home to four of the best barbecue restaurants in a state that's known for its barbecue. The City of Lockhart estimates that approximately 250,000 people a year eat barbecue at this town's 'que restaurants.

getting there

From San Antonio, take I-10 east for 53 miles to US 183 near Luling, then continue on US 183 north for 15 miles to reach Lockhart.

where to go

Caldwell County Museum. 315 East Market St.; no phone. You can't miss this old building—just look for the 5-story redbrick castle. Built in 1908 as the county jail, this imposing structure was designed with Norman-style castellations, giving it almost a fairy tale look. Today the building, which houses items detailing the settlement and history of the region, is operated by the Caldwell County Historical Commission and is open to the public Sat and Sun 1 to 5 p.m.

Dr. Eugene Clark Library. 217 South Main St.; (512) 398-3223; www.lockhart-tx.org/web98/history/dreugeneclarklibrary.asp. Built in 1889, this is the oldest continuously operating library in Texas. Modeled after the Villa Rotunda in Vicenza, Italy, it has stained-glass windows, ornate fixtures, and a stage where President William Taft once spoke. Open daily. Free admission.

Lockhart State Park. (512) 398-3479; www.tpwd.state.tx.us. Go 1 mile south of Lockhart on US 183 to FM 20, then head southwest for 2 miles to PR 10 and continue 1 mile south. This 263-acre park has a 9-hole golf course, the only staff-operated course in the Texas State Park system. You'll also find fishing on Plum Creek, picnic areas, a swimming pool, and campsites for both tents and trailers. Many of the facilities were built by the Civilian Conservation Corps in the 1930s. Open daily.

where to shop

Texas Hatters. 911 South Commerce St. (US 183); (512) 398-4287 or (800) 421-4287; www.texashatters.com. This store's founder, the late Manny Gammage, was "Texas's Hatmaker to the Stars." His hats topped the heads of Roy Rogers, Willie Nelson, Ronald Reagan, Burt Reynolds, and many other celebrities whose pictures decorate the shop walls. Besides the obligatory cowboy hats, this store also sells hand-blocked high-rollers, Panamas, and derbies. Open Tues through Sat 9:30 a.m. to 5:30 p.m.

where to eat

Black's Barbecue. 215 North Main St.; (512) 398-2712; www.blacksbbq.com. This cafeteria-style restaurant is reputedly the oldest barbecue joint in Texas under the same ownership, owned by the Black family since 1932. Beef brisket is the specialty of the house,

lockhart meets hollywood

While its reputation as the Barbecue Capital of Texas has made Lockhart legendary among foodies, its historical architecture and small-town charm has secured this Hill Country community a place in Hollywood history. The Muldoon blue sandstone facade of the Caldwell County Courthouse played a starring role alongside Johnny Depp in a scene from the 1993 drama What's Eating Gilbert Grape? *and the 19th-century structure also appears in the cult comedy favorite* Waiting for Guffman. *Locals filled the bleachers at the high school football field in 1998 for the sci-fi flick* The Faculty, *and residents shop in the same aisles of the Wal-Mart that actress Natalie Portman wandered in 2000 when she filmed the screen adaptation of the best-selling novel* Where the Heart Is.

along with sausage, ribs, chicken, and ham. There's also a fully stocked salad bar. Open Sun through Thurs 10 a.m. to 8 p.m., Fri and Sat 10 a.m. to 8:30 p.m. $–$$.

Chisholm Trail Bar-B-Que. 1323 South Colorado St. (US 193); (512) 398-6027; www .chisholmtrailbbq.com. Opening a barbecue restaurant in Lockhart—home of some of Texas's oldest and most lauded barbecue joints—takes a lot of confidence, but in 1978 Chisholm Trail opened its doors, and they've been busy ever since. This cafeteria-style restaurant serves lots of brisket, sausage, and ribs, but you'll also find fried catfish on Mon, Wed, and Fri. Open daily 8 a.m. to 8 p.m. $–$$.

Kreuz Market. 619 North Colorado St.; (512) 398-2361; www.kreuzmarket.com. Vegetarians, head elsewhere. Kreuz (pronounced "Krites") Market is a meat-intensive kind of place, offering spicy sausage, pork loin, prime rib, and pork ribs, with a few side dishes such as German potatoes and sauerkraut. Open Mon through Sat 10:30 a.m. to 8 p.m. $.

Smitty's Market. 208 South Commerce St.; (512) 398-9344; www.smittysmarket.com. Since 1900 this store was part of Kreuz Market, the no-frills barbecue joint and Texas legend. "Smitty" Schmidt bought the restaurant from its original owner in 1948 and devised the huge pit system for barbecuing. The smokehouse was run first by Schmidt, then by his two sons until 1999, when the family divided the business: Sister Nina Schmidt Sells took the building and brother Rick took the name, moving it to a newer building that houses Kreuz Market. Today the original brick building is home to Smitty's Market, which still operates much as the original did. The specials include brisket, pork chops, and sausage, with ribs on the weekend. Side dishes are also sold here, including potato salad, coleslaw, and beans. Open weekdays 7 a.m. to 6 p.m., Sat 7 a.m. to 6:30 p.m., and Sun 9 a.m. to 3 p.m. $.

cedar creek

Originally a distinct small town, the Cedar Creek area has spread north and now reaches TX 71, where you'll find many of its attractions.

getting there

From Lockhart, head north on US 183 for 10 miles to the intersection of TX 21, then turn east and continue to Cedar Creek.

where to go

The Dinosaur Park. 893 Union Chapel Rd.; (512) 321-6262; www.thedinopark.com. This attraction features, you guessed it, life-size dinosaur replicas in an outdoor setting that kids will enjoy. Other activities include a fossil dig, playground, and picnic area, in addition to the Dinosaur Store. Open Sat and Sun 10 a.m. to 4 p.m.

McKinney Roughs Nature Park. 1884 TX 71, 8 miles west of Bastrop; (512) 303-5073; www.lcra.org. A favorite with both hikers and equestrians, this 1,100-acre park preserves several ecosystems as well as an extensive riverbank. Open Mon through Sat 8 a.m. to 5 p.m. and Sun noon to 5 p.m.

where to shop

Berdoll Pecan Candy and Gift Company. 2626 TX 71 West; (800) 518-3870; www .berdollpecanfarm.com. For nearly 30 years this unique shop on TX 71 has sold all things pecan, from the nuts themselves (grown in Berdoll's own pecan orchards located nearby) to pies, candies, and a myriad of other items. If you happen by when they are closed, never fear—a vending machine on the front porch sells several of their items, including pecan pies! Open daily 9 a.m. to 5:30 p.m. in fall and winter, 9 a.m. to 7 p.m. in spring and summer.

where to stay

Hyatt Regency Lost Pines Resort and Spa. 575 Hyatt Lost Pines Rd., 13 miles east of Austin-Bergstrom International Airport on TX 71; (512) 308-1234; www.lostpines.hyatt.com. Opened in 2006, this luxury resort offers 491 guest rooms and a distinctive Central Texas atmosphere. The hotel spans over 400 acres and features an equestrian center, an Arthur Hills–designed golf course, rafting on the Colorado River, supervised children's programs, a full-service spa, and more. $$$.

bastrop

Bastrop is the heart of the Lost Pines region, evoking comparisons to East Texas or the great pine forests of the southeastern United States. It's one of the oldest settlements in the state, built in 1829 along the Camino Real, also known as the King's Highway or the Old San Antonio Road. This was the western edge of the original "Little Colony" established by Stephen F. Austin. Settlers came by the wagonload from around the country to claim a share of this fertile land and to establish a home in this dangerous territory. Even as homes were being erected, Indian raids continued in this area for many years.

Bastrop is a popular day trip for visitors looking for a chance to shop and savor some quiet country life in a historic setting. Outdoors lovers can enjoy two nearby state parks and also the Colorado River, which winds through the heart of downtown. Canoe rentals and guided trips along the river are available.

getting there

To reach Bastrop, take TX 21 east from Cedar Creek for 5 miles to TX 71; continue east on TX 71 for 6 miles.

where to go

Bastrop "Old Town" Visitor Center. 1016 Main St.; (512) 303-0904; www.visitbastrop .org. Located in the old lobby of the 1889 First National Bank building, this official visitor center has information on Bastrop attractions, accommodations, and special events. Open daily.

Bastrop County Historical Society Museum. 702 Main St.; (512) 303-0057. This 1850 frame cabin contains Indian relics and pioneer exhibits. Open Mon through Fri 1 to 5 p.m. and Sat 10 a.m. to 2 p.m.

Bastrop Opera House. 711 Spring St.; (512) 321-6283; www.bastropoperahouse.com. Built in 1889, this building was once the entertainment center of town. After a major renovation in 1978, it's again the cultural center of Bastrop, the site for live theater ranging from mysteries to vaudeville.

Bastrop State Park. TX 21, 1.5 miles east of Bastrop; (512) 321-2101 for park information or (512) 389-8900 for reservations; www.tpwd.state.tx.us. Beautiful piney woods are the main draw at this 3,500-acre park, the fourth busiest state park in Texas. Facilities include a 9-hole golf course, campsites, and a 10-acre fishing lake. The 1930s-built stone and cedar cabins are very popular and should be booked well in advance. They feature fireplaces, bathrooms, and kitchen facilities. Guided bus tours every other Saturday during summer months introduce visitors to the park's unique ecology and to an endangered resident: the Houston toad.

Central Texas Museum of Automotive History. South on FM 304 to FM 535, then left 1 mile to Rosanky; (512) 237-2635; www.ctmah.org. This private museum is dedicated to the collection and preservation of old cars and accessories. The vehicles on display include a 1935 Rolls-Royce Phantom, a La France fire engine, and a 1922 Franklin. Open Apr through Sept, Wed through Sat 10 a.m. to 5 p.m.; Oct through Mar, Fri and Sat 10 a.m. to 5 p.m. and Sun 1:30 to 5 p.m.

Lock's Drug. 1003 Main St.; (512) 321-2551. This turn-of-the-20th-century drugstore features an antique mirrored fountain where you can belly up for a thick, creamy malt. Built-in cabinets are still labeled with the names of their original contents, and old apothecary tools sit in the front windows. Open daily except Sun.

North Shore Park, Lake Bastrop. Northeast of Bastrop; (800) 776-5272. From Bastrop, travel north on TX 95 for 2 miles, then turn right on FM 1441. Travel approximately 4 miles; the park entrance is on the right. Day travelers and overnight campers are welcome at this park. Facilities include campsites, RV sites, group pavilions, a 2-lane boat ramp, a fishing pier, playgrounds, and trails. Open daily.

Riverwalk. Enjoy this nature walk along the banks of the Colorado River near downtown. Opened in 1998, the 0.5-mile trail features a variety of trees, native plants, and wildflowers. It is accessible from either Fisherman's Park or Ferry Park. Free admission.

South Shore Park, Lake Bastrop. (800) 776-5272. From Bastrop, travel north on TX 95. After about 1.5 miles, take TX 21 east and travel about 3 miles to South Shore Road (CR 352). Turn left on South Shore Road; the park entrance is on the right. This popular LCRA park includes restrooms, showers, a group facility, hike/bike trails, picnic facilities, and a boat ramp. Open daily.

where to shop

Park your car and enjoy an afternoon of browsing through the many antiques and specialty stores along Main Street.

Apothecary's Hall. 805 Main St.; (512) 321-3022. Located in a small frame cottage on a quiet stretch of Main Street near the Colorado River, Apothecary's Hall specializes in antiques and other gift items including glassware, pottery, china, stained glass, handmade quilts and furniture. The shop is open Mon to Fri, noon to 5 p.m. and Sat 10 a.m. to 5:30 p.m.

The Rockin' Tiara. 908 Main St.; (512) 332-0202. Co-owners Misty Williamson and Amy Frank sell a "fun and funky" collection of clothing, jewelry, purses, home accessories, and unique gift items in this boutique in downtown Bastrop. Open Tues through Fri 10 a.m. to 6 p.m. and Sat 10 a.m. to 5 p.m.

where to eat

Maxine's on Main. 905 Main St.; (512) 303-0919; www.maxinesonmain.com. Open for breakfast, lunch, and dinner, Maxine's has become a beloved fixture in downtown Bastrop. The restaurant is known for its griddle cakes, burgers, chili, and homemade pie. Live music is featured every Fri evening. Open Sun through Wed 7 a.m. to 2 p.m.; Thurs 7 a.m. to 9 p.m.; Fri and Sat 7 a.m. to 9 p.m. $–$$.

where to stay

Bastrop State Park. TX 21, 1.5 miles east of Bastrop; (512) 321-2101 for park information or (512) 389-8900 for reservations; www.tpwd.state.tx.us. This park's picturesque stone and cedar cabins were built in the 1930s by the Civilian Conservation Corps from native materials. They feature rustic fireplaces, bathrooms, and kitchen facilities. *Note:* Due to their popularity, cabins should be booked well in advance.

rockne, texas

*Football fans will find a unique community just south of Bastrop, well worth a quick detour. The tiny town of **Rockne** is located south of TX 71. To get there, head south on FM 20, just west of Bastrop, for 6 miles then turn east for a mile on FM 535. This is the only town named for legendary Notre Dame coach **Knute Rockne.***

*Established by German immigrants in the 1860s, this community went through several name changes, but then in 1931, following the death of Coach Rockne, the town's schoolchildren voted to honor him by renaming the town Rockne. Today a statue of Knute Rockne stands in front of the **Rockne Museum.** The local-history museum, open Saturdays from 10 a.m. to 4 p.m., includes artifacts from the town's first Sacred Heart Church, which was built in 1892. It is located in Hilbig Park, home to several pioneer cabins. The **Philip Goertz Cabin** (circa 1860) stands near an outhouse, corn crib, and smokehouse. Just down the street is the current **Sacred Heart Catholic Church,** dedicated in 1892 and rebuilt in 1940 on the same site.*

smithville

This small town is built alongside the railroad tracks at the edge of the piney woods and home of Buescher State Park. Smithville was once a ferry stop on the Colorado River, but in the 1880s the railroad replaced the ferries as the main mode of transportation, and tracks were laid across town. Today the railroad still plays an important part in Smithville's economy.

Smithville was the backdrop for the Sandra Bullock movie *Hope Floats.* Many local citizens had small parts in the film and, even today, you'll see a billboard at the Smithville turnoff proudly proclaiming this the home of the *Hope Floats* movie.

getting there

Continue east from Bastrop for 12 miles on TX 71 to Smithville.

where to go

Buescher State Park. Three miles north of town via TX 71 and FM 2104, or access from PR 1; (512) 237-2241; www.tpwd.state.tx.us. Buescher (pronounced "BISH-er") neighbors Bastrop State Park, but the two have different ecosystems. Oaks dominate this park, along with a few pines. The park is especially popular for its 30-acre lake. Visitors can enjoy ample campsites and screened shelters, as well as a playground and picnic area. Open daily.

Railroad Museum and Depot. 100 West First St.; (512) 237-2313. Built beside the tracks, this park has two cabooses and a depot relocated here from West Point, a community east of town. The chamber of commerce office is housed adjacent to the depot as well. You'll also find an excellent dog park here if you're day tripping with Fido. Open Mon through Sat 10 a.m. to 5 p.m.; park always open. Free admission.

Rocky Hill Ranch Mountain Bike Resort. FM 153, 2 miles northeast of Buescher State Park; (512) 718-8822; www.rockyhillranch.net. Beginner, intermediate, advanced, and expert trails tempt mountain bikers with more than 1,200 acres that include gentle slopes and challenging grades as well as stream crossings. More than 25 miles of trails are available for use by helmeted riders. The ranch includes a casual restaurant with horseshoes, shuffleboard, and beach volleyball; campsites are available along small creeks and spring-fed water holes.

Smithville Heritage Society Museum. 602 Main St.; (512) 237-4545. This 1908 home contains the Smithville archives and a museum of local memorabilia. Open Tues mornings (call for other times). Free admission.

Vernon L. Richards Riverbend Park. TX 71 where it crosses the Colorado River, just north of Smithville; (800) 776-5272 or (512) 237-2343 for campsite reservations; www.lcra .org. The park entrance is located off the highway shoulder on the westbound side of the road. This LCRA park includes restrooms, a group facility, hike/bike trails, a playground, picnic facilities, and a boat ramp. Open daily for day use and camping.

where to shop

Izadora's Antiques & Vintage. 116 Main St.; (512) 237-2600. Izadora's has a unique specialty, vintage garden items, as well as other unusual items from days gone by. Open Thurs through Mon 11 a.m. to 5 p.m.

la grange

Just 4 miles southeast of Smithville on the left side of TX 71 is a scenic overlook that is an excellent place to pull over for a picnic. While you're here you can gaze at the miles of rolling hills and farmland that attracted many German and Czech immigrants a century ago.

Continue on TX 71 to the somewhat infamous community of La Grange. For generations this was a quiet town in the center of a farming region. In the 1970s, however, La Grange caught the public's attention with the revelation of the Chicken Ranch, a brothel

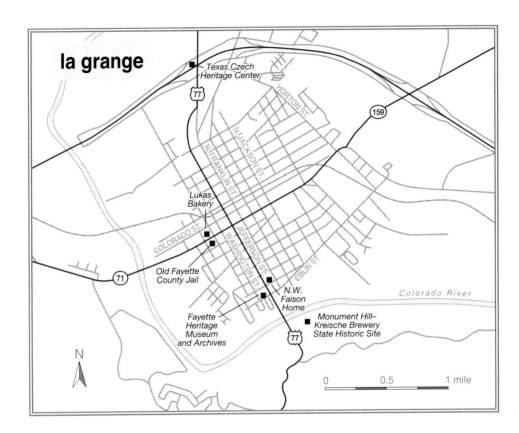

la grange

Texas Czech Heritage Center

HORTON ST.

77

159

N. JACKSON ST.

N. FRANKLIN ST.

Lukas Bakery

COLORADO ST.

WASHINGTON ST.

JEFFERSON ST.

EBLIN ST.

71

Old Fayette County Jail

N.W. Faison Home

Colorado River

Fayette Heritage Museum and Archives

Monument Hill– Kreische Brewery State Historic Site

77

N

0   0.5   1 mile

that became the subject of the Broadway musical and movie *The Best Little Whorehouse in Texas*. Today the Chicken Ranch is gone, but La Grange still has other sights to see.

getting there

From Smithville, continue east on TX 71 for 20 miles to the town of La Grange.

where to go

Old Fayette County Jail and Visitors Center. 171 South Main St.; (800) 524-7264; www .lagrangetourism.com/History/History-Jailhouse.html. Now the home of the La Grange Area Chamber of Commerce, this historic building once housed the Fayette County Jail, serving in that role for a century. Open weekdays 8 a.m. to 5 p.m. Free admission.

Fayette Heritage Museum and Archives. 855 South Jefferson St.; (979) 968-6418. Housed with the public library, this museum contains displays on the area's rich history. Open Tues through Sat; call for hours. Free admission.

Monument Hill/Kreische Brewery State Historic Site. US 77, 1 mile south of La Grange; (409) 968-5658; www.tpwd.state.tx.us. Located on a bluff high above town, this site is home to two combined parks.

Monument Hill Historical Site is the burial site for the Texans who died in the Dawson Massacre and the Mier Expedition, two historic Mexican conflicts that occurred in 1842, six years after the Texas Revolution. The Dawson Massacre took place near San Antonio when La Grange citizen Nicholas Dawson gathered Texans to halt the continual Mexican attacks. Dawson's men were met by hundreds of Mexican troops, and 35 Texans were killed.

The Mexican village of Mier was attacked in a retaliatory move, resulting in the capture of Texas soldiers and citizens by Mexican general Santa Anna, who ordered every tenth man to be killed. The Texans were blindfolded and forced to draw beans: 159 of the beans were white and 17 black. Men who drew white beans were imprisoned; those who drew black ones were executed.

The **Kreische Brewery State Historic Site** recalls a far more cheerful time in Texas history. Heinreich Kreische, who immigrated here from Germany, purchased the hilltop and the adjoining land in 1849, including the burial ground of those Texas heroes, for his brewery site. Before closing the brewery in 1884, Kreische became the third-largest beer producer in the state. Open daily 8 a.m. to 5 p.m. One admission covers both adjacent sites.

the chicken ranch

La Grange drew international attention in 1973 when the story of what many believe was the country's oldest continuously run brothel was exposed by consumer-affairs reporter Marvin Zindler from KTRK-TV in Houston. The report would inspire a Broadway musical and movie as well as lots of curiosity about the site, which was located on 11 acres outside of La Grange. The house, which was added onto many times as the number of women increased, was nicknamed the **Chicken Ranch** *during the Great Depression. When customers grew fewer, the proprietor, a woman known as Miss Jessie, began allowing men to pay in chickens. Soon the ranch was overrun with poultry and eggs, both of which they sold locally.*

As economic times improved, the ranch returned to a cash basis, and ownership changed in 1952 to a madam who became one of La Grange's most generous philanthropists. When the Chicken Ranch closed, the building was moved to Dallas and, for a while, became a chicken restaurant.

N. W. Faison Home. 822 South Jefferson St.; (800) 524-7264. N. W. Faison was a survivor of both the Dawson Massacre and the Mier Expedition in 1842. The Faison family resided in this home for more than 20 years, and today it contains the family's furniture as well as exhibits from the Mexican War. Open by appointment.

Oak Thicket Park. (979) 249-3504; www.lcra.org. From La Grange, travel east on TX 159 for about 7 miles and turn right at the sign for Fayette County Lake. This 65-acre park offers plenty of family-oriented activities: a playground, fishing piers, and a good swimming area on Lake Fayette. Camping is available, as well as 8 cabins.

Park Prairie Park. (979) 249-3504; www.lcra.org. From La Grange, travel 10 miles east on TX 159 to the entrance of the park. Park Prairie is another favorite with families, thanks to volleyball courts, plenty of picnic space, tent camping, and even some pelicans and gulls along the shores of Lake Fayette. Hikers can walk to Oak Thicket Park on a 3-mile trail. Other facilities include restrooms, showers, a group facility, and a boat ramp.

Texas Czech Heritage and Cultural Center. 250 West Fairgrounds Rd.; (979) 968-9399 or (888) 785-4500; www.lagrangetourism.com/History/History-Texas-Czech.html. Located near the fairgrounds, this home, with its original hardwood floors, now contains displays about the region's Czech history. Exhibits are in English and Czech. Plans are under way for the construction of the Texas Polka Music Museum at the site as well, to include costumes and memorabilia relating to the Czech, Polish, and German musicians who entertained in the region. Open weekdays 10 a.m. to 4 p.m. and weekends by appointment.

White Rock Park. On east bank of the Colorado River, just south of La Grange; (979) 968-5805. From La Grange, take US 77 (Jefferson Street) south to Elbin Road and continue about 0.75 mile to Mode Lane (CR 134). Take a right on Mode Lane and travel about 0.25 mile; the park entrance is on the right. This day-use park includes restrooms, hike/bike trails, picnic facilities, and a canoe launch.

where to eat

Lukas Bakery. 135 North Main St.; (979) 968-3052. Since 1947 this landmark bakery has been turning out fragrant delights like breads, kolaches, pigs in a blanket, and ana bars. Open Mon through Sat 5 a.m. to 1 p.m. $.

Prause Meat Market. 253 West Travis St. (US 77) on Courthouse Square; (979) 968-3259. The front of this meat market sells fresh cuts, but it's behind the counter where business is smoking—literally. The barbecue side of this business is hot; so hot, in fact, that when the high demand means they run out of barbecue (and they often do early in the day), these folks just close up shop. Get there early for a chance at some sausage or brisket; you'll be served on butcher paper and can take it into the back room to eat on long tables. Open for lunch Mon through Sat. $.

Weikel's Bakery. 2247 West TX 71; (979) 968-9413; www.weikels.com. The Czech pastry specialties for which this region is known make up many of the offerings at this highway-side bakery. Kolaches and pigs in a blanket are top items; kolaches come in a range of flavors, from pineapple to poppy seed to prune. The bakery may not look like much from the outside (well, actually it looks like a gas station), but it was named one of America's top 10 bakeries by foodies Jane and Michael Stern in *Epicurious,* and for good reason. Open Mon through Thurs 5 a.m. to 9 p.m., Fri through Sun 5 a.m. to 10 p.m. $.

southeast

day trip 01

southeast

>>> **texas history:**
floresville, panna maria, helena,
goliad, fannin

Texas history takes center stage on this day trip that visits not only some of Texas's oldest communities, but also one of the most important sites of the Texas Revolution. Agriculture remains a vital part of this region's economy, and farms and cattle ranches line much of the roadside between these stops.

floresville

This community of 7,000 residents has a long link to agriculture, thanks in part to its growing season of 285 days. Through the years, cattle ranching and farming have been the backbone of the local economy, with crops including flax, cotton, and even peanuts. Today a large peanut statue stands on the courthouse lawn to recognize this important crop, which takes center stage during Floresville's annual Peanut Festival every October.

getting there

From San Antonio, head southeast on US 181 for 29 miles to the agricultural community of Floresville.

where to go

Canary Islanders Cemetery. Intersection of Plum and 10th Streets off US 181, 1 mile west of Floresville. This historic cemetery is ancient by Texas standards. Although its exact

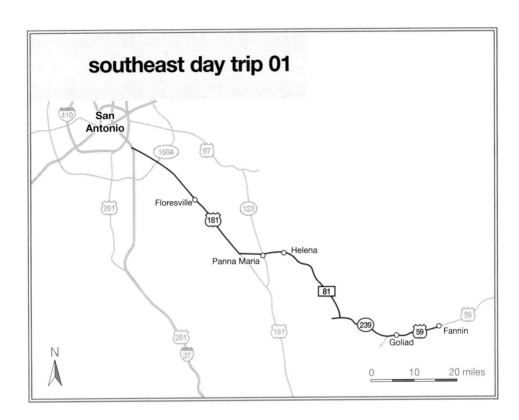

southeast day trip 01

date isn't known, it was established before 1732 by Canary Islanders who settled in this region.

Rancho de las Cabras. Tours meet at River Park on TX 97 to caravan to Rancho de las Cabras; (210) 932-1001; www.nps.gov/saan/planyourvisit/guidedtours.htm. Located near Floresville, the site of Rancho de las Cabras (Goat Ranch) is part of the national parks system thanks to its historic role in supporting the residents of San Antonio's Mission Espada. Today tours of the ranch, with information on the historic vaquero system, are offered at 10 a.m. on the first Saturday of each month; call for information. The ranch itself is undeveloped, and good walking shoes are recommended. Free admission.

panna maria

If you weren't aware of its interesting history, you might just call this another pint-size Texas town, perched on a shady hilltop with a nice breeze and a beautiful view. But there's a lot more to Panna Maria, which means "Virgin Mary" in Polish, than meets the eye. This quiet community was the first Polish settlement in America, and it still maintains a place in the history of Poland, well known among the people of the old country.

This small town was founded in 1854 by 100 Polish families led by Father Leopold Moczygemba. After a nine-week voyage to Galveston, the settlers rented Mexican carts to transport their farm tools and bedding, as well as the cross from their parish church. They made the difficult journey to Central Texas on foot, finally stopping at the hillside that overlooks the San Antonio River and Cibolo Creek. The day was December 24, 1854, and the pioneers offered a midnight mass beneath one of the large hilltop oaks. They settled here.

The year that followed was a grueling one, a time when the pioneers learned the harshness of their new home. A cold winter was followed by a hot, dry summer filled with snakes and insects. Most of the settlers did succeed with their new venture and were soon joined by more Polish immigrants.

getting there

From Floresville, continue southeast on US 181 to the intersection of FM 81. Turn northeast on FM 81 and continue 5 miles to the community of Panna Maria.

where to go

Church of the Immaculate Conception. TX 81, in town; no phone. Within two years of settling in Panna Maria, the pioneers built the Church of the Immaculate Conception, the first Polish church in America. The original church was destroyed by fire and replaced in 1878 by the present structure, which serves as the center of worship for Panna Maria's citizens.

The church is home to a replica of the mosaic of Our Lady of Czestochowa, or the Black Madonna. The original Black Madonna is enshrined at the Monastery of Jasna Gora in Czestochowa, Poland, a city about 65 miles east of the area from which the first Panna Maria pioneers originated. According to tradition, the Madonna was painted by St. Luke and then found in the Holy Land in AD 326 by Saint Helena, mother of Constantine the Great.

This replica, a gift to the United States from Poland, was presented to the town by President Johnson in 1966. It rests on display at the front of the church along with hand-carved chairs and a gold chalice that belonged to Pope John Paul II. These priceless treasures were presented to the people of Panna Maria in 1987.

The church is open daily. Free admission. For a small donation you can purchase a brochure outlining the history of the Black Madonna and Panna Maria's early settlers.

helena

This was once a thriving town on the San Antonio River, founded in 1852 by Thomas Ruckman and Louis Owings (the latter became the first governor of the Arizona territory). Owings named the town after his wife, Helen.

During the Civil War much of the Confederate cotton passed through the town. At the time, Helena even had its own Confederate post office, which issued Helena stamps. Today they're a rare find, worth several thousand dollars each. Helena's existence as a thriving burg came to a halt in 1886 when the railroad bypassed the town. Soon the county seat moved to Karnes City, and the town all but rolled up the sidewalks.

getting there

From Panna Maria, continue on FM 81 for 5 miles to the tiny community of Helena.

where to go

Karnes County Museum. FM 81; (830) 780-3210; www.karnesmuseum.com. This museum is actually a collection of historic buildings from the area, including a post office, jail, farmhouse, and barn. A museum traces the history of Karnes County, including its busy days during the Civil War. The grounds, shaded by large mesquite trees, also provide a picnic area. Open Fri through Mon 11 a.m. to 4 p.m. Free admission.

goliad

Like the Alamo and the Battle of San Jacinto, Goliad holds a special place in Texas history. Founded by the Spanish, Goliad is the third oldest city in Texas. To protect their passage to the Gulf, the Spaniards moved their Mission Espíritu Santo and its royal protector, Presidio La Bahia (Fort of the Bay), to this location in 1749. At that time the community was named Santa Dorotea. Years later the town's name was changed to Goliad, an anagram of the spoken word Hidalgo (the *h* is silent in Spanish), in honor of Father Miguel Hidalgo, a priest who became a hero during the Mexican Revolution.

Goliad was also the birthplace of General Ignacio Zaragoza, who led Mexican troops to victory at the Battle of Puebla, during which Mexico defeated France on the fifth of May, or Cinco de Mayo. Although Cinco de Mayo celebrations take place in Mexico, Texas, and elsewhere, Goliad is considered the official Texas location of this historic celebration.

Few towns have their own flag, but Goliad boasts its own historic, if somewhat gruesome, banner. On October 9, 1835, the Texas colonists made a move in their battle for independence. The settlers took over the presidio and raised the "Bloody Arm Flag," picturing a severed arm holding a sword.

The next year the Texans, led by Colonel James W. Fannin Jr., surrendered at the Battle of Coleto about 9 miles east of town. Approximately 390 soldiers were marched back to the presidio. After a week of imprisonment, all but 20 soldiers (physicians and mechanics) were placed before a firing squad. More than two dozen men escaped during the massacre, but 342 were killed, the largest loss of life during the fight for independence. "Remember Goliad" soon became a cry alongside "Remember the Alamo."

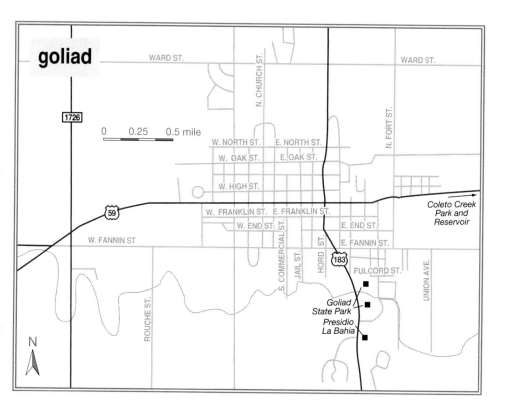

Today the presidio, Mission Espíritu Santo, and several other historic sites are restored and open to the public. You also can visit Colonel Fannin's grave and see the monument that marks the resting place of the Texas soldiers.

Goliad is also popular for its Market Days, held on the second Saturday of each month. These downtown street markets draw over 200 vendors and are considered the largest street markets in South Texas.

getting there

To reach Goliad, continue south from Helena on FM 81 to the intersection of TX 239 at the town of Charco. Take TX 239 south to the intersection of US 59, then head east to the historic city of Goliad.

where to go

Angel of Goliad Hike and Bike Nature Trail. www.texastrails.org. This 2-mile trail winds from the foot of Market Street to the Fannin Memorial Monument. Along the way it passes the Mission Espíritu Santo, Presidio La Bahia, and the San Antonio River. The trail is named in honor of Francisca Alavez, known as the Angel of Goliad for her role in saving many lives during the Goliad Massacre.

Coleto Creek Park and Reservoir. Fifteen miles northeast of Goliad on US 59; (361) 575-6366; www.coletocreekpark.com. This 3,100-acre reservoir surrounded by a 190-acre park is a South Texas mecca for boaters, anglers, birders, and campers. Winter Texans can enjoy an extended stay at these campgrounds.

Fannin Memorial Monument. Just east of Presidio La Bahia; no phone. A large memorial marks the site of the massacre that occurred here on March 27, 1836. (The site where the surrender took place is at a historic site in nearby Fannin.)

Fannin Plaza Park. Market and Franklin Streets, 1 block northeast of the city square. This small park was dedicated in 1885 by the Fannin Monument Association, formed by one of the survivors of the Goliad Massacre. The park includes a small cannon that was used by Fannin's men and monuments honoring the fallen soldiers.

Goliad Paddling Trail. Numerous entry points; www.riverrec.org and www.canoetrail goliad.com. This 6.6-mile trip along a state-designated Inland Paddle Trail winds from US 59 to Goliad State Park on the San Antonio River. The leisurely trip can be started at several points, including Goliad State Park, US 59, and Ferry Street.

Goliad State Park & Mission Espíritu Santo Historic Site. On US 183, 0.25 mile south of town at 108 PR 6; (361) 645-3405; www.tpwd.state.tx.us. The highlight of this 178-acre park is the reconstruction of the Mission Nuestra Senora del Espíritu Santo de Zuniga, better known as Mission Espíritu Santo. This reconstruction was done by the Civilian Conservation Corps in the 1930s and includes displays on life at the mission and ranch, which was one of the first successful livestock operations in North America, with over 15,000 cattle by 1778. The restored mission offers spinning, weaving, and pottery-making demonstrations, primarily on weekends. Park activities feature hiking, picnicking, fishing, and boating. Screened shelters as well as tent and RV camping sites are available year-round. Open daily.

> **Mission Rosario State Historic Site.** Also located on park property are the remains of Mission Nuestra Señora del Rosario. This historic mission was established in 1754; today the remains are being studied and the site is open by appointment only.

> **Zaragoza Birthplace State Historic Site.** Two miles south of Presidio La Bahia off US 183. This modest structure was the first home of Mexican general Ignacio Zaragoza. Under Zaragoza's command, the Mexican army defeated the French at the Battle of Puebla, an event now celebrated as Cinco de Mayo, or "Fifth of May." Today the building is filled with exhibits that depict the general's role in Mexican history.

Market House Museum. 205 South Market; (361) 645-8767. This museum contains exhibits on local history. The building also houses the Goliad Chamber of Commerce, where you can pick up brochures and area maps. Open Wed through Sat 10 a.m. to 4 p.m. Free admission.

Presidio La Bahia. US 183, south of the San Antonio River; (361) 645-3752; www.presidio labahia.org. The presidio holds many distinctions: It is the oldest fort in the West, one of few sites west of the Mississippi that was active in the American Revolution, the only fully restored Spanish presidio, and the only Texas Revolution site with its original appearance intact. The stone garrison is impressive and worth a stop. While you're here, visit the fort chapel, built in the Spanish colonial style. Open daily.

where to eat

Empresario Restaurant. 141 South Courthouse Sq.; (361) 645-2347. Grab a deli sandwich followed by a slice of homemade pie at this eatery that's a favorite with locals. Open for lunch daily and for dinner Thurs through Sat. $–$$.

Hanging Tree Restaurant. 141 North Courthouse Sq.; (361) 645-8955; www.hanging treerestaurant.com. As its name suggests, this restaurant is located near the historic hanging tree on the north lawn of the Goliad County Courthouse. The restaurant serves Texas favorites like chicken-fried steak as well as surprises like mahi mahi platters and chicken fettuccine Alfredo. Open for lunch and dinner daily except Tues. $–$$.

fannin

Fannin, a town of just over 100 residents, was named for James W. Fannin Jr., a hero of the Texas Revolution. The town is home to the Fannin Battleground State Historic Site, a place of interest to those tracing the history of the revolution in towns such as Goliad and Gonzales.

getting there

From Goliad, head northeast on US 59 for 10 miles to the community of Fannin.

where to go

Fannin Battleground State Historic Site. One mile south of town on PR 27; (361) 645-2020; www.visitfanninbattleground.com. Formerly part of the state park system but now administered by the Texas Historical Commission, this site honors the location where Colonel James W. Fannin Jr. surrendered to the Mexican army after the Battle of Coleto Creek. The Mexican commander offered a clemency petition, but General Santa Anna overruled the offer and ordered Fannin and his 342 men to be executed in Goliad. Today the men are remembered with a monument that recalls the actions of March 27, 1836. Picnic and restroom facilities are available at the day-use park. Open daily. Free admission.

day trip 02

southeast

texas crossroads:
stockdale, cuero, victoria

Although Victoria is known as the "Crossroads of Texas," the term could be applied to all the stops on this day trip, each of which is located in the area where the agricultural heartland of Texas meets the coastal plains.

stockdale

This small town, home to just 1,400 residents, has had a few names in its history: High Prairie, Free Timber, Bunker's Store. Eventually the community was renamed in honor of Fletcher Stockdale, who served as lieutenant governor and governor of Texas during the Confederacy. Today the town is an agricultural center, and its most important crop is celebrated every June with an annual Watermelon Jubilee, considered one of the oldest watermelon festivals in the state.

getting there

From San Antonio, head southeast on US 87 for 41 miles to the community of Stockdale.

where to go

Jackson Nature Park. 10422 Old Floresville Rd. (CR 401) at Cibolo Creek, between Floresville and Stockdale; (866) 345-7272. This 50-acre rural park is owned by Wilson County and managed by the San Antonio River Authority. A favorite with birders, hikers, and nature

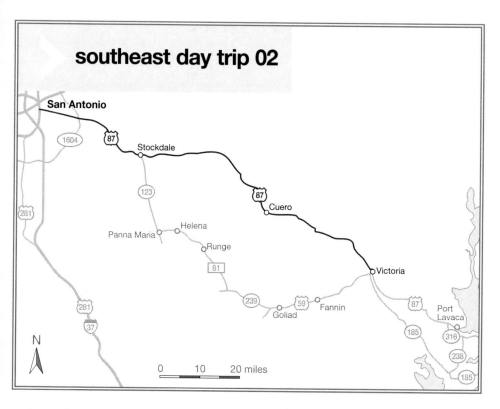

southeast day trip 02

San Antonio

Stockdale

Panna Maria

Helena

Runge

Cuero

Victoria

Goliad   Fannin

Port Lavaca

N

0   10   20 miles

lovers, the park can be enjoyed on self-guided tours or on occasional guided tours as well. Open 9 a.m. to dusk.

cuero

This onetime "Wild West" town, named for the Spanish word for rawhide, has a long history in ranching and farming. Once an important stop on the Chisholm Trail, Cuero (pronounced "KWER-oh") was named by the Texas Legislature as the "Wildflower Capital of Texas" thanks to its 1,000-plus species.

getting there

From Stockdale, continue on US 87 through the communities of Nixon and Westhoff for a total of 47 miles to Cuero.

where to go

Cuero Chamber of Commerce/Cuero Heritage Museum. 124 East Church St.; (361) 275-2112; www.cuero.org. Located in the former Cuero Post Office building, this facility serves as both a visitor center and a museum, with exhibits on Cuero's historic turkey trots and World War II pilots' school. Open weekdays 8:30 a.m. to 5 p.m. (closed noon to 1 p.m.). Free admission.

DeWitt County Museum. 312 East Broadway; (361) 275-6322. Built in 1886, this historic home features displays on the history of DeWitt County and Cuero. Along with the home, the grounds also house a log cabin dating back to 1865. Open Wed through Fri 8 a.m. to 5 p.m.

Reuss Pharmacy Museum. 515 North Esplanade St.; (361) 275-3411; www.reuss pharmacy.com. Reuss Pharmacy is the oldest continuously operated pharmacy in the state of Texas, although it has not always been at the same location. The drugstore originally opened in what's now the ghost town of Indianola in 1845 and moved to Cuero two years later, after the historic hurricane hit the seaport city. It operated in Cuero for 99 years at the same location, then in 1971 the great-grandson of the founding owner moved it to the Esplanade location, preserving the history of the pharmacy in this museum's exhibits. Open Mon through Sat 8:30 a.m. to 6 p.m. Free admission.

victoria

Termed the "Crossroads of Texas," Victoria is located equal distances from San Antonio, Austin, Houston, and Corpus Christi. Named for the first president of Mexico, the city was founded by 41 Spanish families. Later Victoria became one of the first three towns incorporated by the Republic of Texas.

getting there

From Cuero, continue southeast on US 87 for 28 miles to Victoria.

where to go

Coleto Creek Park and Reservoir. Fifteen miles west of Victoria off US 59 South; (361) 575-6366; www.coletocreekpark.com. Swim, picnic, or camp at this year-round park. Sites with electricity are available; the park includes restrooms with showers, laundry facilities, barbecue pits, volleyball courts, and more.

Museum of the Coastal Bend. 2200 East Red River; (361) 582-2511; www.museumof thecoastalbend.org. Tracing the heritage of the entire Coastal Bend region, this museum (located on the campus of Victoria College) includes exhibits on subjects such as Victoria's ranching history and La Salle's first French settlement on Texas soil, Fort Saint Louis. Open Tues through Sat 10 a.m. to 4 p.m.

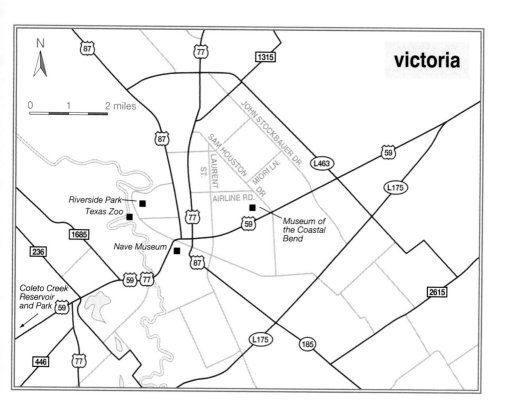

Nave Museum. 306 West Commercial St.; (361) 575-8228; www.victoriaregionalmuseum .com. This neoclassical-style temple was constructed in 1932 to honor Royston Nave, a painter known nationally for his landscapes and seascapes. Today the museum features traveling fine art exhibits, which in the past have included Andy Warhol, Frieda Kahlo, and Mary Cassatt. Open Tues through Sun 1 to 5 p.m.

Riverside Park. East Red River Street; (361) 485-3200. Spanning over 560 acres, this city park borders 4.5 miles of the Guadalupe River. Park amenities include numerous picnic tables, a canoe and kayak trail, a duck pond, and more. Open daily. Free admission.

The Texas Zoo. 110 Memorial Dr.; (361) 573-7681; www.texaszoo.org. Spanning 6 acres within Riverside Park, this distinctive zoo features more than 150 native Texas species of mammals, birds, reptiles, fish, and amphibians as well as animals from other parts of the world. Endangered Texas species are highlighted. Texas species are also showcased in a native plants and wildflower garden. In 1984 the mission of the zoo was recognized by the Texas Legislature, which proclaimed it the "National Zoo of Texas." Open daily 9 a.m. to 5 p.m.

Victoria Memorial Rose Garden. McCright Drive; (361) 485-3200. One of only seven accredited rose gardens in Texas, this serene garden contains over 1,000 rose bushes representing 105 varieties. The garden includes walkways, a fountain, and a gazebo. Free admission.

where to eat

Olde Victoria at the Oak Room. 101 West Goodwin; (361) 572-8840; www.oldevictoria .com. Olde Victoria is perched on the 12th floor of One O'Connor Plaza, providing an elegant setting for this eatery which specializes in continental and Italian dishes. Look for specialties such as the Hickory Spicy Chicken with chipotle barbecue sauce and steamed salmon with potato-garlic sabayon. Open for lunch and dinner. $$$.

Rosebud Fountain and Grill. 102 South Main St.; (361) 573-5111; www.rosebudfountain .com. Named for the Victoria Rosebud, a minor-league baseball team based in the city from the 1920s to 1960s, this restaurant boasts a historic soda fountain theme from decor to menu. Authentic soda fountain malts and shakes accompany burgers, beer-battered fries, Texas-fried shrimp, and more. Open Mon through Sat 11 a.m. to 2:30 p.m. and Fri and Sat 5:30 to 9 p.m. $–$$.

day trip 03

southeast

gulf shores:
port lavaca, indianola, port o'connor

This day trip is an extension of Southeast Day Trip 02 from Victoria, adding the quiet port cities of the Coastal Bend. Perfect for birders, anglers, and beach strollers, this day trip takes in some of the lesser-explored communities of the region.

port lavaca

This community of about 12,000 residents, located on Lavaca Bay, is a center for fishing and agriculture but also contains some visitor attractions. The region is a favorite with bird lovers and beach buffs, who will find miles of beaches at several parks. Birders also enjoy the challenge of this destination, which is home to numerous birding sites along the Great Texas Coastal Birding Trail. Anglers also find plenty of activity with several bay charters.

getting there

From Victoria, continue south on US 87 for 25 miles to the bayside city of Port Lavaca. If you are starting in San Antonio, take US 87 south for 142 miles, a 3 hour drive.

where to go

Formosa Wetlands Walkway and Lighthouse Beach. 700 Lighthouse Beach Rd.; (361) 552-1234. This beach park is a favorite with beach buffs as well as birders, who can view

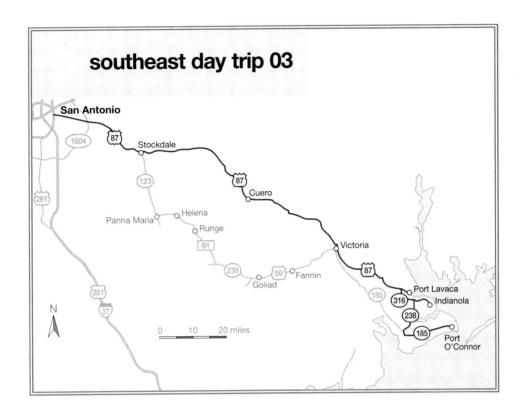

southeast day trip 03

San Antonio

Stockdale

Cuero

Helena
Panna Maria
Runge

Victoria

Fannin
Goliad

Port Lavaca
Indianola

Port
O'Connor

0   10   20 miles

N

species from the 2,200 foot-long walkway and the Alcoa Bird Tower. Open daily. Free admission.

Halfmoon Reef Lighthouse. TX 35 near causeway. This historic structure, a screwpile lighthouse, dates back to 1858, when it stood watch in the waters of Matagorda Bay, perched on high piles. Damaged in 1942 by a hurricane, the hexagonal-shaped building eventually was moved to shore and today stands next to the chamber of commerce, where it serves as a community center.

Magnolia Beach. At the north end of Margie Tewmey Road. One of the most popular beaches in Port Lavaca Magnolia Beach has some modest public amenities including picnic tables and shelters, playground equipment and basketball courts. Locals say that the fishing is good there at times, especially around the Indian Point fishing pier. Farther down the beach, a self-guided birding walk winds through the coastal dunes.

Port Lavaca State Fishing Pier. 202 North Virginia; (361) 552-5311. This state facility, operated by the City of Port Lavaca, extends into Lavaca Bay and offers anglers the chance to enjoy saltwater fishing. The park includes a lighted pier as well as a restroom, snack bar, and fish-cleaning facility. Open daily.

indianola

This port was one of the most prosperous in Texas during its heyday, before it began battling a series of tragedies. The city endured several yellow fever epidemics as well as shelling during the Civil War, only to finally be wiped out during a terrible hurricane in 1875 followed by another just more than a decade later. Today little remains of the ghost town.

getting there

From Port Lavaca, drive south on TX 316 for 14 miles to the ghost town of Indianola.

where to go

Indianola County Historic Park. TX 316. This bayside park is located at the site of the former town and offers picnic sites, camping, fishing, and a boat ramp. Open daily.

La Salle Monument. TX 316. This monument marks the place where French explorer René-Robert Cavelier, Sieur de La Salle, came ashore on February 20, 1685. The memorial is made from granite from Kingsland, located on the Highland Lakes, not far from where the granite for the Texas capitol building was mined.

port o'connor

This coastal community of a little more than 1,000 residents is just about the end of the road: From here, Texas gives way to the Gulf of Mexico. Port O'Connor (also known as P.O.C.) is a destination for many anglers as well as birders.

getting there

From Indianola, return north on TX 316 to the intersection of TX 238. Turn south on TX 238 to FM 1289, then turn south again and continue 11 miles to TX 185 (Adams Street). Turn east and continue to Port O'Connor.

where to go

Matagorda Island Wildlife Management Area. (979) 323-9553; www.tpwd.state.tx.us. Formerly Matagorda Island State Park, this is now a wildlife management area but continues to be operated by the Texas Parks and Wildlife Department. Unlike most parks, this site can only be reached by private or chartered boat. The barrier island offers visitors primitive beach camping and use of several boat ramps. The park itself is little improved, with no electricity or drinking water. Its attractions include the chance to view more than 300 species of birds, including the whooping cranes that migrate through the region. Fishing and relaxing on the beach are also popular activities. Open daily.

south

>>>

day trip 01

feathers & fins:
aransas pass, port aransas,
rockport-fulton

Birders come from around the world to test their skill at spotting some of the nearly 500 species recorded in this area. Anglers and spring breakers also call this region a favorite.

aransas pass

Aransas Pass is more a genuine fishing village and less a tourist destination than many other Texas coastal communities. Most of its 8,000 residents are employed in the fishing industry. Make your first stop the chamber of commerce at 452 Cleveland Blvd.

Nicknamed "Saltwater Heaven," Aransas Pass is a popular stop with anglers eager to try their luck landing a speckled trout, redfish, flounder, black drum, or sheepshead in the bay. Deep-sea excursions are available as well as guides for fishing the saltwater flats and the bay.

getting there

To reach Aransas Pass, take I-37 south from San Antonio for 145 miles to Corpus Christi. (For attractions in Corpus Christi, see South Day Trip 02.) Cross the Harbor Bridge and follow US 181 north to TX 35. Continue to the intersection of TX 361, then turn right to Aransas Pass.

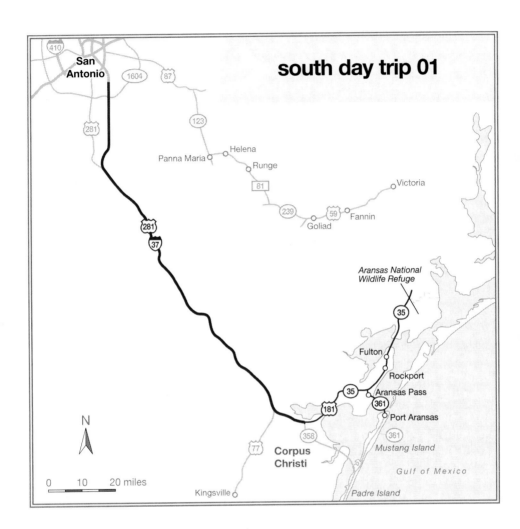

where to go

Aransas Pass Community Park. East Johnson Avenue and South Euclid Street; (361) 758-2750. Although it is located next to the water treatment plant, this park makes a serene getaway for bird lovers, especially during winter migration. Two observation decks here make it easy to view waterbirds in the nearby marshes. Free admission.

Conn Brown Harbor–Aransas Pass Wetlands. TX 361 toward Port Aransas on the Dale Miller Causeway; (361) 758-2750. This site is a favorite for winter birding, when pelicans, American oystercatchers, snowy plovers, sooty terns, and other birds can be spotted. The site includes a marina, home of the region's shrimping fleet, as well as kayaking and fishing. Free admission.

Lydia Ann Lighthouse. Off Redfish Bay Causeway. Although it is privately owned and not open to the public, this picturesque lighthouse is one of the most popular photo spots in Aransas Pass. It is the only lighthouse in Texas that is staffed and operated 24 hours a day.

Newbury Park Hummingbird Garden. Lamont Street and Yoakum Avenue. This day-use park is filled with plants that attract hummingbirds. These small birds arrive by the thousands during the fall and spring migrations. Free admission.

Seaman's Memorial Tower. Bigelow Street at Harbor Park. This memorial was constructed in 1970 to honor fishermen who lost their lives in the Gulf waters. A plaque honoring Coast Guard members who perished in 1973 while trying to rescue a shrimp boat is also located at the site. You'll also see a historic anchor at the tower, one brought up in the Gulf and thought to be from a Civil War gunship.

where to eat

The Butter Churn. 228 West Wheeler Ave.; (361) 758-2300; www.butterchurnrestaurant.com. Friendly service and Texas comfort food are the hallmarks of this modest family-owned cafe. You'll see a lot of locals as well as visiting anglers gathered here most days, enticed by the hand-breaded chicken-fried steak, fried catfish, and the generous salad bar. Two kinds of soups are featured every day, and the banana pudding is just like your mother used to make. Open Sun and Mon 11 a.m. to 3 p.m.; Tues through Sat 11 a.m. to 9 p.m. $$.

port aransas

Port Aransas, or just "Port A" to most Texans, is perched on the northern tip of Mustang Island. Life in the coastal community centers around the Gulf, with its crying gulls, rolling surf, and miles of pancake-colored sand. When the spring-break crowds depart, it's a town that appeals to birders and anglers as much as to bikini-clad sunbathers.

Although Port A is now one of the state's most popular coastal destinations, its history as a hideaway dates from far before the days of sunscreen and surfboards. Some of the island's first residents were the fierce Karankawa Indians, a cannibalistic tribe that greeted later visitors, from pirates to Spanish missionaries. Buccaneer Jean Lafitte reputedly camped on the shores of Mustang Island, building bonfires to lure ships onto the beach to be looted and plundered. Wild horses, evolved from the steeds of Spanish explorers, gave Mustang Island its name.

Just as it was more than 200 years ago, the most common way to reach Port A is by water. As noted previously, you follow TX 361 from Aransas Pass across the Redfish Bay Causeway to Harbor Island. Free ferries run 24 hours daily from Harbor Island across the Corpus Christi Ship Channel to Port Aransas. Tune your radio to 530 AM for ferry traffic conditions during the morning, lunch hour, and late afternoon rush times.

Port Aransas is a small town filled with year-round seaside attractions. During spring break, Port A greets more than 150,000 college students (and an increasing number of families as well) from throughout the Midwest and Southwest. The crowds are very manageable the rest of the year, however. During the winter months, most visitors are anglers and Winter Texans.

Port A tempts travelers with excellent attractions, dining, and shopping, and the best way to enjoy them is aboard the Port Aransas Shuttle. This trolley whisks vacationers from the community's many seaside restaurants and eclectic shops to the beach and Fisherman's Wharf, running from 10 a.m. to 6 p.m. daily.

After a day of surf hopping and sand-castle building, head to the town of Port Aransas itself. Shopping for shirts, shells, or elegant jewelry is a prime activity. So is dining. You can buy shrimp and fresh fish and prepare it in a condo kitchen or visit one of the island's many restaurants.

getting there

To reach Port Aransas, follow TX 361 from Aransas Pass across the Redfish Bay Causeway to Harbor Island.

where to go

Visitor Center. 403 West Cotter; (361) 749-5919; www.portaransas.org. Stop by the visitor center, located just across from the ferry landing, for brochures, maps, and assistance. Open weekdays 9 a.m. to 5 p.m. and Sat 9 a.m. to 3 p.m. Free admission.

Dolphin Watch Nature Tours. Woody's Boat Basin; www.dolphinwatchnaturetours .com. Nature tours and bottlenose dolphin watch cruises are available on two vessels from Woody's Boat Basin. A trawl net pulls up shrimp, fish, crabs, squid, and other small marine creatures for a close-up look at the Gulf's wildlife. Birding tours to Shamrock Island, a protected rookery island, and Pelican Island, the largest brown pelican rookery island in Texas, are other favorite choices. Additional cruises departing from Woody's Sport Center include a sunset cruise and a sightseeing tour with a look at the US Naval Station (home of the largest US minesweeping fleet), the Lydia Ann Lighthouse, and the Intracoastal Waterway. Call for schedule.

Fishing Cruises. Few coastal cities offer more fishing cruises than Port Aransas. In varying seasons, the Gulf is home to mackerel, ling, pompano, marlin, barracuda, grouper, and amberjack. In the calmer bay waters, look for redfish, speckled trout, drum, and flounder.

Large group excursions take as many as 100 passengers and provide bait and tackle. Serious anglers looking for big-game fish such as marlin and shark should book charter excursions for personalized service. Group fishing cruises are available for the bay and the Gulf, ranging in length anywhere from 4 to 24 hours. Trips include bait and tackle and start at about $45 per person.

If you do take a Gulf fishing cruise, be aware that Gulf waters can be very choppy. Except for the bay cruises, most boats travel 15 to 20 miles from shore. Seas are usually calmest in the summer, but even then 4- to 6-foot waves are possible. Seasickness has spoiled more than one vacationer's cruise, so be sure to purchase motion sickness medication or obtain a skin patch from your doctor before your trip.

Contact the tourist and convention bureau at (800) 45-COAST or (361) 749-5919 for more information.

Gulf Beach. The best way to learn about the beach life is to become part of it. And that's just what most visitors do. Armed with sunscreen, beach umbrellas, and folding chairs, they line the Gulf beach. Swimmers and surfers frequent the shallow, warm waters, and beachcombers search for fragile sand dollars, pieces of coral, and unbroken shells. Drivers on the public beach are restricted to a marked lane, and parking requires an annual permit (see www.cityofportaransas.org), available for $12 from the chamber of commerce or at many Port Aransas businesses such as grocery and convenience stores. There is free boardwalk access to the beach from many of the condominiums as well.

Leonabelle Turnbull Birding Center. Off Cut-Off Road on Ross Avenue; (800) 45-COAST. This city is home to the Leonabelle Turnbull Birding Center which is part of the Great Texas Coastal Birding Trail. The center is landscaped with plants to attract migrating hummingbirds and is also home to two 6-foot alligators named Boots and Bags and a family of nutria, members of the rodent family who nest in fallen reeds. The raised boardwalk here is wheelchair accessible; there's also a raised tower (with a free scope) for excellent viewing of the surrounding marshes. Free admission.

Mustang Island State Park. TX 361, southwest of Port Aransas; (361) 749-5246; www .tpwd.state.tx.us. The facilities at this scenic beach include freshwater showers, picnic tables, and tent and RV camping. The area is protected from vehicular traffic. Open daily.

Port Aransas Museum. 101 East Brundrett St.; (361) 749-3800; www.portaransas museum.org. Operated by the Port Aransas Preservation and Historical Association, this museum in the Community Center Complex recalls life on the island in the early days of Port Aransas. Open Thurs through Sat 1 to 5 p.m. Free admission.

Port Aransas Nature Preserve. Port Street. This 1,217-acre park includes 2 miles of hike and bike trails and a tower for viewing the wetlands around Salt Island. Free admission.

San Jose Island. Woody's Boat Basin; (361) 749-5252. Both Port Aransas and Mustang Island State Park beaches are popular with vacationers, but if you're looking for a real getaway, head to nearby San Jose Island (sometimes also called Saint Joseph Island or Saint Joe's Island). You'll feel like pirate Jean Lafitte, whose camp was found on the island in 1834. Large iron rings, thought to have been used to tie up small boats his group used to row ashore, were discovered at the site. Even today the island is accessible only by boat, and there are no public facilities. San Jose is a quiet getaway for fishing, beachcombing, swimming, and especially shelling. Ferries leave throughout the day from Woody's Boat Basin, so you can stay as long as you like. Open daily.

University of Texas Marine Science Institute Wetlands Educational Center. On Ship Channel; (361) 749-6764; www.utmsi.utexas.edu. Students of oceanography, ecology, marine chemistry, and botany train at this branch of the University of Texas, located on 82 beachfront acres. The public is invited to stroll the boardwalks to view migrant and resident bird species. Free admission.

Wharf Cat **Birding Tours.** Fisherman's Wharf; (361) 749-5448 or (800) 605-5448; www.texaswhoopers.com. This 75-foot heated and air-conditioned catamaran departs from Fisherman's Wharf Monday and Tuesday from November through early April for a look at magnificent whooping cranes. (On Wed through Sun, the cruise departs from nearby Rockport.) The cruise leaves Port Aransas for the Aransas National Wildlife Refuge, the winter home of the 5-foot-tall whooping cranes. Binoculars and scopes are provided (although it is best to bring your own), along with checklists of frequently spotted birds. Call for schedule.

where to eat

Barnacle Bill's Pierhouse and Grill. 230 North On The Beach; (361) 749-6200. There's absolutely nothing fancy about this diner that offers breakfast, lunch, and dinner—as well as bait—in its building perched on a pier. The food is tasty, and the atmosphere is fun and coastal. Open daily. $.

The Crazy Cajun. 303 Beach Ave.; (361) 749-5069. This Cajun seafood restaurant's house specialty is a steaming concoction of shrimp, sausage, potatoes, stone crab claws, and crawfish in season. The bowl is dumped onto your butcher-paper tablecloth. The atmosphere is casual and fun, and there's live entertainment many nights. Open for lunch and dinner on weekends, dinner only on weekdays. $$.

Seafood and Spaghetti Works. 710 Alister St.; (361) 749-5666. This excellent restaurant is housed in a geodesic dome. Spaghetti primavera, shrimp and pepper pasta (a spicy dish that could be called Italian Tex-Mex if there were such a thing), filet mignon, and Cajun-style blackened redfish are popular choices. Save room for the Butterfinger cheesecake. Open for dinner only. $$.

Trout Street Bar and Grill. 104 West Cotter; (361) 749-7800; www.tsbag.com. Enjoy the catch of the day and other seafood favorites at this restaurant. Burgers and steaks served along with oysters, shrimp, and the local catch. Open for lunch and dinner daily. $$.

where to stay

You won't find full-service hotels in Port Aransas, but the town does offer everything from luxury condominium complexes to mom-and-pop motels aimed at vacationing anglers. Many condominiums include full kitchens and appliances and easy access to the beach.

Dunes Condominiums. 1000 Lantana; (361) 749-5155 or (877) 296-3863; www.the dunescondos.com. These Gulf-view condominiums include kitchenettes with refrigerators and amenities such as a pool, a beach, and tennis. $$–$$$.

Sand Castle Condominiums. Sand Castle Drive; (800) 727-6201. This 6-story condominium complex is located near the beach. Every room offers a great view and comes with a fully equipped kitchen. (If you can afford it, get a room with a private balcony.) When you've had enough saltwater swimming, take a dip in the large free-form pool in the center of the complex. Minimum stay and deposit required. $$$.

Seashell Village. 502 East Avenue G; (361) 749-4294; www.seashellvillage.com. We love this little Caribbean-style complex of suites and cottages just a short walk from the beach. Large porches, a pool, fully equipped kitchens and kitchenettes, and a family-friendly atmosphere make this place one of our beach favorites. $–$$$.

Tarpon Inn. 200 East Cotter St.; (361) 749-5555 or (800) 365-6784; www.thetarponinn .com. The most historic hotel on the island (and listed on the National Register of Historic Places) is the Tarpon Inn, which dates from 1923. The lobby walls are papered with thousands of tarpon scales, each autographed by the lucky angler. There's even one signed by Franklin D. Roosevelt. Within the last few years, the hotel has been renovated, but it still has a breezy atmosphere with rockers on the verandas. Each of the 24 rooms is decorated and furnished with antiques. $$.

rockport-fulton

The adjoining fishing villages of Rockport and Fulton lie along scenic Aransas Bay and are havens for snowbirds of all varieties, from 5-foot-tall whooping cranes to those in 30-foot-long Winnebagos. Both flock to this part of the Texas coast in late October and remain until the end of March. Rockport residents welcome the feathered snowbirds with several protected refuges, and the RVers have their choice of many well-manicured campgrounds, complete with a friendly small-town atmosphere.

Rockport and neighboring Fulton have quickly caught the attention of the birding world. In the 1940s a feisty and dedicated local amateur birder named Connie Hagar identified hundreds of species. Her research brought Rockport-Fulton to the attention of the National Wildlife Service and other organizations, which eventually recorded nearly 500 species in the area. Today Rockport-Fulton is renowned as one of the finest birding spots in the world.

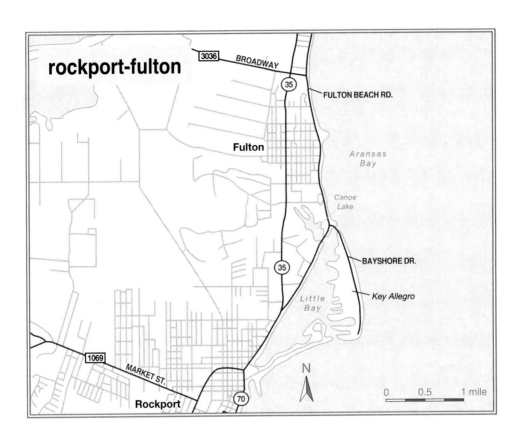

The Connie Hagar Sanctuary, downtown along TX 35 at Little Bay, is a good place to spot pelicans and many shorebirds. Whooping cranes winter at the Aransas National Wildlife Refuge northeast of town, and the drive to the refuge passes many marshes and coastal plains filled with birds.

Numerous birds fly through the area during fall and winter migration. Every September, Rockport-Fulton hosts the HummerBird Celebration to mark the passage of thousands of hummingbirds that stop in Rockport-Fulton on their way south to Central and South America. Bird lovers from around the country come to watch this feeding frenzy, when up to 150 hummingbirds often swarm the same feeder. The annual spring migration each May also brings hundreds of colorful songbirds to the area.

Bird-watching opportunities are available year-round. Contact the Rockport-Fulton Area Chamber of Commerce to order a copy of the "Birder's Guide." It illustrates the most common species found here, such as pelicans, cranes, storks, and laughing gulls. It also features driving tours to 16 birding sites.

Except for year-round boat tours and special bus tours during the HummerBird Celebration, you must depend on self-guided drives to good birding sites. The chamber can give you directions to the best locations outside of town, as well as information about recent spottings.

getting there

To reach the Rockport-Fulton area from Aransas Pass, take TX 35 north for 11 miles.

where to go

Rockport-Fulton Area Chamber of Commerce. 404 Broadway; (361) 729-6445 or (800) 242-0071; www.rockport-fulton.org. Especially if this is your first visit to Rockport, make your first stop the chamber office, where you can load up on free brochures and maps, as well as advice from "charmers"—volunteers representing the "Charm of the Texas Coast."

The Aquarium at Rockport Harbor. 702 Navigation Circle; (361) 729-2328; www.rock portaquarium.com. This nonprofit aquarium exhibits the marine life of the area, from the red drum found in the bays to the sea urchins and sergeants major seen around the jetties. Although nowhere the size of the Texas State Aquarium, this facility is free and a fun choice for families who are curious about the marine life below the surface of Rockport's waters. Open Thurs through Mon 1 to 4 p.m. Free admission.

Aransas National Wildlife Refuge. Forty-five minutes northeast of Rockport; (361) 286-3559; www.fws.gov. Take TX 35 north to FM 774, turn right, and continue to the intersection of FM 2040. Turn right and stay on FM 2040 to the refuge. This 54,829-acre refuge is the prime wintering ground for the endangered whooping crane, plus hundreds of other bird species. The refuge includes several hiking trails and a paved 15-mile loop drive that offer a chance to see some of the 80 mammal species indigenous to the region, including opossum, shrew, bat, armadillo, raccoon, coati, ringtail, mink, weasel, nutria, skunk, bobcat, white-tailed deer, coyote, and even wild boar.

The observation tower is located on the loop drive. From its heights you can view the elegant whooping cranes, whose numbers once dwindled to only 16. Thanks to conservation programs, the present population has increased tenfold. The Wildlife Interpretive Center includes films and exhibits on the annual migration of these 5-foot-tall birds. Across the road, have a look at native alligators resting in a swampy, fenced enclosure. Refuge open daily from sunrise to sunset; the Wildlife Interpretive Center is open daily 8:30 a.m. to 4:30 p.m.

Copano Bay Causeway State Fishing Pier. (361) 729-7762. This park is a favorite with anglers, who will find fishing piers and concessions. There's also a public boat launch ramp. Open daily.

Fulton Mansion State Historic Site. Three miles north of Rockport off TX 35, corner of Henderson Street and Fulton Beach Road; (361) 729-0386; www.visitfultonmansion.com. Built in 1876 by Colonel George Fulton, this grand 4-story home overlooks Aransas Bay.

Formerly a state park and now operated by the Texas Historical Commission, the Fulton Mansion features interesting architecture and surprising modern conveniences. Built at a cost of $100,000, the house included central forced-air heating. A central cast-iron furnace in the basement provided heat through a series of flues to false decorative fireplaces in the main rooms. Hot and cold running water was achieved with a tank located in the tower attic. A gas plant located at the back of the house provided fuel for gas chandeliers.

Visitors are asked to wear flat, soft-soled shoes because of the delicate Axminster and Brussels carpets purchased from New York. Tours of the home's 29 rooms are conducted Tues through Sat 10:30 a.m. to 3 p.m. and Sun 1 to 3 p.m.

Demonstration Garden and Wetlands Pond. Picnic area on east side of TX 35. Stop by this demonstration garden for a look at plants that attract hummingbirds and butterflies. Firecracker bush, cape honeysuckle, Mexican Turk's cap, and lantana are a few of the native plants that help keep Rockport buzzing with winged visitors. Free admission.

Goose Island State Park. TX 35 and PR 13, 21 miles northeast of Rockport; (361) 729-2858; www.tpwd.state.tx.us. This 314-acre park is the home of the "Big Tree," the coastal live oak state champion. The park is also home to a variety of waterfowl and shorebirds. Anglers try for speckled trout, redfish, drum, flounder, and sheepshead. Open daily.

Rockport Beach Park. Downtown, just off TX 35; (361) 729-2213; www.cityofrockport .com. This is a very popular spot, especially during warm weather. The 1-mile beach offers swimming, picnicking, a children's playground, boating, fishing, and crabbing off an 800-foot pier, as well as paddleboat and Jet Ski rentals. There's also a bird-watching platform overlooking an island said to be the home of one of the best colonies of birds in the state. Open daily.

Rockport Center for the Arts. 902 Navigation Circle, across the street from Texas Maritime Museum; (361) 729-5519; www.rockportartcenter.com. This restored 1890 house is now the home of the Rockport Art Association and a good place to buy a painting of a Texas beach scene by a local artist. Look for changing exhibits every month. Open Tues through Sat 10 a.m. to 4 p.m. and Sun 1 to 4 p.m. Free admission.

Texas Maritime Museum. 1202 Navigation Circle, on downtown waterfront; (866) 729-AHOY or (361) 729-1271; www.texasmaritimemuseum.org. This 2-story museum chronicles Texas maritime activities, starting with Spanish shipwrecks off the coast and continuing through today's offshore oil and gas industries. Special exhibits are devoted to shipbuilding, Texans of the sea, the *LaBelle* shipwreck, and fishing. Open Tues through Sat 10 a.m. to 4 p.m. and Sun 1 to 4 p.m.

where to eat

The Boiling Pot. 201 South Fulton Beach Rd.; (361) 729-6972; http://the-boiling-pot.com. Don a bib, grab a Mamba beer from one of the 31 Baskin Robbins–like selections, and sit down. This roadside shack is always noisy, crowded, and fun. The Cajun Combo features blue crab, shrimp, andouille sausage, new potatoes, and corn, all boiled up in a spicy pot and dumped from a metal container onto the paper-covered table. You crack the crab claws with a wooden mallet and dip the succulent flesh in melted butter. Fingers, not forks, are the rule here; dainty eaters need not apply. This is a Texas experience to savor. Open for dinner only Mon through Thurs, lunch and dinner Fri through Sun. $–$$.

Latitude 28° 02' Coast Cuisine & Fine Art. 105 North Austin St.; (361) 727-9009; www .latituderockport.com. This restaurant combines fresh local seafood with a fine-arts gallery representing over 70 artists to create a unique dining experience. Open for dinner Tues through Sun. Reservations are recommended. $$–$$$.

where to stay

Rockport has a selection of accommodations, ranging from fishing cottages to elegantly furnished condominiums. Because of the large number of Winter Texans who call Rockport home during the cooler months, many RV and trailer parks and condominiums lease by the day, week, or month. For a brochure listing all of Rockport-Fulton's varied lodgings, call the chamber of commerce office at (800) 242-0071.

Key Allegro Rentals. 1798 Bayshore Dr., just over Key Allegro Bridge on Fulton Beach Road; (361) 729-3691 or (800) 348-1627; www.keyallegro.com. Key Allegro is a small island linked to Rockport by an arched bridge. The lovely drive here is your first hint of the elegant accommodations awaiting visitors in this area. Nicely appointed condominium units and upscale homes located on the water's edge afford beautiful views of Rockport's fishing

connie hagar

*The eyes (and binoculars) of the birding world were focused on Rockport due to the efforts of the late **Connie Hagar,** a woman who became somewhat of a legend along the Coastal Bend. She migrated to Rockport in the 1930s, drawn by the large number of birds she had seen on an earlier visit.*

*For more than three decades Connie Hagar chronicled the comings and goings of hundreds of species. She was not an ornithologist, but a birder who enjoyed the feathered visitors. Today you can visit the **Connie Hagar Bird Sanctuary** in downtown Rockport at First and Church Streets, a marshy grassland that is a stopping place for many seabirds, not to mention the many birders who sit on the piers and revel at the magnificent great blue herons and pelicans.*

vessels heading out for the day's catch. Rental homes and condominiums are available by the day or week. $$–$$$.

Kontiki Beach Resort. 2290 North Fulton Beach Rd.; (800) 388-0649; www.kontikibeach.com. These hotel rooms and condos offers spacious accommodations that feature a living and dining area, fully equipped kitchen, and separate bedroom, available by the day, week, or month. All take in a view of the water. $$–$$$.

Laguna Reef Condominium Resort. 1021 Water St.; (361) 729-1742 or (800) 248-1057; www.lagunareef.com. This pet-friendly waterfront hotel and condominium resort has an unbeatable view of the bay, especially for early risers who want to watch the gorgeous sunrise. Each fully furnished unit has a private balcony, kitchen, and dining/living room. After a day of sightseeing, take a walk along the complex's beach or down the long fishing pier. The units rent by the day, week, or month. $$.

especially for winter texans

Rockport hosts many special events for Winter Texans, from fishing and horseshoe tournaments to arts and crafts shows to concerts by talented seasonal residents.

The **Paws and Taws Center** on Fulton Beach Road is the site of many gatherings for the winter visitors who stay in Rockport and Fulton. With a hardwood floor, a stage, and kitchen facilities, the center holds weekly square dances, bingo games, AARP meetings, and State Days, with parties for visitors from specific states.

The Rockport area includes many excellent RV parks, with busy clubhouse activities. For more information, call the Rockport-Fulton Area Chamber of Commerce at (800) 242-0071 or visit www.rockport-fulton.org.

day trip 02

coast & cattle:
three rivers, mathis, corpus christi,
padre & mustang islands, kingsville

The interstate highway between San Antonio and Corpus Christi is well traveled during peak periods of spring break and summer vacation, but this coastal getaway makes a fun weekend trip year-round. From sandy strolls on Padre Island to seafood dining in Corpus Christi to tours of a ranch that is truly Texas-size, the stops on this getaway hold plenty of fun for the entire family.

three rivers

Located halfway between San Antonio and Corpus Christi on I-37, the community of Three Rivers is best known as the gateway to Choke Canyon.

getting there

From San Antonio, head south on I-37 and let your cruise control do its thing. You'll roll past a couple small towns, Pleasanton and Cambellton, along the way, but for the most part the views will be of farms and fields. Soon after crossing the Atascosa River at Cambellton, start watching for exit 72 for US 281. Take exit 72 and drive 5 miles south to the Three Rivers city limits.

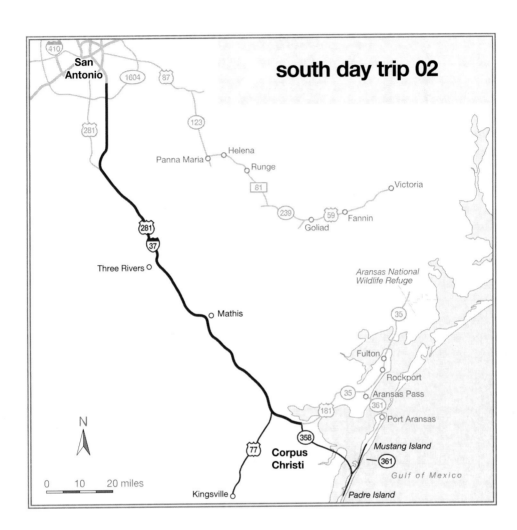

south day trip 02

where to go

Choke Canyon State Park, Calliham Unit. Twelve miles west of Three Rivers on TX 72 to Tilden; (361) 786-3868; www.tpwd.state.tx.us. The larger of the two Choke Canyon parks, this facility sprawls over 1,100 acres. Park facilities include screened shelters, campsites, a sports complex, fishing, tennis, basketball, RV hookups, birding trails, and a wildlife educational center. Open daily.

Choke Canyon State Park, South Shore Unit. Three and a half miles west of Three Rivers on TX 72; (361) 786-3868; www.tpwd.state.tx.us. This 385-acre park offers visitors camping, boating, hiking, birding, a swimming pool, and many recreation areas. This and the nearby Calliham Unit comprise Choke Canyon State Park, named for the extensive reservoir that supplies water to the city of Corpus Christi. The parks are filled with wildlife, ranging from Rio Grande turkey to fox to American alligator. Open daily.

mathis

This agricultural capital is located south of San Antonio and is a popular stop for visitors wishing to boat or fish at Lake Corpus Christi State Park.

getting there

To reach Mathis, drive east on TX 72 from Three Rivers to I-37 and proceed south for 33 miles. The city is located just 22 miles from Corpus Christi.

where to go

Lake Corpus Christi State Park. FM 1068, 4 miles southwest of Mathis, off TX 359; (361) 547-2635; www.tpwd.state.tx.us. This sprawling park surrounds the 21,000-acre Lake Corpus Christi, a favorite with boaters and anglers. Activities here include waterskiing, fishing, swimming, hiking, and birding. Open daily.

Lipantitlan State Historic Site. (361) 547-2635; www.tpwd.state.tx.us. Go south on TX 359 for 31 miles to Orange Grove, then turn east and continue 9 miles on FM 624 and FM 70. This historic park highlights an adobe fort built by the Mexican government in 1833. Today visitors find few facilities here. Open daily. Free admission.

corpus christi

This city of 305,000 residents is a popular year-round destination. During the summer months, the nearby beaches of Padre and Mustang Islands appeal to surfers, families, and sun worshippers. During the winter, this coastal city fills with Winter Texans.

The waters of Corpus Christi Bay are calm, protected from the Gulf of Mexico by the barrier islands of Padre and Mustang, which served as pirate hideouts even after the area was charted in 1519 by Spanish explorer Alonzo Alvarez de Pineda. He bestowed the bay with its name, which means "body of Christ."

Today Corpus Christi is a thriving city, consistently ranking as one of America's busiest ports. The bayfront is a combination fishing village and tourist spot, and the downtown piers are lined with picturesque shrimp boats. High-rise luxury hotels, specialty shops, and seafood restaurants overlook the bay. The heart of Corpus Christi is Shoreline Boulevard, with its proud palms and spectacular views of the water. The handsome boulevard begins as Ocean Drive at the gates of the US Naval Air Station and winds north past grand mansions perched on the bluffs overlooking the bay.

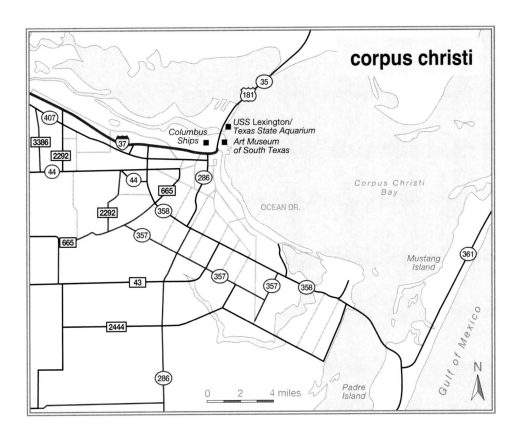

Because of the warm weather and a fairly consistent breeze of about 12 miles per hour, Corpus Christi is known as the unofficial windsurfing capital of the United States. It's not unusual to see the bay dotted with the colorful sails. Ocean Drive's Oleander Park is the only city-sanctioned sailboard park in the world. If you want to give the sport a try, several operators along South Padre Island Drive offer instruction and rentals.

The north section of Shoreline Boulevard contains the huge piers known as Coopers Street L-Head, Lawrence Street T-Head, and Peoples Street T-Head. Each pier bustles with life, from the predawn hours when the shrimp boats leave until midnight; the night cruises offer anglers a chance at trophy tarpon, kingfish, or marlin. Peoples Street T-Head is also home of the *Flagship,* an 85-foot paddle wheeler that offers guided bay tours.

The northern end of Shoreline Boulevard also holds the Art Museum of South Texas, and the Corpus Christi Museum of Science and History, with its ships of Christopher Columbus. At the end of the drive is the Harbor Bridge. Built in 1959 to link the city with the small towns that line the Texas coast, it leads across the ship channel to the Texas State Aquarium.

getting there

Continue south from Mathis on I-37 to Corpus Christi.

where to go

Art Museum of South Texas. 1902 North Shoreline Blvd., Bayfront Arts and Science Park; (361) 825-3500; www.artmuseumofsouthtexas.org. Famous for its stark white architecture, this museum is filled with changing fine-arts exhibits of traditional and contemporary works. Open Tues through Sun.

> **Watergardens.** Bayfront Arts and Science Park; no phone. A man-made stream tumbles from the entrance of the art museum down to a sunken circle of flags and fountains. This is a nice place to take a box lunch. Open daily. Free admission.

Asian Cultures Museum and Educational Center. 1809 North Chaparral St.; (361) 882-2641; http://asianculturesmuseum.org. The museum boasts an extensive collection of Asian cultural artifacts. The original collection was assembled by the museum's founder, Billie Trimble Chandler, a Corpus Christi teacher who spent much of her career teaching in Asia. The permanent collection now includes articles from China, Japan, Korea, Laos, India, Sri Lanka, Thailand, and the Phillippines. In addition, the museum hosts a changing menu of visiting exhibits from around the world. In keeping with Mrs. Chandler's involvement in teaching, the museum conducts regular classes with a curriculum focusing on Asian culture. Classes range from learning to use chopsticks to studying Asian religions. Open Tues through Sat.

Captain Clark Flagship Cruises. Peoples Street T-Head; (361) 884-8306; www.capt clarksflagship.com. Several daily tours take visitors for a look at the shipyards and the bay. Sunset cruises are particularly scenic, with the lights of downtown reflected in the calm bay waters. Open daily in the summer months; weekends only Sept through May.

Corpus Christi Museum of Science and History. 1900 North Chaparral St., Bayfront Arts and Science Park; (361) 826-4667; www.ccmuseum.com. This museum is filled with natural history exhibits, including displays recalling the many Spanish shipwrecks found off the Gulf Coast. Children can climb aboard a re-creation of a 15th-century vessel for a peek at the cramped quarters endured by early explorers. Don't miss the *Seeds of Change* exhibit, designed by the Smithsonian's National Museum of Natural History for the 500th anniversary of the European discovery of America.

After a look at exhibits that tell the story of these explorers and the effects their arrival had on the New World, see for yourself what it was like to make the Atlantic crossing aboard the **ships of Christopher Columbus.** Life-size replicas of the *Pinta* and *Santa Maria* are located in a shipyard repair facility adjacent to the museum (*Nina* is undergoing repairs at a shipyard). These re-creations of the Columbus fleet were built by the Spanish government at the cost of more than $7 million to commemorate the 500th anniversary of the explorer's voyage. You can board the *Pinta,* and adjacent onshore exhibits explain more about sea travel and the Spanish voyages. Open Tues through Sun.

Dolphin Connection. Beneath US 181 bridge to Portland, just before Nueces Bay Causeway; (361) 776-2887; www.dolphinconnectiontexas.com. Two Dolphin Connection boats take visitors into the bay to feed and interact with dolphins. Guides know the wild mammals by name and are glad to explain their habits, family connections, and lifestyle. You can hand feed and pet these remarkable creatures during the hour-long excursion. Open daily Mar through Oct or Nov, when the dolphins leave for the winter.

Heritage Park. 1581 North Chaparral St.; (361) 826-3410; www.ccparkandrec.com. Located a short walk from the convention center, this park contains a collection of historic homes relocated here from around the region and lovingly restored. Tours of the homes that date from the mid-19th century are available Thurs and Fri at 10:30 a.m. Open weekdays. Free (fee for tours).

Selena Memorial. Mirador de la Flor, Peoples Street T-Head and Shoreline Boulevard; no phone. Many music fans make a special stop at this privately erected memorial to Selena Quintanilla-Perez, a very popular Tejano singer who was slain in Corpus Christi in 1995. The life-size bronze statue of the star, sculpted by a Corpus Christi artist, is located on the downtown seawall.

South Texas Botanical Gardens and Nature Center. 8545 South Staples Dr.; (361) 852-2100; www.stxbot.org. Take South Staples Drive toward Kingsville, past Oso Creek; signs mark entrance. These gardens feature native South Texas plants and winding trails through subtropical foliage. Open daily.

Texas State Aquarium. 2710 Shoreline Dr., across ship channel from the downtown area; (800) 477-GULF; www.texasstateaquarium.org. The Texas State Aquarium focuses on sea life of the Gulf of Mexico, the first such facility in the nation. The **Gulf of Mexico Exhibit Building,** a $31.5 million facility, houses 250 species, including groupers, eels, and sharks. This must-see attraction showcases the aquatic animals and habitats indigenous to the Gulf. You'll enter the interpretive center beneath a cascading waterfall, symbolic of the dive into coastal waters. It's a self-guided discovery through exhibits such as *Islands of Steel,* a look at a replica of an offshore oil platform surrounded by nurse sharks, amberjacks, and other marine creatures commonly found around these man-made reefs. Nearby, the *Flower Gardens Coral Reef* exhibit looks at the beautiful coral gardens found 115 miles off the coast, blooming with aquatic life and marine animals such as moray eels, tarpon, and rays. Outdoors, young visitors enjoy touch tanks filled with small sharks and rays; *Otter Creek,* where playful river otters amuse visitors with their antics; and the *Floating Phantoms* exhibit, an 800-gallon display tank allowing safe inspection of jellyfish, sea nettles, and other stinging sea creatures.

High-tech displays feature the use of a video monitor to help you guide the image of an underwater robotic arm. Touch-screen monitors offer a chance for visitors to try their hand at environmental decision-making. When you're finished here, walk outside for a look at the ship channel, the **Harbor Bridge,** and an unbeatable view of the city. Open daily.

Texas Surf Museum. 309A North Water St.; (361) 888-7873; www.texassurfmuseum .com. Tucked into a nicely landscaped pedestrian area next to the Water Street Seafood Company, this 3,000-square-foot museum honors the sport of surfing on the Texas coast. Hundreds of surfing memorabilia pieces fill the museum, including rare surfboards, and a small theater shows surfing movies. A gift shop sells surfing music, T-shirts, and other souvenirs of the sport. The museum is open Mon through Thurs 10 a.m. to 7 p.m.; Fri and Sat 10 a.m. to 10 p.m.; and Sun 11 a.m. to 5 p.m.

Outside the museum, you'll find the **South Texas Music Walk of Fame,** a brick-paved area adorned with stars honoring famous South Texas musicians, among them Kris Kristofferson, Freddy Fender, Doug Sahm, Selena, and Michael Nesmith (of Monkees fame). Each June, six new stars are added to the display during the **Water Street Market Music & Art Fest.**

USS *Lexington* Museum on the Bay. 2914 North Shoreline Blvd.; (800) LADY-LEX; www.usslexington.com. This aircraft carrier is berthed just offshore from the Texas State Aquarium, and visitors have permission to come aboard. Reported as sunk four times by the Japanese in World War II, the ship returned to fight again, taking part in every major naval engagement in the Pacific. Today this carrier, with a main deck larger than three football fields, is a museum open daily for tours. Texas's first flight simulator takes up to 16 passengers on a 3- to 5-minute flight. Hydraulically powered, the "cabin" uses a combination of sight, sound, and movement to give passengers the sensation of riding in either an attack airplane or a helicopter. The USS *Lexington* is open 9 a.m. to 6 p.m. Memorial Day through Labor Day; 9 a.m. to 5 p.m. the rest of the year.

where to eat

City Diner. 622 North Water St.; (361) 883-1643. This fun restaurant boasts a 1950s diner atmosphere. The menu includes all types of American dishes, from chicken to burgers, as well as fresh Gulf seafood. Open for breakfast, lunch and dinner Sun through Thurs 7 a.m. to 9:30 p.m.; Fri and Sat 7 a.m. to 10:30 p.m. $$–$$$.

Landry's Seafood House. Peoples Street T-Head; (361) 882-6666. This restaurant is a restored 2-story barge that sports a casual, fun atmosphere. Huge picture windows offer a great view of the bay. The specialty of the house is Gulf seafood, including shrimp, oysters, and scallops. Open for lunch and dinner daily. $$.

Water Street Seafood Company and Water Street Oyster Bar. 309 North Water Street, Water Street Market; (361) 882-8684. Located just a block from Shoreline Boulevard, this casual restaurant features Cajun-inspired seafood as well as the usual Gulf Coast fare. Open daily for lunch and dinner. $$–$$$.

where to stay

Best Western Marina Grand Hotel. 300 North Shoreline Blvd.; (361) 883-5111; www .marinagrandhotel.net. This high-rise hotel boasts one of the best locations (and some of the best views) in the city, located just across Shoreline Boulevard from the seawall and Lawrence Street T-Head and 1 block east of the Water Street Market area with its bars, restaurants, and the Texas Surf Museum. The dog-friendly 11-story hotel has a fitness room, outdoor pool area, and business center, and offers complimentary breakfast, covered parking, and laundry facilities. $$.

Embassy Suites Hotel. 4337 South Padre Island Dr.; (361) 853-7899 or (800) EMBASSY; www.embassysuites.com. This all-suite hotel is located on the north side of town, 15 minutes from Shoreline Boulevard and Padre Island. The huge open lobby and atrium include a heated pool, hot tub, and sauna, as well as a dining area that serves a free all-you-can-eat breakfast plus evening cocktails. $$.

Holiday Inn Emerald Beach. 1102 South Shoreline Blvd.; (361) 883-5731; www.holiday inn.com. The only hotel in downtown Corpus Christi with a beach (albeit a small one), this property is very popular with families. The 368-room hotel includes a restaurant, pool, exercise room, game room, and playground. $$–$$$.

Omni Corpus Christi Bayfront. 900 North Shoreline Blvd.; (361) 887-1600 or (800) THE-OMNI; www.omnihotels.com. This elegant 475-room hotel overlooks the bay and includes a health club, heated swimming pool, and rooftop dining room. Many of Corpus Christi's main attractions lie within walking distance. $$$.

Omni Corpus Christi Marina. 707 North Shoreline Blvd.; (361) 887-1600 or (800) THE-OMNI; www.omnihotels.com. This bayfront hotel offers 346 guest rooms, a pool, a restaurant, and more. The location, like its sister property the Omni Corpus Christi Bayfront, is excellent for anyone wanting to be right in the heart of downtown. $$–$$$.

Sea Shell Inn. 202 Kleberg Place; (361) 888-5391; www.seashellinnmotel.com. Located on Corpus Christi Beach at the base of the Harbor Bridge, this 26-room property includes many rooms with kitchenettes. The hotel offers beach access and a pool. $–$$.

padre & mustang islands

When you cross the Intracoastal Waterway via the enormous JFK Causeway Bridge, you leave the mainland for Padre Island. This 110-mile barrier island protects much of the Texas coast from hurricanes and tropical storms. Generally, the northern stretch of island paralleling the area from Corpus Christi to Port Mansfield is called Padre Island; from that point south to the tip of Texas, the landmass is named South Padre Island.

Padre and Mustang Islands feature beaches dotted with rolling dunes, clean sand, and flocks of gulls. The surf is usually gentle and shallow enough to walk for hundreds of yards before reaching chest-deep water. Occasionally undertow is a problem, but on most summer days the waves are gentle and rolling, and the water is warm.

Visitors can choose from several parks here, each with its own special charm. One of these, **Padre Balli Park,** is named for the priest who managed a ranch on the island in the early 19th century. It offers a 1,200-foot fishing pier. Continuing south, the **Padre Island National Seashore** has a snack bar, and showers are available at the **Malaquite Beach Visitor Center.** Although vehicles are allowed on most Padre beaches, Malaquite is one where vehicles are not permitted.

Beyond Malaquite lies 66 miles of protected beach in Padre Island National Seashore, accessible only by four-wheel-drive vehicles. Little Shell and Big Shell Beaches are located in this area.

Although much of Padre Island is undeveloped, you'll find many commercial establishments on neighboring Mustang Island. To reach it, turn left off South Padre Island Drive from Corpus Christi onto TX 361. Only 18 miles long, Mustang Island is far smaller than its neighbor to the south, but it shares many of the same attractions. One of the best stops is Mustang Island State Park (361-749-5246), where showers, restrooms, and camping are available. Cars, however, are prohibited on the beach.

Whether you choose Mustang or Padre, follow a few rules of safety. Portuguese man-of-war jellyfish are commonly seen on the beaches. If you are stung, locals claim the best relief is a paste of meat tenderizer and water applied to the bite. A far less dangerous, but very annoying, aspect of the Gulf beaches are tar balls. These black clumps, formed by natural seepage and offshore oil spills, wash up on the beach and stick to your skin and your shoes. Many hotels have a tar removal station near the door to help you remove the sticky substance.

getting there

To reach the islands, head out of Corpus Christi on South Padre Island Drive, also called TX 358. The road is lined with shell shops, windsurfing rentals, bait stands, and car washes. In the shallow waters along the drive, many anglers stand waist deep in salt water alongside tall herons and pelicans looking for a meal.

where to go

Mustang Island State Park. TX 361; (361) 749-5246; www.tpwd.state.tx.us. Mustang Island State Park is clean and enjoyable, perfect for a weekend of RV or tent camping or just a few hours of beachcombing. Freshwater showers are available. Covered picnic tables help keep your gear out of the sand. Open daily.

where to stay

Gulfstream Condos. 14810 Windward Dr., Padre Island; (361) 949-8061 or (800) 542-7368; www.gulfstreamcondos.com. This 132-room property includes a heated pool and Jacuzzi, a game room, and beach access. The 2-bedroom, 2-bath condos have air-conditioning, fully equipped kitchens (including microwave ovens and dishwashers), and balconies with nice view of the sea. $$$.

Holiday Inn North Padre Island. 15202 Windward Dr.; (361) 949-8041 or (888) 949-8041; www.holidayinn.com. Here you can walk from the hotel directly to the beach. When you've had enough salt water, take a dip in the hotel swimming pool. $$.

Island House. 15340 Leeward Dr., Padre Island; (361) 949-8166 or (800) 333-8806; www.ccislandhouse.com. This beachfront condominium resort has well-furnished units, many with beautiful views of the Gulf. Each includes a furnished kitchen, a dining/living room, and 2 bedrooms. Spend the extra money for an oceanfront condo, with sliding glass doors in the living room and the master bedroom. $$$.

kingsville

Perhaps no other destination quite epitomizes "Texas size" like the King Ranch. Larger than the state of Rhode Island, the King Ranch sprawls across 825,000 acres and, even more importantly, stands as a symbol of Texas ingenuity. The ranch has long been known for its role in the American ranching industry and is still a worldwide leader. Many of the practices used industry-wide started here.

Just a few blocks away, the historic downtown is included on the National Register of Historic Places. Kleberg Avenue and King Street are lined with antiques shops and specialty stores.

But the prime attraction in this community is the **King Ranch,** located 39 miles south of Corpus Christi. Visitors can enjoy a guided tour of the ranch in air-conditioned buses. Don't expect reenactments of typical ranch activities here, though—this is the real thing. Cowboys, more often seen riding pickup trucks than horses, work more than 60,000 cattle on this ranch. The ranch also offers nature trails that provide glimpses of white-tailed deer, javelinas, coyotes, and other animals native to this region, first known as the Wild Horse Desert.

King Ranch traces its history to 1853, when it was founded by Captain Richard King, a self-made man who left home at an early age and made his fortune on Rio Grande riverboats. The ranch, still one of the largest in the world, developed the Santa Gertrudis and King Ranch Santa Cruz breeds of cattle, the only two registered breeds developed in the United States, as well as the first registered American quarter horse.

Many fall and winter visitors also come to enjoy a look at the resident and migratory birds. A stop on the Coastal Birding Trail, the ranch is home to more than 300 feathered species. Species such as green jays, pygmy owls, and common paurauque are spotted on different areas of the ranch.

getting there

The ranch is located on the outskirts of Kingsville, 39 miles south of Corpus Christi on US 77. The Kingsville Visitor Center is at the intersection of US 77 and Corral Drive and makes a good stop to pick up area brochures and maps.

where to go

Conner Museum. 905 West Santa Gertrudis St., on the campus of Texas A&M University–Kingsville; (361) 593-2810; www.tamuk.edu. Highlighting the natural and social history of South Texas, the museum includes exhibits on ranching, South Texas ecosystems, and area fossil and minerals. Open Mon through Sat. Free admission.

King Ranch Visitor Center. 2205 TX 141 West; (361) 592-8055; www.king-ranch.com. The center is a gathering place for tours of the King Ranch. A continuously running film about the history of the ranch gives guests an overview of the operation. Visitors also sign up for guided 1.5-hour tours (call for tour times). The guided bus tours begin at the site where Captain King first camped in 1852 and proceed to cover both the history and the modern workings of the ranch. Special-interest tours of cattle operations, feedlots, and other aspects of the ranch are available by appointment. Nature tours, including special programs for birders, are scheduled several times annually. Open daily (afternoons only on Sun). Free (except for tours).

where to shop

King Ranch Saddle Shop. 201 East Kleberg Ave.; (800) 282-KING; www.krsaddleshop .com. The King Ranch Saddle Shop carries on the tradition of saddle making that began after the Civil War when Captain King started his own saddle shop. It produces fine purses, belts, and saddles in downtown Kingsville's John B. Ragland Mercantile Company Building. Open Mon through Sat.

Sellers Market. 220½ East Kleberg; (361) 593-2810. Handmade arts and crafts made by over 100 local artists fill this marketplace. The market is a relaxing change of pace from typical mall shopping and you'll often have the opportunity to meet the artisans, especially if you shop on a Saturday. Open Tues through Sat.

where to eat

CB's Bar-B-Que. 728 North 14th St.; (361) 516-1688; www.cbsbarbque.com. Mesquite-smoked meats are the star attraction at this restaurant once voted South Texas's best by

captain king

*King Ranch traces its history to 1853, when it was founded by **Captain Richard King**, who made his fortune on Rio Grande riverboats.*

This area, which was first called the Wild Horse Desert by early settlers and later became part of the Rincon de Santa Gertrudis Spanish Land Grant, was tamed by Captain King. King first saw the land when traveling from Brownsville to Corpus Christi to attend the Lone Star Fair. He traveled 124 miles north of Brownsville before reaching what must have seemed like an oasis: the mesquite-shaded Santa Gertrudis Creek. Soon he and his friend Texas Ranger Captain Gideon K. "Legs" Lewis set about forming a partnership, a livestock operation headquartered at this creek.

In the ensuing years, King fenced these rugged coastal plains and moved an entire village from Mexico to staff the ranch, people who would become the first cowboys of Texas.

Texas Monthly Magazine. Don't let the geodesic-dome exterior fool you—this is genuine Texas barbecue with a loyal local following. Open for lunch and dinner Mon through Sat. $.

Young's Pizza. 625 West Santa Gertrudis St.; (361) 592-9179; www.youngspizza.com. This Kingsville institution traces its history back to the mid-1960s and bills itself as the "Birthplace of the Texicali," their proprietary sub sandwich. In addition to subs and pizza, Young's offers soups, salads, and desserts. Open for lunch and dinner Mon through Sat. $.

where to stay

Rodeway Inn Kingsville. 3430 South US 77; (361) 595-5753; www.rodewayinn.com. Located just minutes from downtown, this family-style hotel includes a restaurant, outdoor pool, and fitness center, and offers laundry services, free Wi-Fi access, complimentary breakfast, and free local phone calls. Pets up to 40 pounds are allowed for a nominal fee. $$.

southwest

day trip 01

southwest

run for the border:
pearsall, dilley, cotulla, laredo

The 153-mile drive from San Antonio to Laredo via I-35 is a fast one. Although a few small towns appear on this stretch, much of the area remains ranch land.

Much of this day trip is through very small communities that serve area ranches such as Devine, located 32 miles outside of San Antonio on I-35. Founded as a railroad station in 1881 and named for a San Antonio judge, Devine is a quiet town that's best known as an agricultural center. Six miles southeast of the town lies the smaller community of Bigfoot, named for Texas Ranger "Bigfoot" Wallace, a hero of the Texas War of Independence.

pearsall

This home of just fewer than 8,000 residents is the capital of the region's peanut crop. There's even a peanut monument downtown.

getting there

From San Antonio travel down I-35 for 22 miles to the community of Pearsall.

where to go

Frio Pioneer Jail Museum. Cedar and Medina Streets; (830) 334-9414 (chamber of commerce). The stone 2-story Late Victorian structure dates back to 1884 and featured

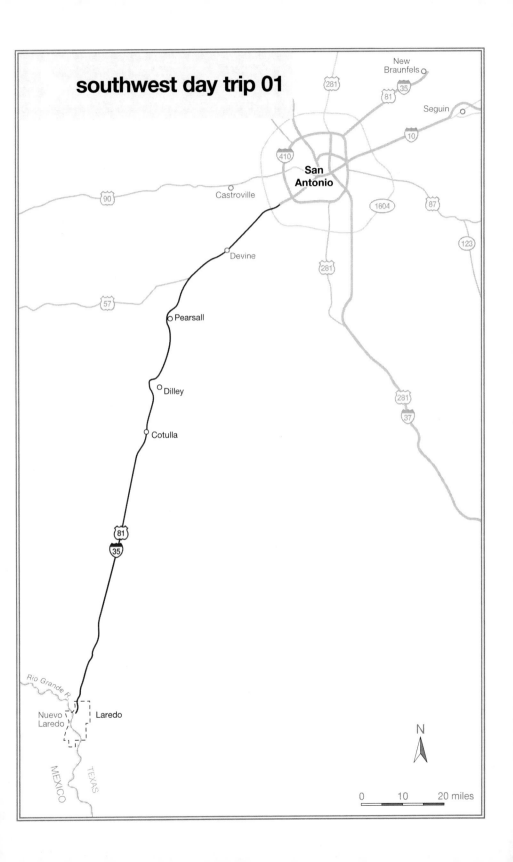

4 cells for men and 2 for women on the second floor. Downstairs, in 5 rooms which were the sheriff's quarters, exhibits focus on local-history artifacts recounting the town's early days as a railroad community. One curiosity is a "pear burner," an early blow torch used by ranchers to burn the spines from prickly pear cactus to enable cattle to eat the plants during drought times when only the tough native plants could survive. The museum hosts an annual Pioneer Day celebration. Open Tues through Sat. Free admission.

dilley

Although peanuts are also grown in this region, here watermelons are king. Dilley's economy has benefited from another resource as well: oil. Many visitors have another reason to visit this community of just 3,000 residents. With more than 250 species spotted, Dilley is known for its excellent birding.

getting there

From Pearsall, drive south on I-35 for 17 miles to Dilley.

where to go

Dilley Chamber of Commerce. Miller and Main Streets; (830) 965-4177. Stop by this office for free information on local attractions and activities throughout the region as well as maps. The office is open Mon through Fri during working hours.

Watermelon Statue. City Park on Main Street. Truly a Texas-size watermelon, this statue is Dilley's favorite photo spot and a reminder of the importance of agriculture in this region. Watermelons remain an important crop here, harvested during the early summer when as many as 15 million pounds of the fruit may be harvested from area fields. The statue of a watermelon (with a big slice taken out) is located in City Park, which includes picnic tables. Open daily. Free admission.

where to eat

Pancho Garcia Cafe. I-35 and TX 117; (830) 965-1493. This expansive diner, popular with bus groups on their way to the border, serves breakfast, lunch, and dinner. Tex-Mex specialties such as enchiladas, quesadillas and chorizo are popular, along with steaks, quail, and catfish. The menu features eight different combination plates and portions are very generous. Each combo includes homemade rice and beans. A kids menu offers hamburgers, french fries and corn dogs. The family-owned restaurant is open daily.

cotulla

Cotulla has been home to several notable residents, including Lyndon Baines Johnson and short-story author William Sidney Porter, better known as O. Henry. The town of just fewer than 5,000 residents is a center for the area's cattle and sheep ranching industries.

getting there

Cotulla is located 16 miles south of Dilley, on I-35.

where to go

Brush Country Museum. 201 South Stewart St.; (830) 879-2326 (chamber of commerce); www.cotulla-chamber.com. This museum, housed in the school where Lyndon Baines Johnson once taught, features local-history exhibits including historic photographs of the town's early days, firearms, tools and household items. There are also several collections of Native American artifacts. One section of the museum is devoted to the town's founder, Joseph Cotulla, a Polish immigrant who came to the area in 1856 to establish a farm and ranch operation. Open Tues and Thurs 10 a.m. to noon and 2 to 4 p.m.; and Wed, Fri, and Sat 1 to 4 p.m. Free admission.

laredo

This city has long been known as a South Texas party spot. It's a popular weekend trip with college students, shoppers, and anyone in search of fun. Built on the banks of the Rio Grande, Laredo dates from 1755. Founded by an officer of the Royal Army of Spain, it was one of the first cities established in this part of the country.

Following the Mexican War (1846–48), many Laredo residents packed up and headed across the border to start their own city in Mexico. They named the fledgling community Nuevo Laredo, or "New Laredo." Healthy trade between the United States and Mexico along with the fact that many families straddle both sides of the border have linked the cities, thus the nickname Los Dos Laredos—The Two Laredos.

To reach Laredo's downtown district, take the Zaragoza Street exit off I-35 and drive along the narrow, one-way avenue. With its old buildings, constant traffic, and stately palms, the venue has a definite Mexican feel. Wholesalers along Zaragoza Street entice shoppers with goods, including electronics, clothing, shoes, jewelry, and perfumes. On the right you'll see the enormous San Agustin Church, founded in 1778.

Beyond the city streets lies a whole other side of Laredo—a place filled with desert wildlife, walking trails, fish-filled lakes, and more. Birders find more than 300 species on record in the brush country, including several rare species. Anglers find plenty of challenge

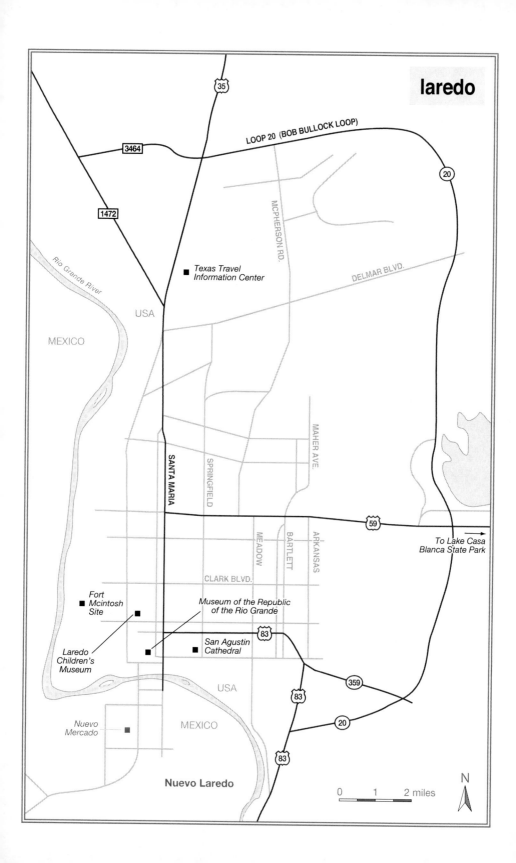

nuevo laredo, mexico

For years Nuevo Laredo, a city far larger than its Texas sister city, was a very popular destination for travelers looking for a day of shopping and dining. Sadly, because of drug cartel violence that is currently plaguing the Mexican border communities, **we no longer recommend travelers visit Nuevo Laredo.** *Although violence has not been aimed at travelers, street shootings have been frequent and the safety situation remains fluid. Please see Appendix A for more on visiting the border communities.*

Most travelers that do visit Nuevo Laredo do so on foot, crossing on International Bridge No. 1 (also called the Old Bridge) to the shopping district and Avenida Guerrero. In the downtown area, every road parallel to Guerrero is an avenue, or avenida; a road running perpendicular to the avenues (and parallel to the river) is a street, or calle.

Four blocks from the International Bridge, the mercado, or market, is far quieter than it was a few years ago. Two blocks away, El Dorado (formerly the Cadillac Bar), on Calle Belden and Avenida Ocampo, was a longtime favorite watering hole for many South Texans and the birthplace of the Ramos Gin Fizz, a concoction of gin, lemon juice, and powdered sugar.

at Lake Casa Blanca, filled with black bass as well as blue and yellow catfish. Not far from the lake lies the Casa Blanca Lake Golf Course, an 18-hole challenge that you can play year-round. And don't forget your walking shoes. Texas A&M International University and Laredo Community College have designated walking trails in the area that take in riverfront property as well as brush country.

Always boasting a fiesta spirit, Laredo really swings into gear every February when, for nearly two weeks, the city is filled with every kind of festival activity in honor of George Washington's birthday. Billed as the largest observance of George Washington's birthday in the nation, the event annually draws close to 400,000 partygoers.

Whether you visit Laredo during the GWB celebration or any other time of the year, you'll find a festive atmosphere in this border community.

getting there

From Cotulla, continue 68 miles south on I-35 to the city of Laredo.

celebrate george washington

Every February for more than a century, Laredo and Nuevo Laredo have cele-
brated George Washington's birthday as a way to spread international goodwill
between the neighboring countries. A Laredo men's organization, the Red Men
and the White Men, holds a mock battle representing a fight for possession of the
city, one that culminates in an unconditional surrender when the mayor gives the
key to the city to Great Chief Sachem.

How does this relate to George Washington? The American leader was named
Sachem by the Sons of Liberty when they disguised themselves as Indians during
their battle for freedom. Because of this, the Laredo organization picked the first
president's birthday as the occasion for the remembrance of this event.

Today **George Washington's Birthday Celebration** *has grown into South*
Texas's largest event, with activities for every age group. Sporting events, a chil-
dren's carnival, dances, parades, and gala balls fill the entire month with revelry.
Events include the WBCA Carnival, popular with families.

George Washington's birthday is known for its fun, food, and fireworks, but
it's also noted for its elegant balls. The Princess Pocahontas Pageant and Ball
features Laredo debutantes wearing Native American regalia, gowns that take as
long as two years to research and prepare. The Society of Martha Washington
Colonial Pageant and Ball, one of the largest social events in South Texas, draws
many spectators.

The days of activities come to a hot climax with the Jalapeño Festival, held
during the final days of the bash. Events range from a "Jello"peño-eating contest
to a jalapeño pizza–eating contest to the popular International Waiters Race,
where waiters from both sides of the border race a course while balancing a tray
with a bottle of champagne and a set of glasses.

where to go

Texas Travel Information Center. I-35 North at exit 18; (956) 417-4728; www.dot.state
.tx.us. This facility on the outskirts of Laredo offers information, maps, and brochures for
locations across Texas. Picnic facilities are available on the grounds.

Imaginarium of South Texas. 5300 San Dario, Suite 505, inside the Mall del Norte; (956)
728-0404; www.imaginariumstx.org. A cornucopia of hands-on learning experiences, the
Imaginarium is a great place for families to let their young ones explore. Kids can create fantastic structures on the Magnetic Wonder Wall, enjoy an extensive model train layout, visit

animals at Critter Corner, and paint glow-in-the-dark masterpieces in the Shadow Room, while the very young can play in the kid-safe Toddler Fun Zone. The museum is sponsored by the National Science Foundation. Open Wed through Sun.

Lake Casa Blanca International State Park. 5102 Bob Bullock Loop, 5 miles east off US 59; (956) 725-3826; www.tpwd.state.tx.us. This park offers fishing, camping and picnic facilities, hiking and biking trails, and a playground. Open daily.

Museum of the Republic of the Rio Grande. 1005 Zaragoza St., adjacent to the La Posada Hotel; (956) 727-3480. Six flags have flown over most of Texas, but Laredo has seen seven, thanks to the short-lived Republic of the Rio Grande. This museum is housed in a 1-story adobe structure that was once the capitol building of the former republic, a country formed when northern Mexico seceded from Mexico in 1839. The new state existed until 1841. The museum contains guns, saddles, and household belongings from that brief period. Open Tues through Sat.

San Agustin Cathedral. 201 San Agustin Ave.; (956) 722-1798. This historic church overlooks San Agustin Plaza, a popular place to just sit and watch the flurry of activity near the bridge. The plaza, with its peaceful gazebo and gas-powered lamps, was the site of one of the West's bloodiest shootouts. In 1886 the Botas (boots) and Huaraches (sandals), two rival political groups, battled here, leaving more than 80 dead when the smoke cleared. Open daily. Free admission.

Walking Tour of Laredo. The streets of Laredo are lined with historic structures, including many old churches and homes built in the Mexican vernacular and Victorian styles. Tours begin and end at the Museum of the Republic of the Rio Grande, 1005 Zaragoza St. For more information, call (956) 727-0977.

where to shop

Mall del Norte. 5300 San Dario Ave.; (956) 724-8191; www.malldelnorte.com. One of the largest indoor malls in the Lone Star State, Mall del Norte boasts over 160 stores anchored by Bealls, Dillard's, Macy's, JCPenney, Mervyn's, and Sears. Plenty of fast-food options fill the food court, and a number of restaurants are located just outside the mall. The Imaginarium of South Texas, a children's science museum, is also located here. Open daily.

Polly Adams. 101 Calle del Norte; (956) 723-2969. For 50 years this upscale store has offered exclusive lines of women's clothing and accessories. Formerly housed in Mall del Norte, the shop relocated to this sprawling store, which spans more than 7,000 square feet. The customer-oriented shop includes large fitting rooms with dressing robes, a living room so customers can take a break from their shopping to visit, and complimentary coffee, tea, and wine. Frequented by many Mexican movie stars as well as discerning shoppers from around Texas, Polly Adams can provide meals for shoppers with advance notice and always has several seamstresses on hand to provide a personalized fit.

San Bernardo Avenue. If you don't want to drive into Mexico, you'll find many large importers on this shopping strip. Wrought-iron furniture, clay products, and vases are popular buys.

Vega's Interiores Mejicanos. 4002 San Bernardo Ave.; (956) 724-8251; www.vegas interiores.com. Mexican home furnishings for every room of the house are sold in this well-stocked store, and much of the furniture is hand-carved. Owned by the same family since 1939, the store's most famous shopper was First Lady Eleanor Roosevelt, who visited in 1939, two days before the Japanese attack on Pearl Harbor.

Zaragoza Street. When Mexicans come into Texas to shop, many make this strip their first stop. Shops here sell the same merchandise, from handbags to headsets, found at many department stores, but at bargain prices. Shops are located throughout the historic district north of Zaragoza Street.

where to eat

Danny's Restaurant. 802 Juarez Ave.; (956) 724-3185; www.mydannys.com. With multiple locations around Laredo, you're sure to find a Danny's when hunger strikes. Since 1983, when this local chain began on Juarez Avenue, Danny's has become one of Laredo's favorites. Danny's specializes in classic Tex-Mex but the extensive menu also includes burgers, sandwiches, and steaks. They even serve breakfast all day. See their website for locations and hours. $$.

El Meson de San Agustin. 908 Grant St.; (956) 712-9009; www.elmesondesanagustin .com. Since 1995 diners in Laredo have flocked to this downtown restaurant for authentic Mexican cuisine. Open for lunch and dinner Mon through Sat. $.

Tack Room Bar and Grill. 1000 Zaragoza St. at La Posada Hotel; (956) 722-1701 or (800) 444-2099; http://laposadahotel.com. This casual restaurant features nightly entertainment and steak and seafood. The upstairs restaurant offers candlelight dining, an exhibition kitchen and grill, and a romantic atmosphere. The building originally housed Laredo's first telephone exchange. $$$.

where to stay

Courtyard by Marriott. 2410 Santa Ursula; (956) 725-5555; www.marriott.com. This 5-story property includes the Bistro Restaurant (open for breakfast and dinner) and a full-service business center as well as an outdoor swimming pool, whirlpool, and fitness center. The hotel offers free on-site parking and Wi-Fi throughout the property. $$.

Holiday Inn Civic Center Hotel. 800 Garden St.; (956) 727-5800 or (888) 465-4329; www .holidayinn.com. This high-rise hotel commands views of the city from its location 1 mile from the International Bridge. Its 203 rooms are nicely decorated and offer free Wi-Fi along with the usual amenities. The Terraza Verde Restaurant and the Covey Lounge offer on-site dining, while the fitness center, outdoor pool, sports court, and Jacuzzi help guests stay in shape. The hotel also offers complimentary shuttle service to the International Bridge and the Mall Del Norte. $$.

La Posada. 1000 Zaragoza St.; (956) 722-1701 or (800) 444-2099; http://laposadahotel .com. This 224-room hotel is the closest accommodation to the Gateway to the Americas International Bridge (International Bridge No. 1) leading from Laredo into Mexico. Two Spanish-style courtyards feature tall palms, blooming bougainvillea, and refreshing pools, one with a swim-up bar. A relaxed lobby restaurant serves Mexican dishes, while two elegant restaurants specialize in steak and continental fare. $$$.

west

day trip 01

>>>
gateway to mexico:
eagle pass

This day trip through the South Texas brush country leads to Eagle Pass and its sister city across the border, Piedras Negras. This route was once popular for San Antonio travelers headed to explore interior Mexico by car; today automobile travel across the border is no longer recommended due to increasing cartel violence (see Appendix A).

eagle pass

Eagle Pass, a city of more than 25,000 residents, was founded after the Texas Revolution when Mexico prohibited all trade with Texas. Smugglers began a new route to the north. The Texas militia set up an observation camp at a crossing called Paso del Aguila (Eagle Pass), named for the birds nesting in the area. As settlers began coming to the area, the US Infantry built Fort Duncan in 1849 to defend the new territory from Indian attack. The fort was used during the Civil War and manned by Confederate soldiers.

Like other border towns, Eagle Pass is bilingual. Many Mexican citizens cross the border to shop at the large Mall de las Aguilas and in the downtown dress and specialty shops.

getting there

From San Antonio, it's 142 miles to Eagle Pass. The drive to Eagle Pass goes quickly, following I-35 south to US 57, which leads through miles of fertile farmland before it hits the

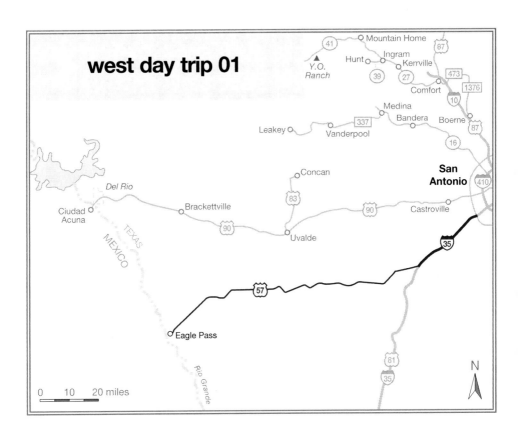

west day trip 01

Mountain Home
41
87
Ingram
Hunt
Kerrville
Y.O.
Ranch
39
27
473
Comfort
1376
10
Medina
Bandera
Boerne
337
Leakey
87
Vanderpool
16
Concan
San
Antonio
410
Del Rio
83
Ciudad
Acuna
Brackettville
90
Castroville
TEXAS
90
MEXICO
Uvalde
35
57
Eagle Pass
81
35
N
Rio Grande
0   10   20 miles

mesquite-filled country near the border. You'll find basic services in Devine, but gas stations are few and far between from this farming community until you reach the border.

where to go

Fort Duncan Park. From Main Street (US 57), turn south on South Adams Street; (830) 773-3224 or (888) 355-3224. Here you can take a self-guided tour of 11 original structures, including barracks and the headquarters building that's home to the Fort Duncan Museum. The museum presents displays on the early history of the old Indian fort and Confederate outpost. The fort saw action from 1890 to 1916, when National Guard units were attached to the command following disturbances in Mexico. During World War II the park's facilities were used as an officers' club for commissioned personnel. Open Mon through Sat afternoons.

Kickapoo Lucky Eagle Casino. 794 Lucky Eagle Dr.; (888) 25-LUCKY; www.luckyeagle texas.com. Located 6.5 miles southeast of Eagle Pass on the Kickapoo Indian Reservation, this 24-hour casino tempts visitors with 1,000 slot machines as well as high-stakes bingo, Kickapoo 21 (blackjack), Seven-Card Stud, and Texas Hold 'Em. Free admission.

piedras negras, mexico

Like other communities along the Texas-Mexico border, **travel to Piedras Negras is no longer recommended.** *This city, named for the "black rock" (anthracite coal) found in the area after flooding on the Rio Grande, is home to more than 100,000 residents and a gateway to interior Mexico.*

For more about the security situation in the border cities, see Appendix A.

where to eat

Charcoal Grill. Mall de las Aguilas, 455 South Bibb, off US 57; (830) 773-8023. This family-style restaurant specializes in charcoal-grilled steaks and burgers, all brought to your table with a bowl of sliced jalapeños. $$.

La Parrilla de San Miguel. 408 South Texas Dr.; (830) 757-3100; http://parrilladesan miguel.com. Offering a more upscale dining experience than the usual Tex-Mex fare, this restaurant specializes in authentic Mexican dishes. An extensive menu includes Filete Monasterio (grilled tenderloin medallions, topped with sautéed shrimp, garlic and white wine), Tampiqueña (grilled sirloin served with refried beans, rice, avocado, 2 enchiladas and grilled onions) and Camarones Pacífico (shimp sautéed in olive oil, white wine and citric herbs). Guacamole and salsas are made fresh daily. $$–$$$.

where to stay

La Quinta Motor Inn. 2525 East Main St. (US 57); (800) 531-5900; www.lq.com. This comfortable family motel, offering a palm-shaded swimming pool, sits just 5 minutes from the border. It offers the usual La Quinta amenities like complimentary breakfast, free Wi-Fi, and free local telephone calls. Small pets are allowed. $$.

Weyrich Farm. 1.5 miles from Eagle Pass in Hopedale; (830) 773-6168; www.wfpecan .com. Weyrich Farm, a commercial pecan orchard, operates a quiet bed-and-breakfast in their guest house. The house contains 3 suites outfitted with antique furniture. Set under 100-year-old pecan trees, the B&B offers an outdoor pool and serves tea and sweetbread in the afternoons and a full Mexican breakfast in the mornings. $$.

day trip 02

west

multicultural miles:
castroville, hondo, uvalde, concan

Settled by over 30 different cultures from around the globe, Texas's diversity is really evident on this day trip. You'll explore Castroville's Alsatian roots, Hondo's Belgian ancestry, and the Spanish and Mexican heritage of Uvalde and Concan.

castroville

Castroville is only a half hour's drive from the Alamo City, but it's another world in terms of mood and atmosphere. This small town serves up a mixture of many cultures: French, German, English, Alsatian, and Spanish. It's best known for its Alsatian roots and sometimes is called the "Little Alsace of Texas."

The community was founded by Frenchman Henri Castro, who contracted with the Republic of Texas to bring settlers from Europe. These pioneers came from the French province of Alsace in 1844, bringing with them the Alsatian language, a Germanic dialect. Today only the older residents of Castroville carry on this mother tongue.

Although the language has dropped out of everyday use, many Alsatian customs and traditions have survived. The city still sports European-style homes with nonsymmetrical, sloping roofs. The Alsatian Dancers of Texas perform folk dancing at many festivals, including the town's St. Louis Day celebration. (See "Festivals & Celebrations" at the back of this book.)

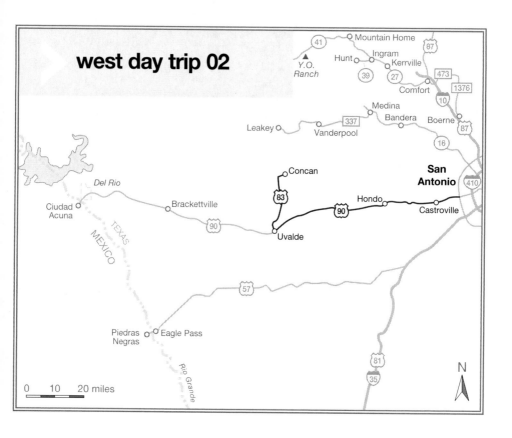

west day trip 02

Castroville is usually busy on weekends, as San Antonio residents come to shop the town's numerous antiques stores, dine in the Alsatian restaurants, and tour the historical sites.

getting there

From San Antonio, drive west on US 90 for 39 miles to Castroville.

where to go

Castroville Regional Park. 816 Alsace Ave., south off US 90; (830) 931-4070. Camp along the banks of the Medina River or enjoy swimming, picnicking, or walking in this park. Fee for camping hookups and picnic table use.

Castroville Walking Tour. (830) 538-3142; www.castroville.com. Pick up a free map from the chamber of commerce (100 Karm St.; 830-538-3142) to see 65 points of interest, from Civil War–era homes to an 1845 church.

Landmark Inn State Historical Site. 402 East Florence St.; (830) 931-2133; www.visit landmarkinn.com. The Texas Historical Commission operates the historic Landmark Inn and museum. The inn was first a home and general store before becoming the Vance Hotel. Robert E. Lee and Bigfoot Wallace, a famous Texas Ranger, were said to have stayed here on the banks of the Medina River. During World War II the hotel was renamed the Landmark Inn. Aside from accommodations (see "Where to Stay"), the inn contains displays illustrating Henri Castro's early efforts to recruit settlers as well as exhibits covering early Castroville life. Tours of the beautifully manicured inn grounds are offered daily.

where to eat

Haby's Alsatian Bakery. 207 US 290 East; (830) 931-2118; www.habysbakery.com. With Castroville's rich Alsatian and German heritage, you know the town has to have a great

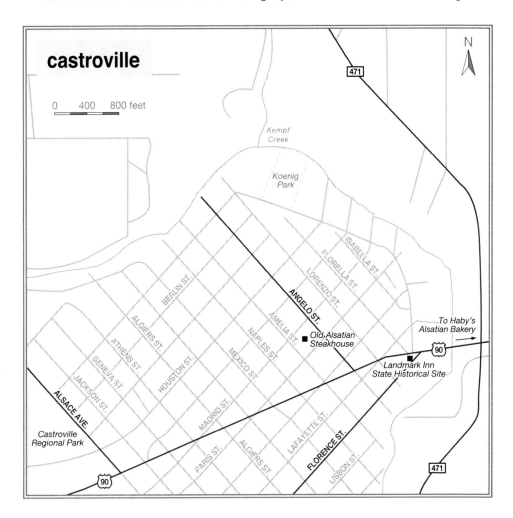

bakery. Well, here it is. You can choose from apple strudel, molasses cookies, and fresh-baked breads. Open Mon through Sat. $.

Old Alsatian Steakhouse. 1403 Angelo St.; (830) 931-3260. Housed in a historic 19th-century cottage typical of the provincial homes of Castroville, this restaurant specializes in Alsatian and German food, including spicy Alsatian sausage, crusty French bread, home-made noodles, and red sauerkraut. Steaks and seafood also are served. If it's a nice day, don't miss the chance to dine outside in the open-air *biergarten*. Open daily for lunch and for dinner Thurs through Sun. $$.

where to stay

Landmark Inn State Historical Site. 402 East Florence St.; (830) 931-2133; www.visit landmarkinn.com. Guests at this historic bed-and-breakfast can stay in one of 10 beautifully appointed rooms or in a separate cottage that may have once served as the only bath-house between San Antonio and Eagle Pass. All rooms have air-conditioning; most rooms come with private baths; none have telephones or television. Make your reservations early, especially for weekends. $$.

hondo

Hondo (which means "deep" in Spanish) is a center for ranching and farming.

getting there

Continue west from Castroville on US 90 to the community of Hondo, once a railroad stop.

where to go

777 Exotic Game Ranch. (830) 426-3476; www.777ranch.com. Take US 90 2 miles west of Hondo to CR 531, then go south on CR 531 for 5 miles and follow signs. The 777 Ranch might look vaguely familiar, even if you've never been to Hondo in the past, thanks to the movie *Ace Ventura: When Nature Calls*. This sprawling ranch, filled with exotic species from around the globe, was used as a set for the Jim Carrey movie; sets from the production can be seen on the property. The ranch is used for hunting, fishing, and photography of exotic species. Reservations required.

uvalde

Spanish settlers came to this area in 1674. A century later they attempted to construct mis-sions to convert the Lipan-Apache Indians, the foremost of the Apache groups in Texas. This plan was soon abandoned because of repeated Indian attacks on the mission. The

Apaches were defeated in 1709 by Spanish military leader Juan del Uvalde in what's now known as Uvalde Canyon.

getting there

Continue west from Hondo on US 90 to Uvalde, located on the Leona River in the last outreaches of the Hill Country.

where to go

Briscoe Art and Antique Collection. 200 East Nopal St.; (830) 278-6231; www.fsbuvalde .com. On display at the First State Bank, this multimillion-dollar art collection was developed by former Texas governor Dolph Briscoe and his wife. Pieces from artists ranging from Rembrandt to Salinas are on display. Tours are available. Open weekdays. Free admission.

Fort Inge County Park. FM 140, 1.5 miles south of Uvalde. This park is located at the site of Fort Inge, a cavalry post that dates from 1849. Travelers find picnic sites as well as hiking trails and camping here, along with good bird watching. The park is located on the Leona River. Open weekends.

Janey Slaughter Briscoe Grand Opera House. 100 West North Austin St.; (830) 278-4184; www.uvaldearts.org. Even if a performance isn't scheduled, this 1891 opera house deserves a peek. Tours can be arranged on weekdays. Free admission.

John Nance Garner Memorial Museum. 333 North Park St.; (830) 278-5018; www .cah.utexas.edu. This was once the home of Uvalde's most famous citizen: John Nance Garner, vice president of the United States during Franklin D. Roosevelt's first and second presidential terms. The museum is filled with reminders of Garner's political career. Open Mon through Sat; extended hours during summer months. Currently, the museum is closed for renovations.

National Fish Hatchery. FM 481, 1 mile south of Uvalde; (830) 278-2419; www.fws.gov. This hatchery specializes in endangered fish species, but visitors will also find good bird watching here as well as hiking and picnicking. Open weekdays. Free admission.

where to shop

Antiques on the Square. 103 North West St.; (830) 278-1294. This downtown antiques emporium houses wares by many dealers. Look for antique furniture, collectibles, jewelry, and gift items. Open Mon through Sat.

South Texas Fine Woods. 4326 East Main; (830) 278-1832; www.mesquiterocker.com. Hand-carved mesquite furniture is showcased in this retail shop. Tours of the workshop are also available. Open Mon through Sat.

where to eat

Evett's Barbecue. 301 East Main; (830) 278-6204. This casual eatery serves traditional Texas barbecue fare—brisket, sausage, and chicken—on picnic tables. Open Tues through Sat. 10:30 a.m. to 4 p.m. $–$$.

Town House Restaurant. 2105 East Main St.; (830) 278-2428. The menu at this casual restaurant offers a taste of several Texas favorites: Tex-Mex, seafood, and, of course, chicken-fried steak. Open for breakfast, lunch, and dinner daily. $$.

Uvalde Rexall Drug and Soda Fountain. 201 North Getty St.; (830) 278-2589. Step back to the days of old-time soda fountains at this favorite eatery. Sandwiches, burgers, and Blue Bell ice cream top the menu. Open Mon through Sat for lunch. $.

where to stay

Holiday Inn Express. 2801 East Main St.; (830) 278-7300; www.hiexpress.com. This 80-room hotel includes a fitness center, pool, and laundry facilities, and offers a complimentary breakfast buffet and free Wi-Fi throughout the property. $$.

concan

Word has it that this town is named for *con quién,* a Mexican gambling game. Today it's a sure bet for outdoor recreation, from swimming to camping.

getting there

Head north on US 83 for 22 miles to the junction with TX 127 to reach tiny Concan.

where to go

Garner State Park. 234 RR 1050; (830) 232-6132; www.tpwd.state.tx.us. Thirty-one miles north of Uvalde on US 83, or 8 miles north of Concan on the Frio River. From US 83, turn east on FM 1050 for 0.5 mile to PR 29. Named for former US vice president John Nance Garner, this beautiful state park is located on the chilly, spring-fed waters of the Frio River (*frio* means "cold" in Spanish). There are campsites, screened shelters, cabins with double beds, an 18-hole miniature golf course, and a 1-mile hiking trail built by the Civilian Conservation Corps during the 1930s. The highlight of the park is the river, filled with swimmers, inner-tubers, and paddleboats during the warmer months.

Other activities include bike riding along a surfaced trail more than 0.5 mile in length and hiking 5.5 miles of trails. Campers can bring their own facilities or rent a screened shelter or cabin. (The park is so popular that travelers who rent a cabin on either Fri or Sat night must take both nights.) Open daily.

where to eat

The Club Grille. 520 Mountain Valley Dr.; (830) 232-4471; www.concangolf.com. Part of the Club at ConCan Golf Resort and Spa, the Grille is the only place in town that's open for lunch every day. Despite its polished decor, the restaurant has a casual feel, with burgers and sandwiches making up most of the menu. This area is "dry," so you'll have to purchase a guest membership to partake at the bar. $.

where to stay

Frio Country Resort. 1801 CR 348; (830) 232-6625 or (888) 926-6226; www.friocountry .com. This sprawling resort on the Frio River boasts over 90 rustic cabins of varying sizes, from basic 1-bedroom cabins up to large cabins with 6 bedrooms. All the lodgings are divided into "subdivisions," with most groupings sharing a common pool; some of the larger cabins have their own pool or hot tub. The property also has 12 RV sites with full electrical hookups, picnic tables, and barbecue pits. The resort's House Pasture Cattle Company Restaurant hosts regular country music events. From May through Sept there is a 3-night minimum stay during the week and a 4-night minimum on weekends. The rest of the year there is a 2-night minimum. $–$$$.

day trip 03

wild, wild west:
brackettville, del rio, seminole
canyon state historical park

This weekend trip has a lot to offer. Take an afternoon dip in Del Rio's San Felipe Springs or visit Texas's oldest winery. The next day, take your choice of Del Rio's historic sites, a cruise on Lake Amistad, or a look at prehistoric drawings in Seminole Canyon.

brackettville

Brackettville is the home of Fort Clark, built by the US Cavalry in 1852 to protect the frontier from hostile Indians. Several important soldiers were stationed here over the years, including General George S. Patton. During World War II, Fort Clark served as a German POW camp. At the conclusion of that war, the fort was deactivated. Although Fort Clark's military days may be over, the compound has taken on a new role as a resort, its stone barracks converted to modern motel rooms. There's also an RV park nearby.

getting there

It's a quick 120 miles down US 90 from San Antonio to Brackettville. (For attractions along this highway, see West Day Trip 02.)

where to go

Kickapoo Cavern State Park. RR 674, 22 miles north of Brackettville; (830) 563-2342; www.tpwd.state.tx.us. The park offers picnic sites, camping, hiking, biking, birding, and

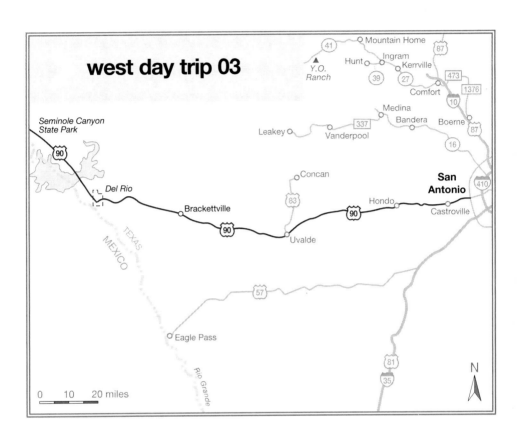

west day trip 03

Mountain Home
41   87
Hunt   Ingram
Y.O.   Kerrville
Ranch   39   27
                 Comfort   473
                             1376
                       10
                 Medina
Seminole Canyon   337   Bandera   Boerne
State Park   87
             Leakey   Vanderpool
90   16

                   Concan   **San**
                              Antonio   410
      Del Rio
                    83   Hondo
         Brackettville   90   Castroville
                90   Uvalde
TEXAS
MEXICO

              57

   Eagle Pass
                            81
                            35   N
0   10   20 miles   Rio Grande

seasonal bat flight viewing. It also contains 15 known caverns, including Kickapoo Cavern. The caves are home to populations of Brazilian free-tailed bats during warm-weather months. The park offers guided tours of the caves for those interested in spelunking; this is not a typical cave tour with lighting and wide paths. For a schedule, visit the park website.

Old Guardhouse Museum. US 90, in Fort Clark Springs; (830) 563-9150. This museum focuses on the famous generals who served at Fort Clark, along with the many troops who passed through the post. Open weekend afternoons.

where to stay

Fort Clark Springs Motel and RV Park. US 90, in Fort Clark Springs; (830) 563-9210; www.fortclark.com. The stone barracks of this 1872 fort have been renovated into modern motel rooms. Guests have access to a pool plus 9- and 18-hole golf courses. $$.

del rio

Del Rio is the most popular border town within reach of San Antonio. It's a year-round paradise for anglers, hunters, boaters, and archaeology buffs. Many Texas border towns serve primarily as overnight stops after a day in Mexico, but Del Rio is its own main attraction. Museums, historic sites, fishing, camping, bird watching, and boating all await within 30 minutes of downtown.

Another feature that separates Del Rio from other border cities is its abundance of water. The town is literally an oasis in the semiarid climate at the edge of the Chihuahuan Desert. Tall palm trees, lush lawns, and a golf course dotted with water hazards are all part of Del Rio. The San Felipe Springs pump 90 million gallons of water daily. The crystal-clear water has drawn inhabitants to this region for 10,000 years, from prehistoric Indians who lived in the canyons west of here to Spanish missionaries who named the area San Felipe del Rio in 1635.

Today the San Felipe Springs provide water for the city of Del Rio, and offer a cool swim on a hot summer day. At the San Felipe Amphitheater, the water is diverted through a stone moat separating the audience from a stage used for concerts and special events.

Del Rio lies 12 miles from the Amistad Dam and Lake Amistad, the result of a cooperative effort between Mexico and the United States.

getting there

Del Rio is located 32 miles west of Bracketville on US 90.

where to go

Pictographs Guided Tours. The Rock Art Foundation conducts tours of the historic pictographs of the Lower Pecos and Lake Amistad regions. This organization was founded by the late James Zintgraff, whose photographs are now the only record of many pictographs that were lost when Lake Amistad was formed. For reservations, call (888) ROCKART or visit the Rock Art Foundation website at www.rockart.org.

Lake Amistad. West of Del Rio on US 90. The construction of Lake Amistad (derived from the Spanish word for friendship) was a cooperative project between the US and Mexico. The 67,000-acre lake was completed in 1969 as a way to control flooding, provide irrigation for South Texas farms and ranches, and offer water recreation. Surrounded by 1,000 miles of shoreline, the reservoir contains 35 species of fish, including striper, bass, crappie, perch, catfish, gar, and sunfish. You must have separate fishing licenses for the US and Mexican areas of the lake. Both Texas and Mexico fishing licenses are sold in the marinas and at many Del Rio stores.

The 6-mile-long Amistad Dam is responsible for the creation of the enormous lake. The observation deck affords a look at the 86-mile-long reservoir. Atop the dam stand two bronze eagles, each 7 feet tall, symbolizing the two participating countries and marking the international border.

Lake Amistad Resort and Marina. US 90, Diablo East Recreation Area; (830) 774-4157. Concessioners at the marina rent small powerboats and large houseboats sleeping up to 10 people. You can cruise to the main part of Lake Amistad or up the Devil's River to some clear, spring-fed swimming holes. Open daily. Free admission; fee for rentals.

Tlaloc, the Rain God. Mexican shore of Lake Amistad, near Amistad Dam. This 23-foot stone statue is a replica of one carved by the Teotihuacán people years before Aztec rule in Mexico. Tlaloc is believed to bring rain. Some swear the statue works, pointing to the higher-than-normal rainfalls in the years following the dam's construction.

Val Verde Winery. 100 Qualia Dr.; (830) 775-9714; www.valverdewinery.com. Italian immigrant Frank Qualia established this winery in 1883, drawn to the area by its flowing springs and fertile land. The oldest winery in Texas, this enterprise is now operated by third-generation vintner Thomas Qualia. Val Verde produces many wines, including award-winning Don Luis Tawny Port. Tours and tastings are available on a drop-in basis. Open daily except Sun. Free admission.

Whitehead Memorial Museum. 1308 South Main St.; (830) 774-7568; www.whitehead museum.org. This museum is best known for its replica of the Jersey Lilly, Judge Roy Bean's saloon and courtroom. (The original Jersey Lilly remains in Langtry, about 60 miles west of Del Rio.) Judge Bean and his son Sam are buried behind the replica of the saloon, their graves marked with simple headstones. The museum boasts more than 20 exhibit sites, including an 1870s store, a windmill, a log cabin, a caboose, and the Cadena Nativity, a cultural folk art exhibit. Open Tues through Sat and Sun afternoon.

judge roy bean

Buried in Del Rio, **Judge Roy Bean,** the self-proclaimed "Law West of the Pecos," was undoubtedly one of the most colorful characters in the American West. From behind the bar of the Jersey Lilly, his saloon in the railroad town of Langtry, Judge Bean served up frontier justice along with beer and whiskey.

Perhaps the strangest story concerns his obsession with the British actress Lilly Langtry, who was popularly known as "The Jersey Lily." Bean named his saloon in her honor and wrote her numerous letters, begging her to visit her namesake town in Texas. So persistent were his entreaties (and his implication that the town was named for her) that after several years Lilly Langtry consented to make a stop there on a 1904 tour. In March 1903, a few months before she arrived, Bean died.

where to eat

Cripple Creek Saloon. US 90 West; (830) 775-0153. Modeled after the original Cripple Creek Saloon in Colorado, this restaurant specializes in prime rib but also serves up a mean sirloin, filet mignon, and rib eye. Seafood, from lobster to coho salmon to swordfish, rounds out the menu. Closed Sun. $$–$$$.

Wright's Steak House. US 90, 3 miles west of the intersection of US 277; (830) 775-2621. This casual steak house features all the usual cuts plus choices like Texas-size chicken-fried steak. Save room for home-baked cheesecake, then work off that big dinner on the dance floor. Dinner only Tues through Sat; lunch and dinner Sun. Closed Mon. $$.

where to stay

Del Rio offers a wide array of accommodations: mom-and-pop motels, popular chains, fishing resorts, and bed-and-breakfasts. For a complete listing, call the Del Rio Chamber of Commerce at (800) 889-8149 or (830) 775-3551; write 1915 Veterans Blvd., Del Rio, TX 78840; or visit www.drchamber.com.

La Quinta Inn. 2005 Veterans Blvd.; (830) 775-7591; www.lq.com. This downtown hotel offers free breakfast, an outdoor pool, and 101 rooms featuring free Wi-Fi, premium TV channels, hair dryers, microwaves, and refrigerators. A host of restaurants are nearby. $.

Ramada Inn. 2101 Veterans Blvd.; (830) 775-1511 or (800) 272-6232; www.ramadainndel rio.com. This popular 183-room motel is conveniently located on the main thoroughfare through town, offering guests a pool, hot tub, workout room, restaurant, and bar. $$.

Villa del Rio. 123 Hudson St.; (830) 768-1100 or (800) 995-1887; www.villadelrio.com. This 19th-century mansion is tucked beneath stately palms and pecan trees. Guests can stroll to Texas's oldest winery or enjoy a leisurely day in one of 4 suites that feature fireplace foyers, hand-painted tiled floors, and an atmosphere that recalls the days of South Texas haciendas. $$.

especially for winter texans

Del Rio has a very active winter-visitor community. The chamber of commerce hosts a Winter Visitors Welcome Party, an arts and crafts fair, and an appreciation party during the season.

The Welcome Party is held during the third week in January and includes a traditional Texas meal. Exhibits introduce newcomers to local attractions, and gold cards offering discounts at area businesses are distributed. The Annual Winter Bazaar kicks off in February, giving participants a chance to sell arts and crafts without the usual booth expense associated with such shows. For more information on winter-visitor events, call the Del Rio chamber at (800) 889-8149 or (830) 775-3551, or visit www.drchamber.com.

ciudad acuña, mexico

As with other Mexican border towns in the region, **travelers to Ciudad Acuña need to check with the US State Department for up-to-date warnings regarding security.** Please see Appendix A for details before crossing the border.

To reach the international border and Ciudad Acuña, take Spur 239 off US 90. Most travelers drive to the Texas side of the International Bridge and pay a small fee for secured parking. From there you can take a cab or a bus across the river or walk across the toll bridge.

A bus takes shoppers from Del Rio across the border to the Acuña (pronounced "a-COON-ya") shopping district. This place is filled with tourist shops, especially along Hidalgo Street.

seminole canyon state historical park

This is a stop archaeology buffs shouldn't miss. During the warmer months, make this an early morning trip because the canyon can be very hot during the afternoon.

Seminole Canyon was occupied by early humans about 8,500 years ago. Little is known of that early culture, but archaeologists believe these people were hunter-gatherers, living on plants and small animals. The former residents left paintings on the caves and canyon walls, but their meaning is still unknown. Sadly, these artifacts are fading, and it is unknown how much longer the images will last. Scientists currently are studying ways to slow the deterioration.

Visitors can see the pictographs on a 90-minute guided tour conducted Wed through Sun at 10 a.m. and 3 p.m. This is a somewhat strenuous 1-mile hike, so bring along a small canteen of water (there are no drinking facilities in the canyon).

In the park campground, both tent and trailer sites are available, along with electrical and water hookups. Open daily. For more information on camping, call (432) 292-4464; write Park Superintendent, Seminole Canyon State Historical Park, P.O. Box 820, Comstock, TX 78837; or visit www.tpwd.state.tx.us.

getting there

To reach the entrance of Seminole Canyon State Historical Park, drive west about 45 miles on US 90 from Del Rio, 9 miles past the town of Comstock.

northwest

day trip 01

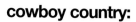

>>> **cowboy country:**
bandera, medina, vanderpool

In the far west reaches of the Texas Hill Country the antelope (well, white-tailed deer) play, cowboys (both real and pretend) ride herd, and brilliant maple trees blaze so brightly in the fall, you'll think you're in New England. The ranches are a little bigger here, the towns a little farther apart, and you'll learn the meaning of the longtime Texas slogan "Drive Friendly," as oncoming motorists are quick to greet you with a welcoming wave.

bandera

Once part of the "Wild West," Bandera Pass, located 12 miles north of town on TX 173, was the site of many battles between Spanish conquistadors and both Apache and Comanche Indians. Legend has it that following a battle with the Apaches in 1732, a flag (or *bandera* in Spanish) was hung at the pass to mark the boundary between the two opposing forces. Today the western heritage lives on in this town well-known for its plentiful dude ranches, country-western music, rodeos, and horse racing.

Bandera has open rodeos weekly from Memorial Day to Labor Day. Typically rodeos are held Tuesday night at Mansfield Park and Saturday night at Twin Elm Guest Ranch. For more schedule information, call the Bandera Convention and Visitors Bureau at (800) 364-3833 or visit www.banderacowboycapital.com.

Today the wildest action in town occurs in the dance halls every night except Monday and Tuesday. Put on your boots, crease your best jeans, and get ready to two-step with locals and vacationers alike.

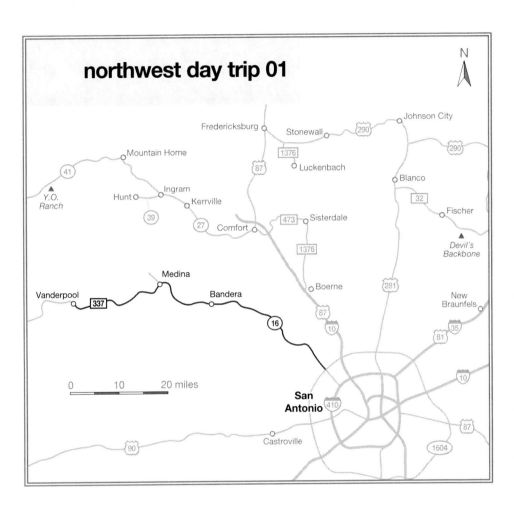

northwest day trip 01

N

getting there

Follow TX 16 northwest of San Antonio for 50 miles to Bandera, the "Cowboy Capital of the World."

where to go

Arkey Blue's Silver Dollar. 308 Main St.; (830) 796-8826; www.arkeyblue.com. Pick up a longneck, grab a partner, and start boot-scootin' at this Texas honky-tonk. Owner and singer Arkey Blue performs country-western hits here as crowds fill the sawdust-covered dance floor.

Frontier Times Museum. 510 13th St., 1 block north of the courthouse; (830) 796-3864; www.frontiertimesmuseum.org. Established in 1927, this museum is a good place to learn more about Bandera's early days. The stone building is filled with cowboy paraphernalia,

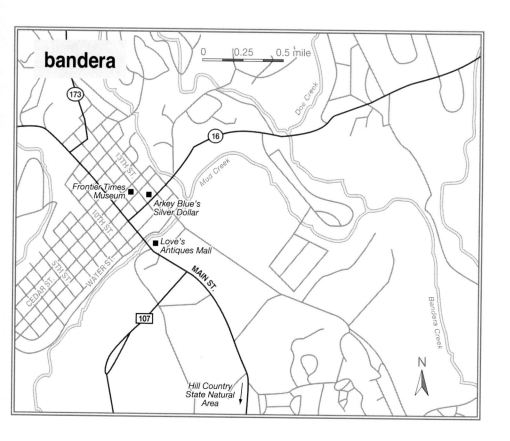

Native American arrowheads, and prehistoric artifacts. Its most unusual exhibit is a shrunken head from Ecuador, part of a private collection donated to the museum. Open Mon through Sat.

Hill Country State Natural Area. (830) 796-4413; www.tpwd.state.tx.us. Go south on TX 173 to FM 1077, then right for 12 miles. This rugged park preserves 5,400 acres of Hill Country land. Only primitive camping is available; you must bring your own water and pick up and remove your own trash. This park was originally open primarily for horseback riding, but today it has become popular with hikers and bicyclists. There are 34 miles of quiet trails and camp areas for backpackers and equestrians. Cool off with a dip in West Verde Creek or fish for catfish, perch, and largemouth bass. Horse rentals are available off-site. Open daily Feb through Oct, Fri through Sun the rest of the year.

Historical Walking Tours. Have a look at the buildings that witnessed Bandera's evolution from a frontier town to a vacation destination with a self-guided tour. Thirty-two sites along the route lead visitors to the county courthouse, the Old Jail, Bandera's first theater, and many homes that date from the community's earliest days. Pick up your free walking-tour brochure at the Bandera County Visitors Center, 1808 TX 16 South.

Medina River. TX 16, east of town. The cypress-lined Medina River is a popular spot during the summer months, when swimmers, canoeists, and inner-tubers enjoy the cool water. The Medina can be hazardous during high water, however, with rocky rapids and submerged trees. There is public access to the river from the TX 16 bridge in town.

Running-R Ranch Trail Rides. Eleven miles from Bandera off FM 1077; (830) 796-3984; www.rrranch.com. Enjoy 1-, 2-, or 3-hour rides with an experienced wrangler. The ranch also offers all-day rides with a picnic and cowboy cookout. Children 6 and up are accepted.

where to shop

Love's Antiques Mall. 310 Main St.; (830) 796-3838. Located in the historic Carmichael and Hay store, this antiques mall features custom-crafted western furniture, wrought iron, sculpture, and collectibles.

where to eat

O.S.T. Restaurant. 305 Main St.; (830) 796-3836. Named for the Old Spanish Trail, this restaurant serves a Texas-size breakfast as well as popular lunches and dinners, featuring Lone Star favorites such as chicken-fried steak, burgers, and fried chicken. Don't miss the bar and its unique barstools—each topped with a saddle. $.

Texaritas Steak House & Mesquite Grill Restaurant. 703 Main St.; (830) 796-9400; www.texassquare.com/texaritas.htm. Part of Old Texas Square, this restaurant offers both indoor and streetside dining featuring Texas favorites, steaks, Tex-Mex, fajitas, and drinks from the adjacent Tequila Rita Cantina. $–$$.

where to stay

The country around Bandera is dotted with dude ranches. Rates usually include three meals daily as well as family-style entertainment and supervised children's programs. Horseback riding is often part of the weeklong package. A minimum stay of two or three days is required at most ranches during peak summer season.

For a complete listing of Bandera's dude ranches, as well as other accommodations and campgrounds, call the Bandera Convention and Visitors Bureau at (800) 364-3833.

Dixie Dude Ranch. (800) 375-YALL; www.dixieduderanch.com. Go south on TX 173 for 1.5 miles to FM 1077, then southwest for 9 more miles. Five generations of the Whitley family have welcomed guests to this ranch since 1937. The Dixie Dude Ranch offers potential cowpokes the opportunity to enjoy a taste of ranch life. Start your morning with a leisurely trail ride followed by a genuine cowboy breakfast, then enjoy a day filled with hiking, hunting for Native American arrowheads, taking country-western dance lessons, fishing, or tossing horseshoes. The ranch includes 19 units made up of individual cottages, duplex cabins, and lodge rooms featuring early Texas architecture. Rates include meals and 2 horseback rides daily. $$$.

Flying L Guest Ranch. (800) 292-5134; www.flyingl.com. From TX 16, turn south on TX 173 for 1.5 miles, then left on Wharton Dock Road. This 542-acre ranch has 38 guest houses, each with 2 rooms, refrigerator, microwave, coffeepot, and TV. You can choose from a variety of packages offering horseback riding, hayrides, and even golf on the ranch's 18-hole course. During the summer there's a supervised children's program. Nightly entertainment ranges from western shows to "branding" parties. $$$.

LH7 Ranch Resort. FM 3240, 5 miles from Bandera; (830) 796-4314; www.lh7ranchresort .com. This 1,200-acre ranch, which raises longhorn cattle, has cottages with kitchenettes, plus RV hookups. There's plenty to keep any cowpoke busy, including angling in a 50-acre lake, hayrides, trail rides, and nature walks. $$$.

Mayan Ranch. TX 16, 2 miles west of Bandera; (830) 796-3312 or (830) 460-3036; www .mayanranch.com. For more than 50 years, this 60-room ranch has entertained vacationers with cowboy breakfasts, cookouts, horseback riding, angling, and hayrides. Summer also brings organized children's programs. Rooms are appointed with western-style furniture. $$$.

Silver Spur Dude Ranch. FM 1077,10 miles south of Bandera; (830) 796-3037; www .ssranch.com. Pull on your boots and grab your Stetson before heading to this 275-acre ranch near Hill Country State Natural Area. You'll stay busy out of the saddle with nearby angling, tubing, canoeing, and golfing, plus swimming in the ranch pool. $$$.

Twin Elm Guest Ranch. Half mile off FM 470 from TX 16 (4 miles from Bandera); (888) 567-3049 or (830) 796-3628; www.twinelmranch.com. This 200-acre dude ranch is on the Medina River. All the usual cowboy activities are available, from angling to horseback riding to horseshoe pitching. May through Sept the ranch hosts a weekly rodeo every Fri. $$$.

especially for winter texans

Besides the dude ranches, Bandera has excellent RV parks. Many weekly activities are of special interest to the Winter Texans who call Bandera home. Country-western dances are held Wednesday through Saturday, and there's bingo on Friday and Sunday. For a complete listing, contact the Bandera Convention and Visitors Bureau at (800) 364-3833.

medina

The tiny community of Medina is best known for its dwarf apple trees that produce full-size fruit in varieties from Crispin to Jonagold.

taking a shine to medina

If there's any truth to the saying "an apple a day keeps the doctor away," the physi-cians of Medina, Texas, better close up shop. This Hill Country community is the capital of Texas's apple industry, a business that's growing by the bushel.

Medina's apple industry took root in 1981 when Baxter Adams and his wife, Carol, moved to Love Creek Ranch outside Medina. Baxter spent 30 years as an exploration geologist before moving to this region, a land of rocky, rugged hills, with fertile valleys irrigated by Love Creek, a cool, spring-fed creek that originates on the ranch.

These valleys gave Adams the idea for an orchard, one that wouldn't take a lot of land. "I don't have much tillable land," Adams once explained to us. "I've got to really make it count. It's a matter of trying to squeeze the most possible dollars out of the smallest possible area."

And that's just what Baxter Adams did.

This Texas version of Johnny Appleseed specializes in dwarf apple trees, which reach a height of only 5 or 6 feet. The Lilliputians boast full-size apples, however, up to 50 pounds per tree, in varieties from Red Delicious to Gala and Crispin.

Baxter and Carol started with 1,000 trees in 1981, and they were soon in the apple business. Unlike the full-size trees that take 7 years to produce a crop, the dwarfs yield fruit in just a year and a half. Another advantage Adams has over the northern producers is his growing season: Texas apples ripen weeks before their northern cousins.

getting there

From Bandera, continue west on TX 16 for 13 miles to Medina.

where to go

Love Creek Orchards. RR 337 west of Medina; (830) 589-2588 or (800) 449-0882; www .lovecreekorchards.com. From May through October these beautiful orchards are open to the public by guided tour only; call to set up a tour time. Free admission.

where to shop

The Cider Mill and Country Store. Main Street (TX 16), downtown; (830) 589-2202; www .lovecreekorchards.com. This shop sells Love Creek apples June through November. But-ter, sauces, vinegars, jellies, syrups, pies, breads, and even apple ice cream are sold here year-round. If you're ready to start your own orchard but you're short on room, you can buy the "patio apple orchard," a dwarf tree grown on a trellis in a wooden planter. Open daily.

vanderpool

Vanderpool is a quiet getaway during all but the fall months. Tucked into the hills surrounding the Sabinal River, this small town is a center for sheep and goat ranching.

getting there

From Medina, turn west on FM 337 and continue for 20 miles. Vanderpool is located just north of the FM 337 and RR 187 intersection.

where to go

Lost Maples State Natural Area. 37221 FM 187; (830) 966-3413 or (800) 792-1112; www.tpwd.state.tx.us/spdest/findadest/parks/lost_maples. Go west on RR 337 to the intersection with RR 187, then turn north and continue 5 miles. This state park is one of the most heavily visited sites in Texas during Oct and Nov, when the bigtooth maples provide

leaf peeping

Are you starting to dream about the feel of a cool autumn breeze? Hearing the crackle of leaves beneath your feet? Smelling the smoke of an evening campfire?

*Central Texas may not have the blazing colors of New England, but with a little looking, you will find a brilliant quilt of fall colors. To find out the status of fall colors, call the **Texas Travel Information Center** at (800) 452-9292 or the **Texas Parks and Wildlife hotline** at (800) 792-1112. The brilliant colors require cold night temperatures, an occurrence that can reach the Hill Country valleys long before the warmer city locations.*

*The top destination for many leaf peepers is **Lost Maples State Natural Area** in Vanderpool. The maples, located so far from other specimens of the beautiful tree, may seem lost, but there's no doubt that the park itself has been found. This state park is one of the most heavily visited sites in Texas during October and November, when the bigtooth maples provide some of the best color in Texas. Weekend visits during this time can be very crowded, and note that the parking here is limited to only 250 cars. The best time to visit is during midweek, when you can enjoy a walk into the park without crowds.*

some of the best color in the state. Weekend visits at this time can be very crowded, so note that parking is limited to 250 cars. The least crowded time to visit is midweek.

There are 10 miles of hiking trails to enjoy all year along the **Sabinal River Canyon.** In the summer visitors can swim and fish in the river. Camping includes primitive areas on the hiking trails and a 30-site campground with restrooms and showers as well as a trailer dump station. Open daily.

Scenic Drive—Camp Wood to Leakey. This drive from Camp Wood to Leakey (pronounced "LAY-key") on RR 337 is often termed the most scenic in Texas and is an excellent spot for fall color. The road climbs to some of the highest elevations in the Hill Country at more than 2,300 feet, and roadside lookouts offer great vistas of reds, greens, and golds. Free admission.

Scenic Drive—Utopia to US 83. West of Utopia, RR 1050 winds its way through the Hill Country, crossing the Frio River before eventually intersecting with US 83 north of Concan. During late fall the drive is dotted with blazing sumacs, sycamores, chinaberries, and cottonwoods. Free admission.

day trip 02

northwest

>>> **western art:**
kerrville, ingram, hunt, y. o. ranch

Head northwest of San Antonio on I-10, and you'll soon see the city fall away and surrender the road to the Hill Country. Not far beyond the loops that lasso San Antonio into a metropolitan corral lies a land of white-tailed deer and oak-dotted hills, a gateway to the Hill Country for I-10 travelers.

kerrville

Kerrville is popular with retirees, hunters, Winter Texans, and campers. The town of more than 22,000 residents was named for James Kerr, a supporter of Texas independence who died in the Civil War. With its unpolluted environment and low humidity, Kerrville later became known as a health center, attracting tuberculosis patients from around the country. The town is still considered one of the most healthful places to live in the nation because of its clean air and moderate climate.

Throughout Kerrville the Schreiner name appears on everything from Schreiner University to Schreiner's Department Store. Charles Schreiner, who became a Texas Ranger at the tender age of 15, came to Kerrville as a young man in the 1850s. Following the Civil War, he opened a dry goods store and started acquiring land and raising sheep and goats. The Charles Schreiner Company soon expanded to include banking, ranching, and marketing wool and mohair. This was the first business in America to recognize the value of mohair, the product of Angora goats. Before long, Schreiner made Kerrville the mohair capital of the world.

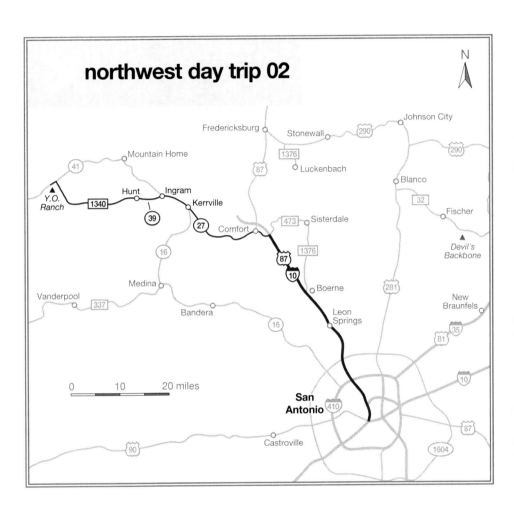

northwest day trip 02

In 1880 Schreiner acquired the Y. O. Ranch, which grew over the next 20 years to more than 600,000 acres, covering a distance of 80 miles. Today the Schreiner family still owns this well-known ranch, located in nearby Mountain Home.

getting there

From San Antonio, drive north on I-10 for 48 miles to TX 27 in Comfort. Follow TX 27 for 19 miles to Kerrville.

where to go

Hill Country Museum. 226 Earl Garrett St.; (830) 896-8633. This local-history museum traces the development of Kerrville. Housed in Charles Schreiner's former mansion, built in 1879, the museum has granite porch columns, wooden parquet floors, and a bronze fountain imported from France. Open Thurs through Sat.

Kerrville-Schreiner Park. 2385 Bandera Hwy., 1 mile southwest on TX 173; (830) 257-5392; www.kerrvilletx.gov. This park offers 8 miles of hiking trails, as well as fishing and swimming in the Guadalupe River. During the summer months, kayaks and canoes are for rent for an afternoon excursion on the river. Mountain bikers will find 6 miles of beginner/intermediate trails. Campsites include water, electrical and sewage hookups, and screened shelters.

Louise Hays City Park. Off TX 16 at Thompson Dr.; (830) 792-8386. Bring your picnic lunch to this beautiful spot on the Guadalupe River. A footbridge spans the river to Tranquility Island, where ducks and cypress trees abound. Open during daylight hours only. Free admission.

Museum of Western Art. 1550 Bandera Hwy. (TX 173); (830) 896-2553; www.museumofwesternart.org. This hilltop museum (formerly the Cowboy Artists of America Museum) features work by members of the Cowboy Artists of America. The building is constructed of 18 boveda brick domes, an old construction method used in Mexico. Western-themed paintings and sculptures fill the museum. Visitors also can take in special programs on the folklore, music, and history of the Old West. Open Tues through Sat as well as Sun afternoons.

where to shop

James Avery Craftsman, Inc. Harper Road, 3.5 miles north of Kerrville; (830) 895-6800; www.jamesavery.com. Since 1954 James Avery has been one of Texas's premier silversmiths. He began crafting silver crosses and religious symbols, but today his work includes gold and silver renditions of many subjects, from prickly pears to dolphins. Retail shop open Mon through Sat; visitor center open weekdays.

art walk

*Many Hill Country communities offer monthly markets featuring arts and crafts, but Kerrville takes their special event one step further. The **Second Saturday Art Trail** offers visitors the chance not only to shop for art, but also to visit the city's growing number of galleries. From 10 a.m. to 6 p.m. on the second Saturday of every month, the city's galleries (now more than two dozen strong) open their doors, provide special demonstrations, serve refreshments, and help introduce all the members of the family to various types of artwork. For more, see www.artinthehills.com.*

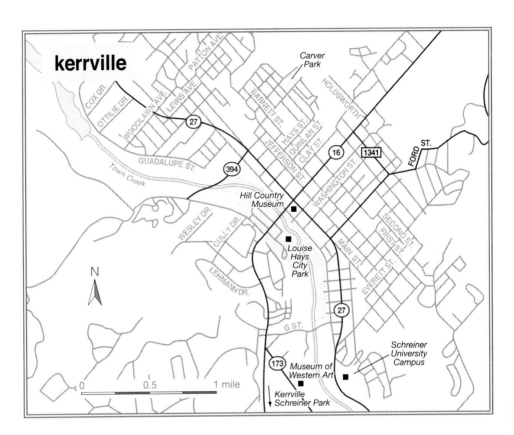

River's Edge Gallery. 832 Water St.; (830) 895-5184; www.riversedgegallery.net. Over 50 regional and nationally recognized artists are showcased at this gallery. River's Edge features western, wildlife, landscape, and other traditional themes in watercolor, oil, mixed media, and digital format. Open Mon through Sat.

Sunrise Antique Mall. 820 Water St.; (830) 895-2414. Kerrville's largest antiques shop is housed in a century-old building that once served as a furniture store. Today the mall features everything from antique furniture to other antiques and artwork. Open Mon to Sat.

where to eat

Bill's Barbecue. 1909 Junction Hwy.; (830) 895-5733; www.billsbbq.net. This barbecue eatery serves up Texas favorites such as brisket, sausage, and chicken with the obligatory side dishes. Open Tues through Sat for lunch and dinner. $$. No credit cards.

Francisco's. 201 Earl Garrett St.; (830) 257-2995; www.franciscos-restaurant.com. Located downtown in the historic Weston Building, this restaurant features steak, seafood, and Mexican dishes. Patrons can choose to dine indoors or alfresco at sidewalk tables. Open Mon through Sat 11 a.m. to 3 p.m. plus Thurs through Sat 5:30 to 9 p.m. $$–$$$.

Hill Country Cafe. 806 Main St.; (830) 257-6665. This diner is a favorite with local citizens as well as travelers looking for a small-town atmosphere. The day starts out with traditional American breakfast as well as specialties such as *huevos rancheros*; for lunch look for burgers and chicken-fried steak. Open for breakfast and lunch weekdays, breakfast only Sat. $$.

Kathy's on the River. 417 Water St.; (830) 257-7811. This restaurant is an excellent spot for outdoor dining with a view of the river. The menu offers a little bit of everything, from traditional chicken-fried steak to dishes with an Asian flair. Open Wed through Sun. $$–$$$.

where to stay

Y. O. Ranch Resort Hotel and Conference Center. 2033 Sidney Baker, at TX 16 and I-10; (830) 257-4440; www.yoresort.com. This 200-room hotel salutes the famous Y. O. Ranch in nearby Mountain Home. The lobby is filled with reminders of the area's major industries—cattle and hunting. Twelve hotel suites include amenities such as fireplaces, furniture covered in longhorn hide, and wet bars. In keeping with the Wild West spirit, the hotel has a bar called the Elm Water Hole Saloon and a swim-up bar dubbed the Jersey Lilly. $–$$.

especially for winter texans

Kerrville is home to over a dozen RV parks, some of which are designated "adults only." For a listing, contact the Kerrville Convention and Visitors Center (800-221-7958; www.kerrvilletexascvb.com). The Kerrville Chamber of Commerce (830-896-1155) can provide a listing of condominium and apartment properties with short-term leases. A welcoming committee greets Winter Texans as well as the many retirees who relocate to the area.

ingram

This small community on the banks of the Guadalupe River was started in 1879 by the Reverend J. C. W. Ingram, who built a general store and post office in what is now called Old Ingram.

Old Ingram, located off TX 27 on Old Ingram Loop, is home to many art galleries and antiques shops. Ingram proper lies along TX 27. It features stores and outfitters catering to white-tailed deer, turkey, and quail hunters. The town is particularly busy during deer season, from November to early January. Hunting licenses are required and are sold at local sporting-goods stores. For more information, call the Texas Parks and Wildlife Department at (512) 389-4800 in Texas or (800) 792-1112 elsewhere, or visit www.tpwd.state.tx.us.

getting there

To reach Ingram, leave Kerrville on TX 27 and continue northwest for 7 miles.

where to go

Hill Country Arts Foundation. 120 Point Theatre Rd. (TX 39), South Ingram, west of the Ingram Loop; (830) 367-5120 or (800) 459-HCAF; www.hcaf.com. The foundation, located 6 miles west of Kerrville in Ingram, is one of the oldest multidisciplinary arts centers in the nation. For more than 35 years, this 15-acre center on the banks of the Guadalupe River has encouraged students in the fields of art, theater, photography, printmaking, and even quilt making. American musicals and plays are performed during the summer months at the open-air Point Theatre; indoor shows entertain audiences at other times throughout the year. A gallery exhibits the work of many artists and is open daily. The Gazebo Gift Shop is a sales outlet for local artists, open Mon through Fri afternoons. Call for a schedule of play times or special events.

Kerr County Historical Murals. At TX 27 and TX 39. Sixteen murals, the work of local artist Jack Feagan, decorate the T. J. Moore Lumber Company building. The scenes portray historical events in Kerr County, starting with the establishment of shingle camps (where wooden roofing shingles were produced in 1846). Other paintings highlight cattle drives, the birth of the mohair industry, and the last Indian raid.

where to shop

Clint Orms Engravers and Silversmiths. 229-B Old Ingram Loop; (830) 367-7949; www .clintorms.com. Clint Orms's works have been purchased for US presidents, top musicians, and other well-known personalities. His silver belt buckle sets are of heirloom quality, using the finest materials.

Don Atkinson Custom Boot and Saddle Maker, 229-C Old Ingram Loop; (830) 367-5400; www.donatkinson.com. Don Atkinson creates custom-made saddles and boots, each intricate works of art. This craftsman's work has been seen in museums and at championship rodeos (the store even features a $10,000 saddle on display) but you'll find everyday wear as well such as belts. The store also runs saddlemaking, chapmaking, and bootmaking schools.

Southwestern Elegance. 207 Old Ingram Loop; (830) 367-4749; www.southwestern elegance.com. This unique store specializes in Mexican collectibles and antiques (especially primitives), Mennonite furniture, and Tarahumara Indian collectibles. Open daily; call for hours.

hunt

The small community of Hunt is best known for its year-round outdoor recreational camps catering to Scouts as well as youth and church groups.

getting there

From Ingram, go west on TX 39 for 7 miles to Hunt.

where to go

Kerr Wildlife Management Area. RR 1340, 12 miles northwest of Hunt; (830) 238-4483; www.tpwd.state.tx.us. Enjoy a driving tour through this 6,493-acre research ranch owned by the Texas Fish and Game Commission. Purchased to study the relationship between wildlife and livestock, the ranch is home to white-tailed deer, javelinas, wild turkeys, bobcats, gray foxes, and ringtails. Pick up a booklet at the entrance or write Kerr Wildlife Management Area, Route 1, Box 180, Hunt, TX 78024. Open daily, but call during hunting season, when the area may be closed for a hunt. Free admission.

y. o. ranch

This ranch dates from 1880 and is part of the 550,000 acres purchased by Captain Charles Schreiner, former Texas Ranger and longhorn cattle owner. Presently the Y. O. spans 60 square miles and supports more than 1,000 registered longhorns, the largest such herd in the nation. Charlie Schreiner III, the original owner's grandson, brought the breed back from near extinction in the late 1950s, founding the Texas Longhorn Breeders Association. The Y. O. hosts a longhorn trail drive at the ranch each spring.

After a devastating Texas drought in the 1950s, the Schreiners began to diversify their ranch, stocking the land with the largest collection of natural roaming exotics in the country, including many rare and endangered species. More than 10,000 animals range the hills, including zebra, ostrich, giraffe, emu, and ibex.

You may visit the Y. O. Ranch by reservation only (1736 Y.O. Ranch Rd., Mountain Home; 830-967-2624 or (800) YO-RANCH; www.yoranch.com). Both day and overnight programs are offered. Day-trippers can enjoy the spread on a lunch tour or photo safari. The ranch also hosts an Outdoor Awareness Program, an environmental education camp that teaches horseback riding, rappelling, gun handling, and wildlife study. Overnight accommodations are available in the 1880s-era cabins; meals are included.

getting there

From Hunt, head west on FM 1340 to TX 41. Turn left, and the Y. O. Ranch will soon appear on your right.

day trip 03

northwest

german heritage:
boerne, comfort, sisterdale

This is an easy day trip from San Antonio, a journey through three small towns that share a strong German heritage. Although the excursion begins on sleek I-10, it includes some curving farm-to-market (FM) roads that are very susceptible to flooding. If it's raining heavily, save this trip for another day!

boerne

Boerne, on the banks of Cibolo Creek, was founded in 1847 by German immigrants, members of the same group who settled nearby New Braunfels. They named the town for author Ludwig Börne, whose writings inspired many people to leave Germany for the New World.

During the 1880s Boerne (pronounced "Bernie") became known as a health spot, and vacationers came by railroad to soak in mineral water spas and enjoy the clean country air. Although no mineral spas remain today, Boerne still offers a quiet country atmosphere and dozens of antiques shops.

Boerne is also home to the Boerne Village Band. For more than a century, this German band (the oldest continuously active German band in the country and the oldest in the world outside of Munich) has entertained residents and visitors with its old-world sound. This group can be heard at many local festivals and at Boerne's own Abendkonzerte, summer concerts scheduled for selected Tuesday nights throughout the summer on the Main Plaza.

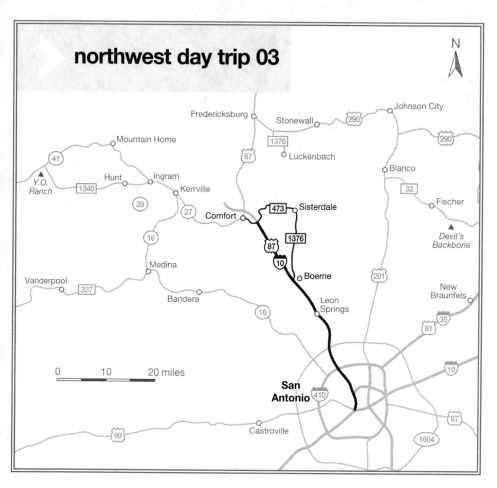

northwest day trip 03

getting there

To reach Boerne, take I-10 northwest from San Antonio for 22 miles to a spot filled with history, antiques, and natural attractions.

where to go

Boerne Convention and Visitors Bureau. 1407 South Main St.; (888) 842-8080; www .visitboerne.org. Stop here for brochures and maps to Boerne attractions and shopping areas. Open 9 a.m. to 5 p.m. Mon through Fri, and Sat 10 a.m. to 2 p.m.

Agricultural Heritage Center. TX 46, 1 mile from Main Street; (830) 249-6007; www .agmuseum.us. This museum features farm and ranch tools used by pioneers in the late 19th and early 20th centuries, including a working steam-operated blacksmith shop. Six acres surrounding the museum are covered with hand-drawn plows, wagons, early tractors, and woodworking tools. Open Sat 10 a.m. to 4 p.m. and by appointment.

Cascade Caverns. (830) 755-8080; www.cascadecaverns.com. From I-10, take exit 543 and follow signs on Cascade Caverns Road. This family-owned cavern, located in a 105-acre park, has a 100-foot waterfall, an unusual underground sight. Guided tours take 45 minutes. Open daily.

Cave Without a Name. 325 Kreutzberg Rd.; (830) 537-4212; www.cavewithoutaname .com. Guided tours take groups through 6 rooms of this family-owned cavern. A subterranean river and numerous cave formations fill the tour. Open daily.

Cibolo Wilderness Trail. Boerne City Park, TX 46 at Cibolo Creek; (830) 249-4616. Enjoy grassland, marshland, and woodland in this park that offers a slice of the Hill Country. The wilderness area includes both reclaimed prairie and reclaimed marsh, with walking trails that range from 0.25 mile to 1 mile in length. Free admission.

Guadalupe River State Park. PR 31, 13 miles east of Boerne off TX 46; (830) 438-2656; www.tpwd.state.tx.us. The star of this park is the clear, cold Guadalupe River. Camp, swim, hike, or just picnic on its scenic banks. On Sat mornings, take an interpretive tour of the Honey Creek State Natural Area to learn more about the plants and animals of the region.

Honey Creek State Natural Area. PR 31, Spring Branch, 13 miles east of Boerne off TX 46; (830) 438-2656; www.tpwd.state.tx.us. Use of this park is limited to those on guided tours. A 2-hour guided look at the park's history and ecology is offered every Sat morning at 9 a.m.; reservations aren't necessary, but call first to confirm that a tour will be offered. Access to the park is through Guadalupe River State Park.

Kuhlmann-King Historical House and Graham Building and Museum Store. Main Street and Blanco Road; (830) 249-7277. The Kuhlmann-King House was built by a local businessman for his German bride in 1885. Today the 2-story stone home is staffed by volunteer docents. The Graham Building, located next door, is home to the Boerne Area Historical Preservation Society and exhibits on local history. Open by appointment. Free admission.

where to eat

Limestone Grill. 128 West Blanco St. at Ye Kendall Inn; (830) 249-2138; www.yekendall inn.com. In 1859 the owners of this 2-story structure began renting rooms to stagecoach travelers, eventually developing the property into an inn. Over the years its famous guests have included Confederate president Jefferson Davis and US president Dwight D. Eisenhower. Along with 7 bed-and-breakfast rooms furnished with period antiques, the inn includes a restaurant with adjoining bar that serves favorites such as burgers, salads, and soups along with specialties like the yellowfin tuna stack, chicken-fried steak, and the cowboy rib eye. Open daily for lunch and for dinner Mon through Sat. $$.

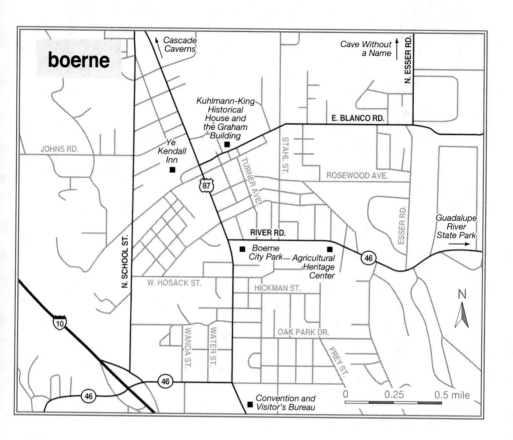

Little Gretel. 518 River Rd.; (830) 331-1368; www.littlegretel.com. European dishes fill the menu at this upbeat restaurant. Dine inside or on the patio while enjoying German and Czech specialties like bratwurst, Wiener schnitzel, and sauerbraten. You can also choose from Italian dishes as well as American favorites like burgers and Ruben sandwiches. Open for breakfast and lunch Mon through Sat and for dinner Wed through Sat. Sunday brunch is served from 9 a.m. to 5 p.m. $$.

where to shop

Calamity Jane's Trading Company. 404 South Main St.; (830) 249-0081; http://calamity janestradingco.com. Located in a historic home on Boerne's Main Street, Calamity Jane's offers an eclectic array of household furnishings imported from all over the world, including one-of-a-kind furniture items, lighting fixtures, pottery, and fine art.

Sun of a Brave. 126 South Main St.; (830) 249-5766; www.sunofabrave.com. This shop offers a variety of unique items, including jewelry, kachinas and fetishes, pottery, dream catchers, and paintings. All are the creations of American Indian artisans. The store prides itself on its commitment to ethical business practices and is a member of the Indian Arts &

Crafts Association, an organization that protects the artists who create the works and also the consumers who buy them.

where to stay

Ye Kendall Inn. 128 West Blanco St.; (800) 364-2138; www.yekendallinn.com. This historic inn offers 36 antiques-filled guest rooms, suites, and cottages. Amenities include a restaurant (see "Where to Eat"), a bar, a spa, and easy access to downtown shops. $$$.

comfort

This small community is big in history and attractions. The downtown area is a National Historic District, filled with homes and businesses built by early settlers.

Comfort was founded in 1854 by German pioneers who wanted to name the town Gemütlichkeit, meaning peace, serenity, comfort, and happiness. After some deliberation, though, they decided on the easier to pronounce Comfort instead.

Today Comfort offers tourists numerous historic buildings to explore, filled with antiques shops and restaurants. Many of the buildings on High Street, such as the Comfort Common (now a B&B), were designed in the late 1800s by noted British architect Alfred Giles. Weekends are the busiest time to visit, but even then the atmosphere is relaxing, unhurried, and, well, comfortable.

getting there

From Boerne, continue northwest on I-10 for 17 miles to road marker 524 and exit to the town of Comfort.

where to go

Bat Roost. FM 473, on private land; (830) 995-3131. As you leave Comfort for Sisterdale, this historic structure sits 1 mile from town on the right side of the road behind private gates. While it's generally known now that bats feed on disease-spreading mosquitoes, the folks here have known about the importance of these furry mammals since 1918, when Albert Steves constructed hygieostatic bat roosts in an experimental attempt to control malaria. The roosts were intended to encourage the area's large bat population to remain in the region. Only 16 such roosts were built in the country, and this is the oldest of 3 known still to exist. Free, but just to view from the road.

Bat Tunnel. Old Highway 9, 15 miles northeast of Comfort off TX 473; (830) 995-3131. View the evening flight of 1.2 million Mexican free-tailed bats from this abandoned railroad tunnel now managed by the Texas Parks and Wildlife Department. Closed Oct to May. Free admission.

Treue der Union (True to the Union) Monument. High Street, between Third and Fourth Streets; (830) 995-3131. During the Civil War, German residents of Comfort who did not approve of slavery and openly swore their loyalty to the Union were burned out of their farms. The Confederates responsible also lynched locals who refused to pledge their allegiance to the movement. Several German farmers refused but were caught by Confederate soldiers and killed on the banks of the Nueces River, their bodies left unburied.

Finally retrieved in 1865, the remains were returned to Comfort and buried in a mass grave. A white obelisk, the oldest monument in Texas and the only monument to the Union located south of the Mason-Dixon Line, was dedicated here in 1866. One of only six such sites in the country, the shrine recently received congressional approval to continually fly the flag at half-mast. The flag that waves here has 36 stars, the same number it had when the marker was dedicated in 1866. Free admission.

where to shop

The Comfort Common. 717 High St.; (830) 995-3030; www.thecomfortcommon.com. This combination bed-and-breakfast inn and indoor shopping area is located within the historic Ingenhuett-Faust Hotel. Several buildings behind the hotel display antique primitives and furniture. Open daily.

Wilson Clements Antiques. 405 Seventh St.; (830) 995-5039; www.wilsonclements.com. Specializing in primitive antique items, this expansive store offers household accessories, furniture, and architectural pieces from Mexico and Western Europe. Open Mon through Sat 10 a.m. to 5 p.m. and Sun noon to 3 p.m.

where to eat

Cypress Creek Inn Restaurant. 408 West TX 27; (830) 995-3977; www.cypresscreekinn .com. Cypress Creek Inn is the oldest restaurant in Comfort, operating since the 1950s. Order up traditional Texas fare such as chicken-fried steak and T-bones, or lighter dishes such as seafood and sandwiches at this casual restaurant. Open Mon through Sat for lunch and dinner. $–$$.

where to stay

The Comfort Common. 717 High St.; (830) 995-3030; www.thecomfortcommon.com. A bed-and-breakfast operating within the 1880 Ingenhuett-Faust Hotel, Comfort Common's 5 suites are variously decorated in English country, American country, or Victorian decor. All rooms include private baths and period furnishings. The backyard Gorman Cottage has a fireplace and complete kitchen. All rates include breakfast. As rooms book quickly for weekends, consider a midweek stay. $$.

sisterdale

This burg, like nearby Boerne, was settled by a group of intellectuals. Today the population has dwindled to a handful of residents, and you have to look carefully to keep from passing right through town.

getting there

From Comfort, head out on FM 473 to nearby Sisterdale, best known as the home of a small winery.

where to go

Sister Creek Vineyards. FM 1376, off FM 473; (830) 324-6704; www.sistercreekvine yards.com. These vineyards thrive in "downtown" Sisterdale, located between the East and West Sister Creeks. The winery, a restored cotton gin, produces traditional French wines. Open daily for self-guided tours. Free admission.

Sisterdale Dancehall. 1210 Sisterdale Rd.; (210) 508-0344; www.sisterdaledancehall .com. A historic structure dating to the mid-1800s, the Sisterdale Dancehall is one of the oldest buildings in town. Over the years it has been a fort, an opera house, and a community center as well as a dance hall. Now restored, it retains its historic features and again hosts live music on weekends in addition to special events. The management operates a bed-and-breakfast next door.

where to eat

Sisterdale Saloon. 1211 FM 473; (830) 324-6767. Part dancehall, part general store, this historic bar has served generations of thirsty customers for over a century. Live music is featured on Tues, Fri, and Sat nights when the dance floor gets busy. Out back, an outdoor beer garden overlooks the bucolic Hill Country landscape. In addition to beer, soda, and Sister Creek Wine, the bar serves pizza and snacks. Open Mon through Wed from noon to midnight; Thurs and Fri from 11 a.m. to midnight; Sat 11 a.m. to 1 a.m. and Sun 11 a.m. to midnight.

regional information

north

day trip 01

Blanco Chamber of Commerce
312 Pecan
P.O. Box 626
Blanco, TX 78606
(830) 833-5101
www.blancochamber.com

Wimberley Chamber of Commerce
14100 RR 12 North
P.O. Box 12
Wimberley, TX 78676
(512) 847-2201
www.wimberley.org

day trip 02

Johnson City Chamber of Commerce
P.O. Box 485
Johnson City, TX 78636
(830) 868-7684
www.johnsoncity-texas.com

Stonewall Chamber of Commerce
250 Peach St.
P.O. Box 1
Stonewall, TX 78671
(830) 644-2735
www.stonewalltexas.com

Luckenbach, Texas
412 Luckenbach Town Rd.
Fredericksburg, TX 78624
(888) 311-8990 or (830) 997-3224
www.luckenbachtexas.com

Fredericksburg Convention and Visitors Bureau
302 East Austin
Fredericksburg, TX 78624
(888) 997-3600 or (830) 997-6523
www.fredericksburg-texas.com

northeast

day trip 01

New Braunfels Chamber of Commerce
390 South Seguin Ave.
P.O. Box 311417
New Braunfels, TX 78130
(800) 572-2626
www.nbjumpin.com or www.nbcham.org

Gruene Historic District
(830) 629-5077
www.gruenetexas.com

day trip 02

San Marcos Chamber of Commerce
202 North C.M. Pkwy.
P.O. Box 2310
San Marcos, TX 78667
(512) 393-5900
www.sanmarcostexas.com

Buda Area Chamber of Commerce
203 Railroad St., Suite 1C
P.O. Box 904
Buda, TX 78610
(512) 295-9999
www.budachamber.com

day trip 03

Austin Convention and Visitors Bureau
301 Congress Ave., Suite 200
Austin, TX 78701
(800) 926-ACVB or (512) 474-5171
www.austintexas.org

east

day trip 01

Seguin Convention and Visitors Bureau
116 North Camp St.
P.O. Box 710
Seguin, TX 78156
(800) 580-7322 or (830) 379-6382
www.visitseguin.com

Luling Area Chamber of Commerce
421 East Davis St.
P.O. Box 710
Luling, TX 78648
(830) 875-3214
www.lulingcc.org

day trip 02

Flatonia Chamber of Commerce
208 East North Main
P.O. Box 610
Flatonia, TX 78941
(512) 865-3920
www.flatonia-tx.com

Schulenburg Chamber of Commerce
618 North Main
Schulenburg, TX 78956
(866) 504-5294
http://schulenburgchamber.org

day trip 03

Gonzales Chamber of Commerce
Visitor Center at Old Jail Museum
414 St. Lawrence St.
P.O. Box 134
Gonzales, TX 78629
(888) 672-1095 or (830) 672-6532
www.gonzalestexas.com

Shiner Chamber of Commerce
817 North Avenue East
P.O. Box 221
Shiner, TX 77984
(361) 594-4180
www.shinertx.com

Yoakum Area Chamber of Commerce
P.O. Box 591
Yoakum, TX 77995
(512) 293-2309
www.yoakumareachamber.com

day trip 04

Lockhart Chamber of Commerce
631 South Colorado St.
P.O. Box 840
Lockhart, TX 78644
(512) 398-2818
www.lockhartchamber.com

Bastrop Chamber of Commerce
927 Main St.
Bastrop, TX 78602
(512) 303-0558
www.bastropchamber.com

Smithville Area Chamber of Commerce
100 First St.
P.O. Box 716
Smithville, TX 78957
(512) 237-2313
www.smithvilletx.org

La Grange Chamber of Commerce
171 South Main St.
La Grange, TX 78945
(800) LAGRANGE or (979) 968-5756
www.lagrangetx.org

southeast

day trip 01

Floresville Chamber of Commerce
910 10th St.
Floresville, TX 78114
(830) 393-0074
http://floresvillecoc.com

Panna Maria Historical Society
P.O. Box 52
Panna Maria, TX 78144
(830) 780-4471
www.pannamariatexas.com

Goliad Chamber of Commerce
231 South Market St.
P.O. Box 606
Goliad, TX 77963
(800) 848-8674 or (361) 645-3563
www.goliadcc.org

day trip 02

Stockdale Chamber of Commerce
700 West Main St.
P.O. Box 578
Stockdale, TX 78160
(830) 996-0021
www.stockdaletx.org

Cuero Chamber of Commerce
124 East Church St.
Cuero, Texas 77954
(361) 275-2112
www.cuero.org

**Victoria Convention and Visitors
Bureau**
3404 North Ben Wilson St.
P.O. Box 2465
Victoria, TX 77902
(800) 926-5774 or (361) 573-5277
www.visitvictoriatexas.com/vcvb

day trip 03

Port Lavaca Chamber of Commerce
2300 Highway 35 North
Port Lavaca, TX 77979
(800) 556-PORT or (361) 552-2959
www.portlavacatx.org

Port O'Connor Chamber of Commerce
P.O. Box 701
Port O'Connor, TX 77982
(361) 983-2898
www.portoconnor.com

south

day trip 01

**Aransas Pass Chamber of Commerce
and Visitors Center**
130 West Goodnight
Aransas Pass, TX 78336
(800) 633-3028 or (361) 758-2750
www.aransaspass.org

**Port Aransas Tourist and Convention
Bureau**
421 West Cotter
Port Aransas, TX 78373
(800) 45-COAST or (361) 749-5919
www.portaransas.org

Rockport-Fulton Area Chamber of Commerce
404 Broadway
Rockport, TX 78382
(800) 242-0071 or (361) 729-6445
www.rockport-fulton.org

day trip 02

Three Rivers Area Chamber of Commerce
P.O. Box 1648
Three Rivers, TX 78071
(888) 600-3115 or (361) 786-4330
www.threeriverstx.org

Mathis Area Chamber of Commerce
211 East San Patricio Ave.
Mathis, TX 78368
(361) 547-0289
www.mathischamber.org

Greater Corpus Christi Convention and Visitors Bureau
101 North Shoreline Blvd., Suite 430
Corpus Christi, TX 78401
(800) 678-OCEAN, (800) 766-2322, or (361) 881-1888
www.visitcorpuschristitx.org

King Ranch Visitor Center
Highway 141 West
P.O. Box 1090
Kingsville, TX 78364
(361) 592-8055
www.king-ranch.com

Kingsville Convention and Visitors Bureau
1501 US 77
Kingsville, TX 78363
(800) 333-5032 or (361) 592-8516
www.kingsvilletexas.com

southwest

day trip 01

Pearsall Chamber of Commerce
317 South Oak
Pearsall, TX 78061
(830) 334-9414
www.pearsalltexas.com

Cotulla–LaSalle County Chamber of Commerce
290 North I-35
Cotulla, TX 78014
(800) 256-2326 or (830) 879-2326
www.cotulla-chamber.com

Laredo Convention and Visitors Bureau
501 San Agustin
Laredo, TX 78040
(800) 361-3360 or (956) 795-2200
www.visitlaredo.com

west

day trip 01

Eagle Pass Chamber of Commerce
400 Garrison St.
P.O. Box 1188
Eagle Pass, TX 78853
(888) 355-3224 or (830) 773-3224
www.eaglepasstexas.com

day trip 02

Castroville Area Chamber of Commerce
100 Karm St.
P.O. Box 572
Castroville, TX 78009
(800) 778-6775 or (830) 538-3142
www.castroville.com

Hondo Area Chamber of Commerce
1607 Avenue K
Hondo, TX 78861
(830) 426-3037
www.hondochamber.com

Uvalde Chamber of Commerce
300 East Main St.
Uvalde, TX 78801
(830) 278-3361
www.uvalde.org

day trip 03

Del Rio Area Chamber of Commerce
1915 Veterans Blvd.
Del Rio, TX 78840
(800) 889-8149 or (830) 775-3551
www.drchamber.com

northwest

day trip 01

Bandera County Convention and Visitors Bureau
P.O. Box 171
Bandera, TX 78003
(800) 364-3833 or (830) 796-3045
www.banderacowboycapital.com

day trip 02

Kerrville Convention and Visitors Bureau
2108 Sidney Baker
Kerrville, TX 78028
(800) 221-7958 or (830) 792-3535
www.kerrvilletexascvb.com

West Kerr County Chamber of Commerce
P.O. Box 1006
Ingram, TX 78025
(830) 367-4322
www.wkcc.com

day trip 03

Greater Boerne Area Chamber of Commerce
126 Rosewood Ave.
Boerne, TX 78006
(888) 842-8080 or (830) 249-8000
www.boerne.org

Comfort Chamber of Commerce
Seventh and High Streets
P.O. Box 777
Comfort, TX 78013
(830) 995-3131
www.comfort-texas.com

festivals & celebrations

Texas undoubtedly has more festivals than any other state. Regardless of the weekend, you'll find some town whooping it up with parades, music, and lots of food. There are festivals for every interest, whether yours is pioneer heritage, German food, or watermelons.

For a quarterly list of Texas's annual events, write the Texas Department of Transportation at P.O. Box 5064, Austin, TX 78763-5064; call (800) 8888-TEX or (512) 452-9292; or pick up a free copy at one of the Texas Travel Information Centers.

You can also view a free annual events calendar from the Texas Festivals and Events association at www.tourtexas.com and at the Texas Tourism site, www.traveltex.com. You'll also find an online calendar on the *Texas Highways* magazine site, www.texashigh ways.com.

february

Celebration of Whooping Cranes. Port Aransas; (800) 45-COAST; www.portaransas .org/cranes.asp. This festival includes seminars, workshops, and tours dedicated to the endangered whooping cranes that winter at the Aransas National Wildlife Refuge. The special event includes birding tours, boat trips, and craft shows.

George Washington's Birthday Celebration. Laredo and Nuevo Laredo; (956) 722-0589; www.wbcalaredo.org. Since 1898 the border towns of Laredo and Nuevo Laredo have celebrated this holiday. Festivities run Tues through Sat with a *charro* rodeo, games, and a general party atmosphere.

march

Festival of the Arts. Corpus Christi; (361) 826-3494; www.ccfestivalarts.org. This event draws participating artists from around the state to show their artwork and demonstrate the techniques used in their creation.

Frio Freedom Fest. Concan; (830) 232-6580. Visitors to this Uvalde County community enjoy its annual ode to the Lone Star way of life with a BBQ cook-off, horseshoe and washer-tossing tournaments, and a 5K race as well as a carnival, live music, and an arts and crafts area.

Fulton Oysterfest. Fulton; (361) 463-9955; www.fultonoysterfest.org. Spend the first weekend in Mar downing fried or raw oysters to celebrate the culmination of the oyster harvest. Besides oyster eating and shucking contests, there are games, entertainment, and dances.

Goliad County Fair and Rodeo. Goliad; (800) 848-8674 or (361) 645-2492. Cowboys and cowgirls compete in this rodeo that features precision riding, live entertainment, and more.

Goliad Massacre Reenactment. Goliad; (361) 645-3752; www.presidiolabahia.org. This annual event re-creates Colonel Fannin and the Texas revolutionaries' occupation of the region and their battle with the Mexican army.

International Friendship Festival. Eagle Pass; (888) 355-3224. This event, with celebrations on both sides of the international border, includes a parade, carnival, and plenty of children's fun. Held in Shelby Park.

Star of Texas Fair and Rodeo. Austin; (512) 919-3000; www.rodeoaustin.com. Held at the Travis County Exposition and Heritage Center east of the city, this 2-week event features nightly rodeos, live entertainment, and a livestock show.

SXSW (South by Southwest). Austin; (512) 467-7979; http://sxsw.com. This event, held in mid-March, attracts more than 3,500 people from the music industry to the capital city for music conferences and nighttime entertainment. During the 4-day festival, more than 400 acts perform at clubs throughout town. Wristbands permit music lovers to take in show after show, from rock to blues to Cajun music.

april

Art City Austin. Austin; (800) 926-2282; www.artallianceaustin.org. This celebration of Austin's vibrant art scene takes place in multiple venues around the downtown cultural district. Over 20,000 visitors come to experience artwork produced by many different types of artists during this Apr event.

Buccaneer Days. Corpus Christi; (800) 678-OCEAN; www.bucdays.com. Near the end of Apr, Corpus Christi's swashbuckling days are relived with pioneer parades, a terrific fireworks display over the bay, and a huge carnival.

Eeyore's Birthday Party. Austin; (512) 448-5160; www.eeyores.com. Held the last Sat of Apr, this is one of Austin's wackiest festivals, paying tribute to Eeyore of Winnie the Pooh fame. Outrageous costumes, live entertainment, food, drink, and games are featured at this unique celebration of springtime.

Great Texas Birding Classic. Port Aransas; (800) 45-COAST; www.gcbo.org. Sponsored by the Gulf Coast Bird Observatory and the Texas Parks and Wildlife Department, this event challenges teams to see who can spot and record the most bird species in a given time period.

Here's to the Heroes Fest & Cookout. Kerrville; (800) 370-1198. Held at Flat Rock Lake Park, this event features a chili and brisket cook-off, live music, and an egg hunt.

River Rendezvous. La Grange; (800) 524-7264. This event draws canoeists from around the state. Visitors paddle down the Colorado River and enjoy camping, fun, food, and old-fashioned storytelling.

Round Top Antiques Fair. Round Top; (888) 368-4783; www.roundtoptexasantiques .com. Held the first weekend of April, this show features dealers from across the nation. It has been called the best antiques show in the state.

SandFest. Port Aransas; (800) 45-COAST; http://texassandfest.com. This event ranks as the largest master sand-sculpting event in the United States, spanning 3 days and showcasing 200-plus sand sculptors and over 100,000 spectators.

Smithville Jamboree. Smithville; (512) 237-2313; www.smithvillejamboree.com. This longtime event includes parades; a livestock show; softball, volleyball, and horseshoe tournaments; nightly dances; an antique car show; and a carnival.

Springs Fest. San Marcos; (512) 393-5900. Fast becoming an annual rite of spring, an array of paddling enthusiasts gather on the first weekend of Apr for a 3-day salute to aquatic activities, including kayak and canoe classes, a kayak polo tournament, kayak slalom races, and a sport originating in San Marcos, the Sladeo (a combination of slalom racing and rodeo).

Texas Ladies' State Chili Cookoff. Seguin; (830) 379-6382. Women from around the state test their skills at this chili cook-off. Along with taste tests, visitors enjoy live entertainment.

Wildflower Tour. Cuero; (361) 275-2112; www.cuero.org. Self-guided driving maps of the best places to view the 1,000-plus species of wildflowers found in DeWitt County are available at the chamber office at 124 East Church St. Throughout the month of Apr, the area celebrates with many special events, including a 5K walk/run, a bicycle race, and photo exhibits.

Yesterfest and Salinas Art Festival. Bastrop; (512) 303-0904; www.bastropdba.com. Return to pioneer days on the banks of the Colorado River and try your hand at quilting, corn shucking, candle dipping, and doll making.

may

Cinco de Mayo. Del Rio; (800) 889-8149 or (830) 775-3551. This border city celebrates its "Best of the Border" binational heritage at historic Brown Plaza.

Fredericksburg Crawfish Festival. Fredericksburg; (830) 997-6523; www.tex-fest.com/ crawfish. Foodies flock to Fredericksburg in May to enjoy a taste of the Big Easy. A gumbo cooking competition and zydeco music add to the New Orleans vibe.

Funtier Days. Bandera; (830) 796-3280; www.banderacountyartists.com. If they had festivals back in the Wild West days, they must have looked like this one. Professional Rodeo Cowboys Association (PRCA) rodeo, arts and crafts, country-western dances, fiddlin' contests, and an Old West parade draw crowds during this weekend late in May.

Kerrville Folk Festival. Kerrville; (800) 221-7958 or (830) 257-3600; www.kerrville-music .com. This is one of the biggest outdoor music festivals in the state. For 18 days Quiet Valley Ranch is filled with music lovers who come to hear both local and nationally known performers.

Memorial Day Pow Wow. Laredo; (800) 361-3360. This annual event, held on the Laredo Civic Center grounds, showcases Native American food, dance, music, arts and crafts, and more.

Old Pecan Street Festival. Austin; (512) 474-5171; www.oldpecanstreetfestival.com. A Sixth Street staple for more than three decades, the Old Pecan Street Festival is the largest juried art festival in Central Texas, welcoming a throng of more than 300,000 for a free, biannual ode to originality and inspiration. Music and children's activities add to the fun.

Pun Off World Championships. Austin; (512) 472-1903; www.ci.austin.tx.us/ohenry/ punoff.htm. Held on the grounds of the historic O. Henry Home in downtown Austin, this annual event celebrates wordplay along with live music, a barbecue, and a book sale.

Texas State Arts and Crafts Fair. Kerrville; (830) 896-5711; www.tacef.org. Every Memorial Day weekend this festival opens its gates on the grounds of the River Star Arts and Event Park. Founded by the State of Texas, this enormous show features the paintings, sculptures, jewelry, and other artwork of more than 200 Texas artists, all available to answer questions about their work. A special children's area includes crafts instruction and a petting zoo. Musical entertainment rounds out the day.

Viva! Cinco de Mayo and State Menudo Cook-off. San Marcos; (888) 200-5620; www .vivacincodemayo.org. This festival is held on the weekend closest to Cinco de Mayo (May 5), the celebration of the Mexican victory over the French at the Battle of Puebla. Besides a carnival and musical performances, there's plenty of Mexican food, including menudo, a dish made from tripe, hominy, and spices.

june

Boerne Berges Fest. Boerne; (888) 842-8080; www.bergesfest.com. This festival, held Father's Day weekend, includes arts and crafts, live music, and a celebration of summer.

Chisholm Trail Roundup. Lockhart; (512) 398-2818; www.chisholmtrailroundup.com. Relive the Battle of Plum Creek, where the Texas militia joined forces with Tonkowa Indians to defeat a band of Comanches. You can also enjoy a dance, a parade, and a carnival.

Night in Old Fredericksburg. Fredericksburg; (830) 997-6523; www.nightinoldfredericks burg.com. This annual event, held in Market Square, showcases the town's German culture through arts and crafts, food, dance, and more.

Peach JAMboree. Stonewall; (830) 644-2735; www.stonewalltexas.com. The Peach Capital of Texas shows off its crop on the third Friday and Saturday of June. The local peach-pit-spitting record is more than 28 feet.

Watermelon Jubilee. Stockdale; (830) 996-0021; www.stockdaletx.org. Always held the third weekend in June, this 3-day event dates back to 1937, making it one of the state's oldest watermelon festivals. A parade, rodeo, carnival, dog show, arts and crafts fair, and more mark the event held in Stockdale Park.

Watermelon Thump. Luling; (830) 875-3214; www.watermelonthump.com. On the last Thurs through Sun in June you can enjoy seed-spitting contests, watermelon-eating con-tests, and champion melon judging. There's also an arts and crafts show, carnivals, live entertainment, and street dances. A Guinness World Record was set here in 1989 for spit-ting a watermelon seed almost 69 feet.

july

Deep Sea Roundup. Port Aransas; (800) 45-COAST; www.deepsearoundup.com. Anglers come from everywhere for a chance at the purse in the biggest fishing tournament on this part of the coast, held the week after the Fourth of July. Stay at the pier and watch the competitors weigh in their catch.

Fourth of July Celebration. Round Top; (979) 249-4042. One of the oldest celebrations of Independence Day winds through Round Top. For more information, write the Round Top Chamber of Commerce, Round Top, TX 78954.

Freedom Fiesta. Seguin; (800) 580-7322; www.freedomfiesta.com. Get ready for a red, white, and blue party known as the biggest small-town Fourth of July parade in Texas. The annual Freedom Fiesta has been drawing onlookers and participants since the early 1900s. The activities start with the patriotic parade, followed by food booths, arts and crafts, family entertainment, and kiddie rides for an old-fashioned street-fair atmosphere. In the evening, a street dance from 8 p.m. to midnight keeps the mood festive, as does the grand fireworks display in Max Starcke Park.

Half Moon Holidays. Shiner; (361) 594-4180; www.shinertx.com. On the first weekend in July, Shiner celebrates summer with a brisket cook-off, barbecue dinner, fireworks, a carnival, a horseshoe-pitching tournament, dancing, and lots of music.

Summerfest. San Marcos; (512) 393-5900; www.summerfestsanmarcos.com. This free, family-friendly Fourth of July celebration is held each year at San Marcos Plaza near the river. Activities include a children's parade with prizes for the best costume, live music, fireworks show, and food vendors.

august

Gillespie County Fair. Fredericksburg; (830) 997-6523; www.gillespiefair.com. This event holds the record as the longest running county fair in the state. The festivities include old-fashioned family fun, from carnival rides to food booths.

Grape Stomping Harvest Celebration. Tow; (512) 476-4477. Jump in a bin of red grapes and start stomping during this late Aug festival. Other activities include a cork toss, grape walk, hayrides, and music.

St. Louis Day. Castroville; (800) 778-6775; www.castroville.com. Since 1889 this Alsatian town has celebrated the feast day of St. Louis with a feast of its own on the Sun closest to Aug 25. Local residents pitch in to prepare barbecue, Alsatian sausage, cabbage slaw, and potato salad, all served picnic-style in Koenig Park. The afternoon is filled with a country auction, arts and crafts, singers, and performances by Alsatian dance groups.

september

Austin City Limits Music Festival. Austin; (888) 512-SHOW. Inspired by the popular PBS TV series, the Austin City Limits Festival has become one of the most important music events in the United States. Big- name acts like Pearl Jam, Coldplay, and Van Morrison share the spotlight with new artists on multiple stages in Zilker Park.

Bayfest. Corpus Christi; (800) 242-0071; www.bayfesttexas.com. Along the bayfront, the city of Corpus Christi celebrates fall with boat races, fireworks, and a parade.

Comal County Fair. New Braunfels; (800) 572-2626; www.comalcountyfair.org. This long-running fair ranks as one of the largest (and one of the oldest) in the state. The event includes everything from a rodeo to carnival rides to children's play areas.

Deis y Seis de Septiembre. Del Rio; (800) 889-8149 or (830) 775-3551. First named San Felipe, Del Rio celebrates its historic past with Mexican food, Mexican bingo, and plenty of music.

Fiesta de Amistad. Del Rio and Ciudad Acuña; (800) 889-8149 or (830) 775-3551; www.drchamber.com. The friendship between Del Rio and Ciudad Acuña is celebrated with a Miss Fiesta Pageant, bike race, arts and crafts festival, and international parade—the only one that starts in one country and ends in another.

Flip Flop Festival. Port Lavaca; (361) 552-2959; www.portlavacatx.org. Live music, horseshoe pitching, arts and crafts, and even a "flip flong" contest fill this 1-day festival in early Sept.

HummerBird Celebration. Rockport; (800) 242-0071 or (361) 729-6445; www.rockport hummingbird.com. Thousands of migrating hummingbirds stop to refuel in Rockport, which celebrates the event with 4 days of lectures by birding authorities, arts and crafts displays, boat tours, and Audubon-guided bus tours to sites swarming with hummingbirds.

Kerrville Wine and Music Festival. Kerrville; (830) 257-3600; www.kerrville-music.com. This Hill Country town celebrates fall with performances by Texas musicians and tastings of Texas wines. Held at Quiet Valley Ranch, the site of the Kerrville Folk Festival in the spring.

october

Come and Take It Days. Gonzales; (830) 672-6532. This reenactment of the famous "Come and Take It" skirmish that started the Texas Revolution takes place the first weekend in Oct. More than 30,000 visitors come to enjoy the battle as well as the games, a carnival, a *biergarten,* helicopter rides, and a street dance.

Czhilispiel. Flatonia; (512) 865-3920; http://flatoniachamber.com. When tiny Flatonia needed a doctor years ago, local citizens decided to send a hometown girl to medical school. To fund her education, they began this chili cook-off (now the second largest in Texas) and festival held in late Oct. There's lots of music, a parade, the "World's Largest Tented *Biergarten,*" and a barbecue cook-off as well.

Halloween on Sixth Street. Austin; (800) 888-8AUS; www.austintexas.org. In the capital city, October 31 is not just for kids. The treat is the sight of thousands of revelers in wild costumes parading through the Sixth Street entertainment district. After the late-night bacchanalian outing, the trick may be getting up the next morning.

Mesquite Art Festival. Fredericksburg; (830) 997-6523; www.texasmesquiteassn.org. Visitors have the opportunity to shop for one-of-a-kind woodwork at this annual show, a gathering of more than 50 artists who work primarily in mesquite wood. The festival showcases collectibles, cabinets, mantels, sculptures, musical instruments, and other artwork made from the often maligned tree.

Missions Tour de Goliad. Goliad; (800) 848-8674; www.goliadcc.org. Bicyclists from around the state compete in this race. Riders select from 4 races ranging from 10 to 85 miles in length.

Oktoberfest. Fredericksburg; (830) 997-6523; www.oktoberfestinfbg.com. On the first weekend in October you can head to the "old country" by driving to this German Hill Country town. You'll find polka dancing and sausage galore, as well as arts and crafts, a street dance, and rides for the kids. Runs Fri through Sun.

Peanut Festival. Floresville; (830) 393-0074; www.floresvillepeanutfestival.org. Always held the second full weekend in October, this popular event celebrates the importance of the peanut to regional agriculture with a parade, family-friendly events, and more.

Rockport Seafair. Rockport; (800) 242-0071; www.rockportseafair.com. For more than three decades this coastal village has celebrated Columbus Day weekend with food and festivities. Crab races, kayak races, live music, and a gumbo cook-off keep the weekend busy.

Round Top Antiques Fair. Round Top; (888) 368-4783; www.roundtoptexasantiques .com. Called by some the best such show in the state, this extravaganza features antiques dealers from across the United States. Held the first weekend of the month, it attracts shoppers from around the country.

Turkeyfest. Cuero; (361) 275-2112; http://turkeyfest.org. Held the second weekend in Oct, this event includes turkey races as well as dances, washer pitching, horseshoe throwing, arts and crafts, and more.

november

Austin Celtic Festival. Austin; www.austincelticfestival.com. Bagpipes beckon each fall as the annual Austin Celtic Festival gets under way at Fiesta Gardens on Ladybird Lake. Kilt-clad participants carry on a tradition reaching back to 12th-century Scotland as they compete in Highland games like the caber toss and other tests of agility and strength. Kids can participate in their own mini-version of the games. Tartan twirls onstage as dancing troupes move to the music of bagpipes and bodhrans. If the beat inspires you to move your feet, there are free dance workshops for all ages.

Fredericksburg Food and Wine Fest. Fredericksburg; (830) 997-6523; www.fbgfoodand winefest.com. In late October the Fredericksburg Food and Wine Fest highlights the top wineries of Texas. Along with award-winning vineyards, the event showcases more than 40 vendors who offer a taste of Texas through spices, salsas, cheeses, and more. Two stages offer plenty of musical entertainment, and the whole family finds plenty of just-for-fun activities such as grape stomping and cork tossing.

Old Gruene Market Days. Gruene; (830) 832-1721; www.gruenemarketdays.com. Shoppers flock to this community during Old Gruene Market Days. The event includes plenty of arts and crafts, a farmers' market, and lots of live entertainment from 10 a.m. to 5 p.m. More than 100 vendors give you the chance to make holiday purchases along the streets in 25 shops and at the arts and crafts tent. Look for one-of-a-kind quilts, pottery, wreaths, jewelry, and other special items. During the Christmas Market Days, visitors will find plenty of activity celebrating the season. Enjoy live music at Gruene Hall on Sat from 1 to 5 p.m. and Sun starting at noon; admission is free.

Smithville Music Festival. Smithville; (512) 237-2313; www.smithvillemusicfestival.org. Held on the banks of the Colorado River in Smithville's Richards Riverbend Park, this festival features family-friendly activities and some great live music on 2 stages. There's also a horseshow tournament and a chili cook-off.

Wurstfest. New Braunfels; (800) 221-4369 or (830) 625-9167; www.wurstfest.com. Pull on your lederhosen, take out your beer stein, and join the fun at this celebration of sausage making. One of the largest German festivals in the country, Wurstfest features oompah bands and great German food.

december

Armadillo Christmas Bazaar. Austin; (512) 477-1605; www.armadillobazaar.com. This 10-day event at Palmer Events Center is one of Austin's best-loved Christmas traditions. Since 1976 it has drawn thousands of visitors who come to browse hundreds of booths selling unique arts and crafts, listening to live music while they shop for one-of-a-kind gifts.

Christmas in Goliad. Goliad; (800) 848-8674; www.goliadcc.org. This celebration gives the Christmas season a unique South Texas flavor that includes Pony Express stamp cancellation for cards, local arts and crafts, and a Las Posadas procession.

A Dickens Christmas. Lockhart; (512) 398-2818; www.lockhartchamber.com. The spirit of Christmas Past leads visitors on a trip back in time in this Caldwell County community's annual holiday celebration. Costumed characters from the Dickens novel stroll through decorated streets, and choirs serenade passersby. At night a traditional Yule log is lit as the "Lord High Mayor" proclaims the arrival of the festive season.

Fiesta de las Luminarias. San Antonio; (800) 447-3372; www.visitsanantonio.com. This beautiful ceremony dramatizes Las Posadas, Joseph and Mary's search for an inn, with costumed children leading a procession down the River Walk. Holiday music selections are sung in English and Spanish.

Harbor Lights Festival. Corpus Christi; (800) 678-OCEAN; www.harborlightsfestival .com. The Christmas spirit starts in Corpus Christi with the Christmas Tree Forest at the Art Museum of South Texas, with all trees decorated with a special theme. Santa Claus arrives to flip the switch at the tree-lighting ceremony, and the bayfront twinkles with thousands of tiny lights. The highlight is the Illuminated Boat Parade, with dozens of decorated watercraft plying the bay.

Lights Spectacular. Johnson City; (830) 868-7684; www.johnsoncity-texas.com. One of the biggest displays in the state, this dazzling event features more than 600,000 lights illuminating homes, businesses, and churches, transforming this quiet Hill Country community into a glittering wonderland. The largest light display is on the Blanco County Courthouse, a historic building aglow with more than 100,000 tiny white lights. Maps available at the courthouse lead you on a self-guided drive by Johnson City's fantastic home light displays, erected by local citizens who play a big part in spreading the holiday spirit.

Old Fashion Christmas. Castroville; (830) 538-3142; www.castroville.com. Held on the first Saturday in December, this event features a large arts and crafts show, food booths, and a visit from Santa Claus.

Texas Hill Country Regional Christmas Lighting Trail. Johnson City, Llano, Fredericksburg, Kerrville, Burnet, and Marble Falls; www.tex-fest.com The Hill Country joins together for this trail of Christmas lights and festivities. In Kerrville over 100,000 lights illuminate the entire downtown area, and Marble Falls celebrates with a walkway of lights every evening. Fredericksburg puts on a Kinderfest, St. Nikolausmarkt, and candlelight tours of homes. Llano features "Starry Starry Nights," and Johnson City, the boyhood home of LBJ, is aglow with more than half a million lights.

appendix a:
visiting mexico

Until just a few years ago, visiting the Mexican border communities was a favorite activity for day-trippers. Shopping, dining, fishing, and other activities were year-round draws to these communities, each located an easy walk or taxi ride across the international bridges that cross the Rio Grande.

Sadly, we can no longer recommend travel to the Mexican border cities. Drug cartel violence has erupted in many places along the border. Although it is not aimed at tourists, street shootouts are commonplace and can erupt without warning.

We recommend that all travelers check the **US Embassy in Mexico,** http://mexico.usembassy.gov, and the **US Department of State,** http://travel.state.gov, for up-to-date information on the safety of visiting the border cities.

At present the State Department warns:

Since 2006, large firefights have taken place in towns and cities in many parts of Mexico, often in broad daylight on streets and other public venues. Such firefights have occurred mostly in northern Mexico, including Ciudad Juarez, Tijuana, Chihuahua City, Nogales, Nuevo Laredo, Piedras Negras, Reynosa, Matamoros and Monterrey. Firefights have also occurred in Nayarit, Jalisco and Colima. During some of these incidents, US citizens have been trapped and temporarily prevented from leaving the area.

The situation in northern Mexico remains fluid; the location and timing of future armed engagements cannot be predicted. US citizens are urged to exercise extreme caution when traveling throughout the region, particularly in those areas specifically mentioned in this Travel Warning.

Travel alerts can also be obtained by calling (888) 407-4747 toll-free in the United States and Canada. Travelers in Mexican border cities who experience problems should contact the **US Embassy Consulates.** In Nuevo Laredo the consulate office is located at Calle Allende 3330; phone (011) 52-867-714-0512. Piedras Negras has a Consular Agency; it is located at Abasolo #211, Zona Centro; phone (011) 52-878-782-5586. The Consular Agency in Ciudad Acuña has been closed until further notice.

Visitors to Mexico will need a valid US passport to return to the United States after traveling in Mexico. For information on obtaining a US passport, see the US Department of State website, www.travel.state.gov.

appendix b: especially for winter texans

If you're among the many lucky travelers who've adopted the Lone Star State as their winter home, welcome to Texas. You've chosen a destination where you can enjoy the excitement of the West, the zest of Old Mexico, the tranquility of the Gulf, and the history of a rambunctious republic, all in one journey. Some of the best seasons and reasons to see the state include the changing leaves in fall, the glittering Christmas festivals, and the often sunny Texas winter days.

Texas has an excellent network of state parks, most of which provide campsites with hookups. Generally there is a 14-consecutive-days limit for camping at each park. The central reservation number for all Texas state parks is (512) 389-8900, Mon through Fri 9 a.m. to 6 p.m. You may also make reservations online at www.tpwd.state.tx.us/business/park_reservations.

Winter Texans will also be interested in state park passes. The **Texas Parklands Passport** (which is also called a Bluebonnet Pass) is for those who meet one of these eligibility requirements:

- If you are 65 years of age or older and a Texas resident, you can receive 50 percent off entry. Residents and nonresidents born on or before August 31, 1930, are entitled to waived entry fees at state parks.

- Veterans of the US armed services with a 60 percent or more service-connected disability receive waived entry fees to state parks.

- Travelers who have been medically determined to be permanently disabled as a result of a mental or physical impairment (including blindness) are entitled to 50 percent off entry.

To get the Texas Parklands Passport, you'll need to apply at any state park or at the headquarters in Austin.

If you don't qualify for the Parklands Passport, you can purchase an annual pass called the **Texas State Parks Pass.** It's valid for 12 months and is presently priced at $60 for a one-card membership or $75 if you would like two cards for the family. The Texas State Parks Pass waives entrance fees at state parks.

appendix c: guide to tex-mex food

You'll find Tex-Mex food everywhere you go in Central and South Texas. It's a staple with all true Texans, who enjoy stuffing themselves at least once a week with baskets of tostadas, a Mexican plate (an enchilada, taco, and rice and beans), and cold *cerveza*. Unlike true Mexican food, which is not unusually spicy and often features seafood, Tex-Mex is heavy, ranges from hot to inedible, and can't be beat.

cabrito—young, tender goat, usually cooked over an open flame on a spit. In border towns, you'll see it hanging it many market windows.

cerveza—beer.

chalupa—a fried, flat corn tortilla spread with refried beans and topped with meat, lettuce, tomatoes, and cheese.

chiles rellenos—stuffed poblano peppers, dipped in batter and deep-fried.

enchiladas—corn or flour tortillas wrapped around a filling and covered with a hot or mild sauce. The most common varieties are beef, chicken, and cheese. Sour cream and shrimp are sometimes offered.

fajitas—grilled skirt steak strips, wrapped in flour tortillas. Usually served still sizzling on a metal platter, with condiments (pico de gallo, sour cream, cheese) on the side.

flautas—corn tortillas wrapped around shredded beef, chicken, or pork and fried until crispy; may be an appetizer or an entree.

frijoles refritos—refried beans.

guacamole—avocado dip spiced with chopped onions, peppers, and herbs.

margarita—popular tequila drink, served in a salted glass; may be served over ice or frozen.

menudo—a soup made from tripe, most popular as a hangover remedy.

mole ("MOLE-ay")—an unusual sauce made of nuts, spices, and chocolate that's served over chicken enchiladas.

picante sauce—a Mexican staple found on most tables, this red sauce is made from peppers and onions and can be eaten as a dip for tortilla chips; ranges from mild to very hot.

pico de gallo—hot sauce made of chopped onions, peppers, and cilantro; used to spice up tacos, chalupas, and fajitas.

quesadillas—tortillas filled and covered with cheese and baked; served as a main dish or an appetizer.

sopapillas—fried pastry dessert served with honey.

tamale—corn dough filled with chopped pork, rolled in a corn shuck, steamed, and then served with or without chile sauce; a very popular Christmas dish.

tortillas—flat cooked rounds of flour or cornmeal used in many main dishes and also eaten like bread along with the meal, with or without butter.

verde—green sauce used as a dip or on enchiladas.

appendix d:
texas state parks

Texas has an excellent system of state parks offering camping, fishing, hiking, boating, and tours of historical sites. Amenities range from those with hiking trails, golf courses, and cabins to others that are largely undeveloped and exist as an example of how the region once looked.

Reservations are recommended for overnight facilities. Pets are permitted if they are confined or on a leash shorter than 6 feet and with proof of vaccinations within the past year. The central reservation number for all Texas state parks is (512) 389-8900, Mon through Fri 9 a.m. to 6 p.m. See www.tpwd.state.tx.us/business/park_reservations for online, e-mail, and fax reservations.

If you are 65 or older, a veteran with at least a 60 percent service-related disability, or a frequent state park visitor, you may want to consider purchasing a Texas Parklands Passport or a Texas State Parks Pass. For details, see Appendix B, "Especially for Winter Texans."

For more information on Texas state parks, call the **Texas Parks and Wildlife Department** at (800) 792-1112 or (512) 389-4800 in the Austin area, Mon through Fri during working hours. See also www.tpwd.state.tx.us.

appendix e: lcra parks

When it comes to parks, Central Texas travelers have only one problem: selecting from a long list of excellent facilities. Many of these parks are the products of the **Lower Colorado River Authority (LCRA),** a conservation and reclamation district that generates and transmits electricity produced by the powerful Colorado River. The LCRA also manages the waters of the river and assists riverside and lakeside communities with their economic development.

Among travelers, the LCRA is best known for its parks. These sites, which vary from unimproved sites along the riverbanks to full-fledged parks with boat ramps, fishing piers, and camping, are favorite summer destinations. Scattered from the shores of Lake Buchanan down through the rest of the Highland Lakes and along the riverbanks of the Colorado River all the way to Matagorda County on the Gulf Coast, these reservoirs offer vacationers a great place to relax.

For more information on LCRA parks, call (800) 776-5272 or visit www.lcra.org.

index